ANATOMY OF A METROPOLIS

166

1-229

NEW YORK METROPOLITAN REGION STUDY

Raymond Vernon, *Director*
Max Hall, *Editor*

Undertaken by the Graduate School of Public Administration, Harvard University, for the Regional Plan Association, Inc.

These books constitute the most thorough existing analysis of the present economic condition, the indicated course of development, and the probable future of the New York Metropolitan Region, the archetype of the American metropolitan community. The findings are meaningful for metropolitan areas throughout the United States, since they deal with the most urgent problems confronting American communities today.

1. *Anatomy of a Metropolis* by Edgar M. Hoover and Raymond Vernon

2. *Made in New York* by Roy B. Helfgott, W. Eric Gustafson, and James M. Hund, with an introduction by Max Hall

3. *The Newcomers* by Oscar Handlin

4. *Wages in the Metropolis* by Martin Segal

5. *Money Metropolis* by Sidney M. Robbins and Nestor E. Terleckyj, with the collaboration of Ira O. Scott, Jr.

6. *Freight and the Metropolis* by Benjamin Chinitz

7. *One-tenth of a Nation* by Robert M. Lichtenberg, with supplements by Edgar M. Hoover and Louise P. Lerdau

8. *1400 Governments* by Robert C. Wood

9. *Metropolis 1985* by Raymond Vernon

To be published:

Technical supplement: *Projection of a Metropolis* by Barbara R. Berman, Benjamin Chinitz, and Edgar M. Hoover

All books in the New York Metropolitan Region Study are published by the Harvard University Press, Cambridge 38, Massachusetts

Edgar M. Hoover is Professor of Economics at the University of Pittsburgh and is now directing an economic study of the Pittsburgh Metropolitan Region. While participating in the New York Study he was Visiting Professor of Economics at Harvard. He is the author of several books and articles on economics. His most recent book (with Ashley J. Coale) was *Population Growth and Economic Development in Low-Income Countries* (Princeton University Press, 1958).

Raymond Vernon is Director of the New York Metropolitan Region Study and was recently appointed Professor of International Trade and Investment at the Graduate School of Business Administration, Harvard University. He has held various positions in the Securities and Exchange Commission, in the Department of State, and in private business, and he is the author of a number of works in the fields of corporation finance, international trade, and urban economics.

ANATOMY
OF A METROPOLIS

THE CHANGING DISTRIBUTION
OF PEOPLE AND JOBS WITHIN
THE NEW YORK METROPOLITAN REGION

EDGAR M. HOOVER
and
RAYMOND VERNON

With the assistance of
Milton Abelson, Alan K. Campbell, Lionel Lerner,
Harvey H. Segal, Peter Stone, and Robert J. Wolfson

ANCHOR BOOKS
DOUBLEDAY & COMPANY, INC., GARDEN CITY, NEW YORK

FOREWORD

This is one of a series of books on the forces that shape metropolitan areas. In particular, the series has to do with the forces that shape the largest and most complex metropolitan area in the United States, a 22-county expanse which takes in parts of three states but which, for convenience, we have termed the New York Metropolitan Region.

In 1956, the Regional Plan Association, Inc., a nonprofit research and planning agency whose purpose is to promote the coordinated development of these 22 counties, requested the Graduate School of Public Administration of Harvard University to undertake a three-year study of the Region. The challenging task was to analyze the key economic and demographic features of the Region and to project them to 1965, 1975, and 1985.

The resulting studies are reports to the Regional Plan Association. At the same time, they are designed to be of service to a much broader audience. Most Americans now live in metropolitan areas; indeed, ever-increasing proportions of the world's populations are gravitating to metropolitan clusters. Their well-being depends to a considerable extent on how these areas develop. Yet the scholar's understanding of the currents underlying the rise of such areas seems grossly inadequate.

As a study of these underlying currents, this project is neither a blueprint for action nor an analysis of metropolitan government. It has no recommendations to make about the physical structure of the Region or about the form or activities of the governmental bodies there. At the same time, it is a necessary prelude to future planning studies of the Region and to well considered recommendations for governmental action. Its end product is an analysis of the Region's probable development, assuming that the economic and demographic forces in sight follow their indicated course and assuming that the role of government is largely limited to existing policies.

The results of the Study, it is hoped, will be applied in many ways. Governments and enterprises in the Region should be in a better position to plan their future programs if they become more closely aware of the economic environment in which they may expect to operate. Other metropolitan areas, it is already evident, will benefit from the methodology and the conclusions which the Study has developed.

From the first, there has been a general recognition that the main part of the Study would have to be done by a group located within the New York Metropolitan Region and devoted exclusively to the project. Such a group was assembled in New York. The work that followed was a complex partnership. The New York staff functioned in close harness with members of the Harvard University faculty. It drew on the faculties of other universities, including Columbia University, Fordham University, Hofstra College, New York University, and Rutgers University. It obtained the help of dozens of governmental organizations in the Region and literally hundreds of private groups and individuals. It made use of the materials which the Regional Plan Association had painstakingly pulled together in prior years.

Each book in the series has a place in the total structure of the Study; yet each is designed to be a complete work in itself. The final report, containing the synthesis and projections of the Study, is published under the title, *Metropolis 1985*.

It is not easy to account for all the elements that went into the making of this book or the others in the series. The Regional Plan Association performed an indispensable function in conceiving and sponsoring the idea of a study. The Ford Foundation and the Rockefeller Brothers Fund generously provided the financial support. The usual formula in such a situation obviously applies: credit for the Study's results must be shared with those who helped to bring it about, but the onus of error or omission lies with us.

The several volumes in the series bear the names of their principal authors. The undertaking as a whole has been under the direction of Raymond Vernon. He is responsible for the final report and for substantial parts of other studies, and his guidance is evident throughout the series.

The present volume traces the changing distribution of jobs and homes within the Region, and it probes for the critical forces in the Region which are likely to change that distribution in the future. While designed to stand on its own feet, the volume nevertheless carries the earmarks of its origins as one of a series. For instance, companion studies explore the impact of developments in the national scene upon the Region and deal more exhaustively with various specialized aspects of the Region's structure such as the role of labor, of transportation, and of government finance and regulation.

In the present volume, written jointly by Edgar M. Hoover and Raymond Vernon, Mr. Hoover was responsible for the chapters on population, and Mr. Vernon was responsible for the remainder of the book. They were assisted by those named on the title page. Of that group, Mr. Abelson did the statistical analyses and estimates relating to the number and location of jobs, Mr. Campbell worked on taxes, Mr. Segal on personal income, Mr. Stone on real estate, and Mr. Wolfson on consumer trade and services. Mr. Lerner assisted Mr. Abelson during part of the Study. Besides those who appear on the title page, many others participated; Patricia Likert Pohlman, in particular, was of inestimable value to Mr. Hoover in preparing data for the chapters on population.

Edward S. Mason
for The Graduate School
of Public Administration,
Harvard University

CONTENTS

CHARTS

TABLES

MAPS

1

CITIES AND SUBURBS

This book is concerned with 6,914 square miles of real estate, covering 22 counties in three states and supporting nearly 7 million jobs and about 16 million people—an area we have termed the New York Metropolitan Region.[1] No other metropolitan area in the United States approaches it in population, employment, or wealth. But the book is not about the position of the Region in the nation. Our focus is the Region's changing internal structure, especially the changes which arise out of forces operating within the Region itself. We seek to understand the relations between the great cities of the Region and their suburbs, and between various groups of counties such as the 9 counties in New Jersey and the 13 counties in New York State and Connecticut. We want to know how the jobs and the homes are distributed in the whole territory —from Dutchess County far up the Hudson Valley to Monmouth County down the Jersey seacoast, and from hilly Morris County on the west to sandy Suffolk on the eastern end of Long Island. Finally, we are interested in what is likely to happen to this internal distribution of jobs and residents during the next 25 years.

THE METROPOLITAN REGION AS AN ENTITY

The disposition to think of a metropolitan area as a meaningful unit for study is a comparatively recent phenomenon. Time was, only four or five decades ago, when the city—not the metropolitan area—was a sufficient unit for analysis. Though urban development sometimes wandered a little beyond the city limits, this phenomenon was far from universal. Most large cities had a "downtown" section and residential and industrial neighborhoods, all of them built up at fairly high densities. Somewhere out near the political boundaries, short of the ends of the trolley lines, city development ended rather abruptly. Just beyond were open fields, dirt roads, and occasional amusement parks, set up to generate week-end traffic on the trolleys.

Here and there, the pattern was punctured by the impact of a high-speed interurban trolley or a suburban railway; where these existed, the houses and neighborhood stores were strung out a little farther beyond the city limits or clustered tightly about the passenger stations. But the distinction between "urban places" and "rural places" was sharp enough for most purposes.

Today, metropolitan areas spill beyond their central cities, embracing smaller cities and towns, and surrounding numerous semirural patches. In the New York Metropolitan Region, the development radiating outward from New York City engulfs a number of old cities which once were the business and cultural centers of the countryside surrounding them and which even today manage to retain some of these attributes. If we think of the Region as a huge conical structure, in which altitude represents the concentration of human activity, we find Newark, Jersey City, Paterson, Elizabeth, Yonkers, and Bridgeport—each with a population over 100,000—protruding as lesser peaks from its sloping flanks. Yet by any measure one cares to devise, the apex of the whole structure is on the island of Manhattan.

Map 1 gives a general impression of the degree to which the population of the Region is concentrated at the center. The black portions on the map, where the dots run together, are principally in New York City.[2] Other dark spots to the left represent cities in New Jersey.

If the dwelling units of the Region are clustered at their densest in Manhattan, the jobs are clustered even more densely there. As we travel outward through the Region, employment becomes progressively less dense, though not with perfect regularity, all the way to the periphery.

MAP 1
Population Distribution in New York Metropolitan Region, 1954

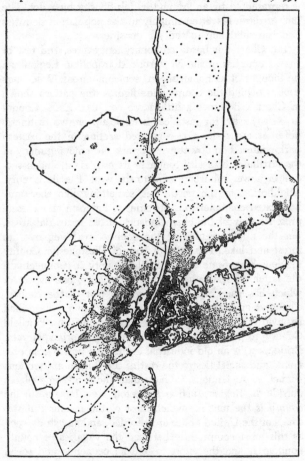

Each dot represents approximately 1,000 persons.
Source: Regional Plan Association, Inc.

Chart 1 gives a rough idea of how population density and job density fall off with the increase of distance from the Empire State Building. Each county's population density is represented by an "x" and its job density by a dot. The line of dashes is fitted roughly to the population densities and the solid line to the job densities.

But Chart 1 is based on county aggregates, and few of the 22 counties of the New York Metropolitan Region can be thought of as homogeneous economic areas. When one probes behind the county-wide figures, the pattern shown in Chart 1 becomes a little more complex. Essex County in New Jersey, for instance, is made up of two distinctly different areas—an old, congested section in the eastern part, centered on downtown Newark and enjoying many of the attributes of a city center in its own right, and a section of newer suburban areas to the west. Passaic County, neighboring to the north, has something like the same bifurcated characteristics; its cities of Paterson and Passaic present many of the characteristics of old industrial areas, but the upper reaches of the county are given over to forest and lake. The same is true of Westchester County in New York State and Fairfield County in Connecticut; the latter especially has a dual personality, one aspect of which has very little relation to the rest of the Region. Though significant numbers of the "exurbanites" described so vividly by A. C. Spectorsky travel daily from Fairfield County to New York City, the county's principal city, Bridgeport, is an old industrial center and port whose economic and social ties to the rest of the Region are tenuous —much more tenuous, in fact, than those of some places outside the Region, such as Princeton, New Jersey. But the *county* is the unit for which most of the meaningful statistics of the United States are afforded, and any study such as this must compromise between the vagaries of county boundaries and the effort to find an economic and social entity for study.

The fact is that the jobs and homes of the people of the Region are still so highly concentrated in a few counties down toward the geographic center of the Region that the scope of the study and its principal conclusions would

CHART 1

Density of Population and Jobs in Counties at Various
Distances from Manhattan, 1956

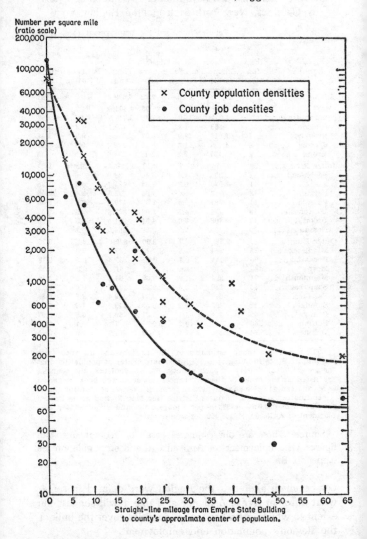

Number per square mile
(ratio scale)

× County population densities
● County job densities

Straight-line mileage from Empire State Building
to county's approximate center of population.

Source: Table 1.

TABLE 1   Estimated Distribution of Population and Jobs
by Counties, New York Metropolitan Region, 1956

	Miles from Manhattan[a]	Population (April 1)			Employment (March 15)		
		Thousands	Per cent of Region	Thousands per square mile	Thousands	Per cent of Region	Thousands per square mile
Entire Region .	..	15,375	100.0	2.22	6,699.8	100.0	0.97
Core	..	8,236	53.6	26.96	4,301.5	64.2	14.08
Manhattan[b] .	..	1,811	11.8	80.85	2,717.5	40.6	121.32
Hudson	4	653	4.3	14.29	289.1	4.3	6.33
Brooklyn	7	2,616	17.0	33.07	664.9	9.9	8.41
Queens	8	1,729	11.2	15.13	398.4	5.9	3.49
Bronx	8	1,427	9.3	32.43	231.6	3.5	5.26
Inner Ring	..	4,573	29.7	3.18	1,572.3	23.5	1.09
Richmond ...	11	208	1.4	3.44	38.8	0.6	0.64
Essex	11	970	6.3	7.64	424.7	6.3	3.35
Bergen	12	713	4.6	3.04	222.5	3.4	0.95
Passaic	14	387	2.5	1.99	170.1	2.5	0.88
Westchester .	19	724	4.7	1.66	229.8	3.4	0.53
Union	19	466	3.0	4.54	201.5	3.0	1.96
Nassau	20	1,105	7.2	3.89	284.9	4.3	1.00
Outer Ring	..	2,566	16.7	0.50	826.0	12.3	0.16
Middlesex ...	25	354	2.3	1.13	137.2	2.0	0.44
Rockland	25	111	0.7	0.65	30.9	0.5	0.18
Morris	25	210	1.4	0.45	61.4	0.9	0.13
Monmouth ..	31	294	1.9	0.62	68.8	1.0	0.14
Somerset	33	119	0.8	0.39	38.7	0.6	0.13
Fairfield	40	614	4.0	0.97	249.4	3.7	0.39
Suffolk	42	493	3.2	0.53	112.7	1.7	0.12
Orange	48	174	1.1	0.21	58.1	0.9	0.07
Putnam	49	27	0.2	0.01	7.1	0.1	0.03
Dutchess	64	170	1.1	0.20	61.7	0.9	0.08

[a] These are our rough estimates of the straight-line distance from the Empire State Building to the approximate center of population (not the geographical center) of each county. For convenience, the counties are listed in the order of these distances. Later in the book, nearness to Manhattan will also be presented in terms of average commuting times.

[b] Manhattan's central business district (see Map 3) had an estimated population of 620,000, or 67,000 per square mile, and an estimated employment of 2,475,000, or 266,000 per square mile.

Source: These are our estimates based on federal and state figures. On employment see Appendix A, and on population see Appendix B.

not be much altered if the Region were defined in somewhat different terms. A glance at Table 1 will suggest the extent to which just a handful of counties cover the bulk of the Region's population and employment.

More than half of the Region's inhabitants live in five

counties, designated as the *Core*. The seven counties immediately surrounding the Core, the *Inner Ring*, house about 30 per cent of the total, and the *Outer Ring* of the Region accounts for the remainder. As for the jobs, two out of every three in the Region are located in the Core, with Manhattan alone providing 40 per cent of the Region's job opportunities. The inclusion or exclusion of two or three counties at the periphery does little to disturb the nature of the entity with which we are to deal here.

The concept of a Core, an Inner Ring, and an Outer Ring corresponds faithfully with the groupings that one would get by classifying the counties in accordance with the degree of their land development. The Core contains the five most highly developed counties, the Inner Ring those that are the next most highly developed, and the Outer Ring the ones with the lowest development. Thus, in the middle 1950's only 9 per cent of the Core's land suitable for development was still vacant; the comparable figure was 45 per cent for the Inner Ring and 80 for the Outer Ring.[3]

Map 2 shows how the Core, Inner Ring, and Outer Ring appear on a map. It will be observed that the division of the Region into its three main zones is indifferent to certain political boundaries. Hudson County, which lies in New Jersey, joins four of New York City's counties—Manhattan, the Bronx, Queens, and Brooklyn—to form the Core.* Richmond (Staten Island), the maverick among the five counties of New York City, is split away from the others and classified in the Inner Ring. This arrangement crosses political boundaries, but it is supported by the degree of land development in the counties involved. On the other hand, we have no desire to be trapped by our own classification. For some purposes, it will be convenient to stray from the classification suggested here; when taxes are being considered, for instance, there is virtue in regrouping

* Though we use the familiar borough names in this book, New Yorkers will recognize that two of the boroughs have different names when considered as counties. The Borough of Manhattan is New York County, and the Borough of Brooklyn is Kings County.

MAP 2

The Three Main Zones of the Region

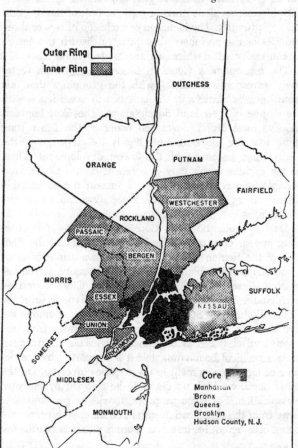

the counties to take cognizance of political jurisdictions. Besides, regrouping will sometimes be required by the exigencies of statistical presentation. But whenever there is no good reason to the contrary, we shall use the three-way breakdown depicted on the map.

THE CORE OF THE REGION

The five Core counties contain 54 per cent of the Region's population and 64 per cent of its jobs. The Core is nearly all congested but is far from being all alike; its various parts differ widely in the kinds of economic pursuits in which they specialize and in the kinds of people who inhabit them.

JOBS IN THE CORE

It is traditional with analyses of the New York Metropolitan Region that they begin by discussing a small segment of the Core, Manhattan's central business district, which we have mapped in Map 3. Nor is the emphasis substantially misplaced. For the central business district is of such considerable importance to the economy of the Region that one might have been justified in giving it the status of a separate zone alongside the rest of the Core and the two Rings.

This minuscule area of nine and one-third square miles with its familiar skyline, lying between the lower tip of the island and Central Park, is the area on which most of the Region's mass transit facilities are designed to converge; the area where its daytime populations are densest; and the area whose activities gave the Region its economic pre-eminence in the nation. Though figures on employment in the central business district are fragmentary and can only be crudely approximated, it appears that the district contains about 37 per cent of the Region's jobs, if we lump all kinds of jobs together. But certain types of activity have a much higher degree of concentration in the district; for example, far more than half of the Region's employment in wholesale trade, finance and other office activities, theatrical pursuits, printing, publishing, and garment-making

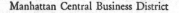

MAP 3

Manhattan Central Business District

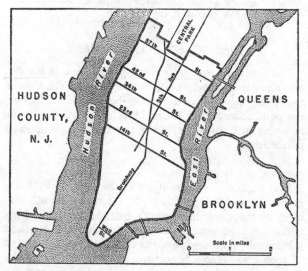

Northern boundary (left to right) follows 66th Street, Amsterdam Avenue, 62nd, Central Park West, Central Park South, Fifth Avenue, 63rd, Third Avenue, 64th, York Avenue, and 63rd. In estimates of commuter flow, reported in later chapters, the boundary is simply considered to be 61st Street. In discussing retail trade (Chapter 5), we use a smaller district which, for clarity, we term the "central shopping area" (see Table 21).

is found here. Table 2 shows how the jobs in each major category of employment are distributed among various parts of the Region. The employment figures are given in greater detail in Appendix A.

Many of the jobs in the central business district—whether they be in manufacturing, in wholesaling, in retail trade, or in some office activity—have a common quality. They are, on the whole, jobs whose dominant locational requirement is that they must be a part of a great cluster of economic activity. This requirement stems from an overriding need to communicate face-to-face with persons outside the firm; from a need to draw on short notice from a

TABLE 2   Distribution of Employment in New York
Metropolitan Region by Categories of Industries,
March 1956

	Number of employees (thousands)	Percentage shares of Region's employment (NYMR = 100)			
		Manhattan central business district	Rest of Core	Inner Ring	Outer Ring
Total employment	6,699.8	37.0	27.2	23.5	12.3
Manufacturing	1,889.9	27.4	29.3	27.5	15.8
Wholesale trade	453.5	58.3	20.6	15.6	5.5
Financial community ...	320.2	66.7	13.0	16.0	4.3
Other office workers in office buildings	895.6	59.3	19.0	14.9	6.8
Consumer trades and services	1,244.0	29.7	31.7	25.7	12.9
Contract construction ...	241.8	22.5	28.0	32.5	17.0
Other employment	1,654.8	30.2	32.0	24.2	13.6

Source: Appendix A, Table A–1.

common pool of rentable space, labor, skilled subcontractors, or other such facilities outside the firm; and from a
variety of other factors rooted in history.

All of these concepts will be developed in later chapters.
For the present it is enough to note that the special role
of the central business district has left its mark in numerous ways. From our rough approximations, it appears that
the district has about 435 times as many jobs per square
mile as the rest of the Region. These jobs are commonly
organized in tight little subdistricts—a group of blocks, a
single street, or even a single building—devoted to some
specialized pursuit. In manufacturing, the Garment Center
is the classic illustration; in wholesaling, illustrations are
provided by toys, millinery, handbags, textiles, and hardware; in advertising, Madison Avenue; in finance, Wall
Street; in entertainment, Times Square; in diamonds, the
47th Street center; and so on.

Retail trade in the central business district also has distinctive traits. The emphasis here is on "unstandardized"
merchandise with which are connected the elements of
fashion, variety, and specialty. Apparel, accessories, and
department stores are highly concentrated in the central

business district. Eating places also cluster heavily there, feeding the excess populations by day and entertaining them by night.

The rest of the Core possesses some of the job character-istics that distinguish the central business district, though in more dilute form. Industrial areas of Brooklyn, Queens, the Bronx, and upper Manhattan, and to a lesser extent those of Hudson County beyond the Holland and Lincoln tunnels, attract industries whose "communication" needs require close-in locations but not locations so central as those offered by the central business district proper. In these areas, one finds many of the "contract shops" of the apparel industry, with strong umbilical ties to the Garment Center in Manhattan; here, too, are numerous electronics plants, conducting their business by an intricate web of contracting and subcontracting with other plants in the Region. And these counties are the sites of some of the major wholesaling distribution points and trucking termi-nals, whence merchandise fans out to the Region's various corners.

The Core counties outside the central business district are distinguished by still another feature—the noisome in-dustrial enclaves which they embrace. It was only four or five decades ago that Hunts Point in the Bronx, the moist Jersey Meadows in Hudson County, and Newtown Creek washing between Brooklyn and Queens lay on the edges of the main population masses inside the New York Met-ropolitan Region. These areas seemed peculiarly attractive to manufacturers whose processes were peculiarly *unat-tractive* to the citizenry—abattoirs, stench-producing or waste-generating metal refineries or chemical plants, and the like. Though the total employment of such manu-facturers was not great, their decisions to settle where they did—usually well before the first zoning laws—helped to set the tone for the development of the neighborhoods con-cerned.

PEOPLE IN THE CORE

The people who reside in the Core tend to differ from those in the rest of the Region in various critical ways: in the incomes they earn, in their ethnic identities, in their family composition, and in their living conditions.

A century ago, Manhattan's central business district harbored most of New York City's populations, and vestiges of its former role still persist. The district, for instance, includes some of the oldest and most dilapidated residential structures in the Region. But residential population has been thinning out in the central business district since the turn of the century, and the approximately 600,000 people now living in that area are only half the number that lived there in 1905. At the same time, demolitions and new construction have been upgrading the building stock of the district.

In the rest of the Core, the oldest residential structures do not date back as far as those within the central business district. Yet many of them are also old and some of them have become slum dwellings by any standards. Nor has the purging effect of demolitions been so marked in these areas. Running through Manhattan's upper West Side and Harlem, through the middle Bronx, through the Bedford-Stuyvesant section of Brooklyn, and through Jersey City and other cities of Hudson County are belts of dense population, where humanity has crowded into old structures in numbers for which they were never designed. Brownstones have been subdivided into rooming houses, and apartments have been sublet to two or more families. These are the "new" slums, displacing the ancient lower East Side, the Mott Haven area in the Bronx, and the oldest portions of Brooklyn.

In these "newer" areas, Negroes and Puerto Ricans are represented much more heavily than elsewhere in the Region. One-fifth of the residents of Manhattan are Negro, and elsewhere in the Core counties one-tenth are Negro. Puerto Ricans comprise one-sixth of Manhattan's population and one-twentieth of the people in the other Core counties. Indeed, New York City altogether contains about 80 per cent of the Puerto Ricans in the continental United States.

Housing priced for middle-income groups and containing the amenities they demand still exists in the Core, particularly in its outer areas. Upper portions of the Bronx, middle and eastern Queens, and considerable sections of Brooklyn contain great quantities of such housing, much of it built since World War II. Even Manhattan still has some housing acceptable to middle-income groups, but Manhattan is more notable for its heavy representation of the poor and the rich. Besides its slums and its low-income housing developments, Manhattan contains the most expensive rental accommodations of the City—indeed of the whole Region. Manhattan is also the mecca of the small family, the childless couple, and the adult living apart from his family. The 1950 census, for instance, shows about as many "unrelated" individuals in Manhattan as it does families.

One last point about the general characteristics of the Core counties: the ratio of employment to population varies strikingly among them, suggesting some of the ties which bind the Core into an economic unit. Chart 2 shows this ratio for every county of the Region. Manhattan's jobs, of course, outnumber its residents; indeed the central business district has four times as much employment as it has population. But elsewhere in the Core counties, the reverse is true; the Bronx, Queens, Brooklyn, and upper Manhattan, linked to the central business district by the extraordinary rapid transit facilities which New York City affords, are the real "bedroom communities" of the Region by this standard, even more so than the classic suburban county of Westchester in the Inner Ring. Richmond, it is well to note, shares this "bedroomy" trait of the Core counties, sending a considerable portion of its population to other counties to work. Hudson County gives the appearance of a more self-sufficient area, though there is a good deal of commuting both into and out of the county which is cancelled out in the net figures represented by the ratio of employment to population.

THE INNER RING COUNTIES

The counties of the Inner Ring can be thought of as an arc which begins with Richmond on the south, moves over

CHART 2

Ratio of Employment to Population in New York
Metropolitan Region, by Counties, 1956

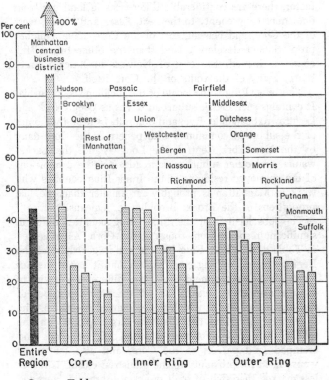

Source: Table 1.

into New Jersey and northward through Union, Essex, Passaic, and Bergen, thence eastward across the Hudson River to Westchester, and finally southeastward to Nassau. The arc envelops Hudson County and New York City, and is in turn ringed by an outer loop of more sparsely settled counties. In the arc of the Inner Ring lie 30 per cent of the residents and 24 per cent of the jobs of the

New York Metropolitan Region. There are four cities above 100,000 population and more than twenty others above 25,000.

Though the Inner Ring differs generally from the Core in the sense that space is not so obviously the restraining factor, there are considerable differences in land use from one Inner Ring county to the next. Essex and Union, west of the Core, and Nassau, east of the Core, have a higher proportion of developed land than the other Inner Ring counties. Indeed, the city of Newark in Essex County shares many of the traits of the Core itself.

The Inner Ring is the locale of the sociologists' Suburbia. It contains such classic suburban towns as Great Neck and Levittown, Scarsdale, Rye, and Summit. In it lie the homes of the suburban commuters who penetrate the Core daily by the New York Central, the Long Island, the Lackawanna, and other suburban railroads. Yet the proportions of the employed residents of the Inner Ring counties who work in Manhattan is probably far smaller than the like proportions in the Bronx, Brooklyn, or Queens.

The jobs located in the Inner Ring counties differ in significant respects from those in the Core. As indicated in Table 2, the Inner Ring has a much larger share of the Region's manufacturing employment than it has of the Region's office employment. But the differences begin to emerge even more clearly as we examine the types of manufacturing jobs in which these counties specialize. The Inner Ring provides the sites for larger plants, on the whole, than those crowded into the loft buildings and cramped land parcels of the Core, and also for plants whose need for proximity to the industrial cluster is rather less marked than that of the Core establishments. Here too —on the New Jersey side of the Inner Ring, at any rate— are the great plants reliant on rail connections for the shipment or receipt of their materials.

The people who live in the Inner Ring counties, true to their general characterization as suburbanites, differ in some ways from those in the Core. With some notable exceptions such as Newark and Passaic, the Inner Ring areas do not yet contain large quantities of housing so obsolete or so dilapidated that those with low incomes can command them. There are many apartment buildings in southern Westchester and other spots in the Inner Ring, but in general multifamily dwellings are not so important as they are in the Core. The average number of residents per acre of residential land in the Inner Ring is 14, as contrasted with 104 in the Core.[4] By and large, overlooking some major exceptions to the pattern, the Inner Ring is the home of middle-income and upper-income groups.

THE OUTER RING COUNTIES

If there is one trait the Outer Ring counties have in common, it is the large quantities of land available for eventual use. If all the vacant usable land were developed on the same pattern as that which is already developed, the population of the Outer Ring conceivably might be 14 or 15 million instead of the present 2½ million.

Once again, however, we are obliged to dwell upon the differences *within* the zone. On the whole, these are remote areas—remote from one another and remote from Manhattan. Far to the south lies Monmouth County, edged with seaside resorts like Sea Girt and Asbury Park—resorts already famous in the nineteenth century—as well as new industrial centers and colonies of modest homes like those surrounding Red Bank. A patient commuter might conceivably make his way from these areas to a job in Jersey City or downtown Newark, using the Garden State Parkway or the declining railroad facilities of the Jersey Central. But a daily commuting trip to Manhattan from these areas would be intolerable for most people.

Swinging clockwise around the outer arc, we come to rapidly industrializing Middlesex, then to Somerset and Morris, containing some of the Region's few refuges for fox-hunting clubs and genteel country living. These counties, too, are remote from New York City in time and distance; high-speed highways penetrate parts of them, while suburban rail connections service other limited portions. Rockland, Orange, Dutchess, and Putnam to the north, as well as the northern portions of Westchester County, have long been regarded as the milk-shed and vacation areas for the populations of the New York Metropolitan Region and as a favorite base for the "exurbanites." To be sure, there have always been spots of industrial activity in these counties, spots whose ties to the New York Metropolitan Region were drawn rather thin. Nyack and Poughkeepsie, for instance, for a long time have had clusters of plants drawing workers from the local population. But the New York State Thruway and the promise of other high-speed highways which will converge on the Core and Inner Ring are bringing an obvious change in these Outer Ring areas, one which is beginning to link them more clearly to the Region.

This brings us to Fairfield County—an area, we have already observed, with two very distinct personalities. Bridgeport, where 27 per cent of the county's people live, is an industrial center specializing in the manufacture of aircraft and parts, metal-working machinery, electrical appliances, and industrial apparatus. According to the 1950 census, over half of Bridgeport's employed residents were working in manufacturing industries. Along most of the Fairfield County shore and in the county's more sparsely inhabited interior, the residents have higher incomes, on the average; more of them hold professional and technical jobs; and more of them are home-owners. To many of these people the Core of the New York Metropolitan Region offers jobs or a cultural and social base.

One other county remains: Suffolk County in the eastern part of Long Island. The western end of this county is getting to be very much like its populous neighbor, Nassau, but most of Suffolk is otherwise. Though the Long Island Railroad makes valiant efforts to serve the county and though the new Long Island Expressway will strengthen Suffolk's link with the Region's complex, most of the county lies outside the commuting range which current technology defines. Here we are in seashore vacation territory, intermixed with potato farms, a few large aircraft plants, Brookhaven's formidable atomic laboratories, and a sprinkling of little manufacturing plants.

The Outer Ring as a whole, notwithstanding its commuters to the Inner Ring and the Core, is a zone still touched with the attributes of rural living; its per capita income is lower than that of the Inner Ring, and its proportion of single-family dwellings higher. Though big changes may come in another generation, today much of the Outer Ring is *in* the Region but not yet altogether *of* it.

FROM JOBS TO PEOPLE

With this brief survey of our 6,914 square miles and their 16 million people, we are ready to try to unravel the complex forces which have shifted jobs and homes from one part of the Region to the other in past decades, and which promise to bring more changes in the future.

Jobs and homes, of course, have a good deal of influence on each other in a locational sense. But there are large and dynamic sectors in the Region's employment whose location is determined without much regard for the distribution of homes. These sectors are manufacturing, wholesaling, certain types of office work, and a few consumer trades and services. Their shifting within the Region has immense importance for the Region's development, including its residential patterns. Thus, before we analyze the movements of the metropolitan population it will be well to explore those economic sectors and discover what *does* determine their location.

Some types of jobs in the Region will be explored hardly at all, because they are moved by forces too transparent to detain us. The Region's 242,000 construction jobs, for instance, transfer from place to place as new construction requires, and our analysis of the locational motivations of the people and enterprises that order new construction will point the way to the location of the construction workers. The Region's approximately 170,000 domestic workers also need little discussion, for the distribution of their jobs chiefly follows the distribution of high-income residents. So, too, with the 350,000 public utility workers outside of office buildings—the meter men, linesmen, bus drivers, trainmen, and others constantly on the move; to the extent that their jobs have a "location" in the Region, that location depends largely on the whereabouts of the homes and jobs of others.

There are still other jobs on which little or nothing will be said in the chapters that follow—not because of transparency but because of murkiness. There seem to be about 350,000 self-employed persons working in places outside of office buildings or consumer outlets. Though it is possible to estimate where they are in the Region, there is no real basis for determining what they are doing there.

The dynamic forces altering the Region's structure are found in the other sectors, the ones that shift location fairly independently of the shifts in homes. And the largest of these is manufacturing.

PART II

THE JOBS

2

LOCATIONAL PRESSURES ON MANUFACTURING

The New York Metropolitan Region is many things: a headquarters for business, a center for culture, a gathering place for international diplomacy, a great port. What is sometimes overlooked, however, is the fact that it is also the nation's largest industrial center and that its manufacturing workers in factories and lofts outnumber its white-collar corps of office workers.

Some 1,900,000 people hold manufacuring jobs in the Region. The industries in which they work run almost the whole range of the industrial lexicon, from airplanes to zippers. In fact, of the approximately 450 industries listed by the federal Bureau of the Census in its detailed breakdowns of the nation's manufacturing economy, some 420 appear in the New York Metropolitan Region.

The pervasive impression of the Region's manufacturing economy is one of diversity—diversity of product, of process, and of environmental needs. Yet, despite this diversity, the general locational pattern of manufacturing jobs within the Region has been changing steadily and persistently from one decade to the next. And the forces which have

Note: Earlier versions of a few passages that appear in this chapter and the three following chapters have already been published as part of a pamphlet written by one of the authors. See Raymond Vernon, *The Changing Economic Function of the Central City* (Committee for Economic Development, New York, 1959).

CHART 3

Distribution of Manufacturing Production Workers in
New York Metropolitan Region, 1869–1956

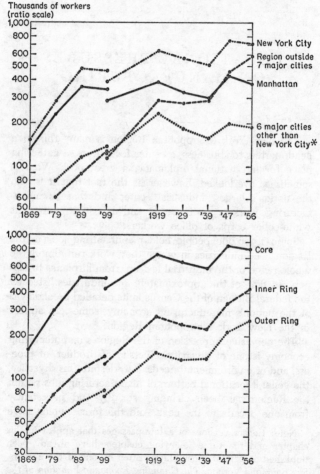

For notes and sources see foot of page 23.

produced these locational changes are not obscure. Once identified, they offer a clear lead to the pattern in which the Region's manufacturing activity is likely to be distributed in the decades ahead.

Chart 3 traces patterns of change in the location of manufacturing jobs in the Region. One characteristic predominates. Though in absolute terms there has been a considerable growth in manufacturing jobs in most parts of the Region, the oldest city centers have grown much more slowly than the other areas.

In this respect Manhattan has been conspicuous. Its industrial expansion was arrested earlier than that of the other areas of the Region. And in the period after World War II the absolute number of manufacturing jobs in Manhattan was not growing at all, but was actually shrinking. The rest of New York City, on the other hand, has managed to maintain its percentage share of the Region's manufacturing employment, throwing open its undeveloped spaces in the Bronx, Brooklyn, and Queens to accommodate the growth.

The six next largest cities of the Region after New York City have behaved more like Manhattan than like the rest of New York City; their percentage share as a group has been experiencing a long-run decline, going back 40 years or more. Old settlements like Yonkers and Newark—with little unencumbered land left for industry—have led the decline. And, like Manhattan, such areas have begun to show losses in absolute numbers in recent years, in a period when other parts of the Region have been growing rapidly.

The effect of these trends has been to shift manufacturing employment outward from the Region's center. After

---

NOTES FOR CHART 3

* Newark, Jersey City, Bridgeport, Yonkers, Paterson, and Elizabeth. Note: "Neighborhood, hand and building" industries were included before 1899 and excluded after 1899. For 1899, however, the figures were available both ways.

Source: For 1869 to 1947, U.S. *Census of Manufactures;* for 1956, data collected by state departments of labor under unemployment insurance programs, adjusted for comparability to the Census series.

1889, both the Inner and Outer Rings began to register relative increases as the Core showed a relative decline. Since then, the outward shift toward the Inner and Outer Rings has been uninterrupted and has proceeded faster than ever since the end of World War II. Of late, the construction of new plants has been overwhelmingly concentrated in the "new" areas of the Region; indeed, in the three-year period running through 1956, roughly 90 per cent of the new plants constructed in the Region, measured by value, were located outside New York City.

The history of the New York Metropolitan Region in this regard is paralleled in most major metropolitan areas in the United States. Major central cities have declined steadily as manufacturing centers of their corresponding metropolitan areas. In some cases these relative declines in the central cities have been so marked as to emulate Manhattan's pattern and to produce an absolute decline in number of jobs. In the period from 1947 to 1954, for instance, this has been the case for Boston, Philadelphia, Chicago, Detroit, Pittsburgh, St. Louis, and San Francisco. The fact that the outward shift of manufacturing jobs from big cities has been so common suggests that the underlying forces, whatever they may be, are of some general sort which is not unique to the New York Metropolitan Region and which can be expected to operate in any large metropolitan area.

For all the simplicity of the trends portrayed in Chart 3, the forces behind the trends are complex. In the first place, the shift of manufacturing within the Region takes place in a number of ways. It takes place through the decisions of manufacturers—for example, a decision to close down a city plant, or to open a suburban one, or to move a plant from city to suburb. And if a manufacturer decides to leave the Region altogether, this decision too affects the distribution of the industry as between different parts of the Region, reducing the share of the part he is vacating. But the intra-Regional shifts also take place independently of the immediate decisions of manufacturers, for the economic advantages of some localities cause existing enterprises there to grow relative to enterprises in less advantageous localities. And these differing rates of change affect each locality's share of the Region's manufacturing jobs just as surely as the migration of firms.

In the second place, whether manufacturing shifts through conscious decisions or in some other way, there are always reasons for the shift, and these reasons are usually multiple and not susceptible to precise evaluation. When a businessman chooses a site, his aim is both to increase sales and to hold down costs, that is, to generate the largest margin for the firm. When he is already operating on a site, he will tend, by and large, to grow if the site has advantages over those of firms at other locations. In one way or another, therefore, each industrial site— whether being considered by a manufacturer or already being used by him—undergoes some sort of test for its effect on such costs as labor, transportation, space, and taxes. What we see in Chart 3 is largely the outcome of that complex process of testing.

THE SEARCH FOR SPACE

Whenever a businessman who has chosen the suburbs over the city is asked to say what prompted the decision, the odds are very high that he will answer the question in terms of a "search for space." There is scarcely a survey of industrial migration in metropolitan areas which has not placed this factor high on the list of migration causes. The theme appears in the earliest accounts of industrial relocation.[1] More recent studies have stressed the same point.[2] What is more, the stress on space has not been confined to studies focused on the New York Metropolitan Region. The emphasis has been almost universal, wherever studies of the migration of plants from cities have been conducted.

There is not much doubt that the contrast in growth rates between the Region's old cities and its suburbs and open areas is a product of this perennial search. One can see a reflection of the force of this factor, for instance, in two periods—one from 1929 to 1939, the other from 1947 to 1956—when data can be had to compare the locational

behavior of growing industries in the Region with the behavior of declining industries.* As Table 3 shows, industries whose aggregate employment in the Region was growing in the 1929–1939 period showed a marked outward
shift from New York City to the Inner and Outer Rings;
by contrast, the industries whose employment was shrinking in the Region barely changed their proportion in New
York City during the ten years. Exactly the same performance was repeated in the period from 1947 to 1956.[3]
Once again New York City lost ground in the growing industries while holding its own in the shrinking ones.

There is no mystery in the tie between the search for
space and the outward shift of industry, particularly in recent decades. It has not been simply a question of finding

TABLE 3   New York City's Percentage Share of Metropolitan Area's Employment in Growing and Declining
Manufacturing Industries,[a] 1929–1939 and
1947–1956

	N.Y. Industrial Area[b] (12-county total = 100)			N.Y. Metropolitan Region (22-county total = 100)		
	1929	1939	Change in percentage points	1947	1956	Change in percentage points
Growing industries[c] ..	72.8	64.9	−7.9	46.3	38.4	−7.9
Declining industries[c] .	49.1	49.2	+0.1	48.3	51.4	+3.1

ᵃ Excludes industries in certain special categories to be discussed in
Chapter 3. This table covers industries with aggregate 1956 employment
of 1,310,000 in New York Metropolitan Region and 549,000 in New York
City.

ᵇ New York Industrial Area consists of New York City's five counties,
Westchester County in New York, and Bergen, Essex, Hudson, Middlesex,
Passaic, and Union Counties in New Jersey.

ᶜ Growing and declining industries were classified according to their
absolute change in employment in the New York Industrial Area for
1929–1939, and in the New York Metropolitan Region for 1947–1956.

Source: New York Metropolitan Region Study estimates, based
on the following: For 1929 and 1939, U.S. *Census of Manufactures.* For 1947 and 1956, data collected by state departments
of labor under unemployment insurance programs. See Appendix
A for exceptions and further details.

* Here and throughout this chapter, we have omitted certain
special industries from data on the distribution of jobs within the
Region. These special industries are discussed in the next chapter.

more factory room for more machines; such a need could be provided in many cases by adding a floor or two to existing factory structures. Rather, the structures themselves are no longer the right type. As the capacity of existing facilities has been reached, manufacturers have been faced with the question whether they could afford to hang onto outmoded structures on inadequate sites. For obsolescence has set in upon most factory structures well before the structures themselves have worn out.

The forces of obsolescence have differed somewhat for different lines of manufacture but some common features have been evident. One of the most universal changes in factory processes over the past 30 or 40 years has been the widespread introduction of continuous-material-flow systems and of automatic controls in processing. In food factories, for instance, refrigeration tunnels and bake ovens with moving floors commonly run many hundreds of feet on a straight line; often, they run longer than the normal city block.

In light of these developments, the disadvantages of operating in a less-than-ideal structure have grown rapidly. Today, the common practice in many lines of manufacture is to find a site which imposes the least possible restraints on the shape of the structure; to plan a production layout suitable for modern processes; and then to "wrap" the building around the layout. The shape of the building is determined by the process rather than vice versa. The shape and size of city block grids, therefore, have become a powerful restraint on factory location.

The effects of new processes on land requirements in recent years have been phenomenal. The extent of the change is suggested by a survey of space used in 1956 in 239 plants in the New York Metropolitan Region located outside of the old cities of the Region.[4] The pre-1922 plants stand on 1,040 square feet of plot space per worker, while the plants built from 1922 to 1945 occupy 2,000 square feet and those built after 1945 occupy 4,550 square feet of plot space per worker.[5]

Yet, the need for tailor-made structures alone is hardly enough to account for the comparatively rapid growth rates outside the cities of the New York Metropolitan Region. Not all manufacturing lines could benefit from such structures; many could do well in standard factory floor space, old or new. Besides, when the actual relocation of a plant was involved in boosting suburban growth, the plants which left their old sites were obliged to absorb large losses in connection with such a move—the junking of considerable fixed equipment, the trauma of rehiring and retraining part of the work force, the costs of developing new suppliers and subcontractors.

Added to the need for tailor-made structures were the special difficulties created by zoning in the city areas. It is true that industrial plants are commonly found in residential neighborhoods of Queens, Brooklyn, the Bronx, Jersey City, Newark, and Passaic—a heritage of the free and easy periods when zoning standards did not exist or when they bent readily under pressure. But plants in mixed neighborhoods cannot easily obtain permission to expand. Indeed, in such places as the waterfront area on the East Side of Manhattan and the Ironbound district of Newark, one now finds such plants hemmed in among housing developments, parks, and schools, hopelessly handicapped in any effort to meet expanding needs. Even where zoning problems can be overcome, there is the time-consuming and chancy task of assembling a site large enough to house a factory addition—a task difficult to achieve in most parts of the Region's old cities even with condemnation powers and almost impossible to achieve without them. In Manhattan and Newark, for instance, city blocks have typically been subdivided into small parcels, as many as 20 to the acre. Accordingly, years of patient planning are usually required for the acquisition of a site, and the developer who tries it is always haunted by the risk of being gouged by the last holdouts. Here, obviously, is one field in which a change in public policy might have a material effect on the Region's development patterns.

But there is still another difficulty in expanding within the old cities, namely, the high cost of acquiring a site, even without the complications of acquisition. If one were to attempt to locate a modern metal-working plant on a typi-

cal gridiron block in Manhattan's lower West Side, for instance, the cost of the site might be in the neighborhood
of $2,300,000 more than that for a suburban site suitable
for the same purpose.[6] In other high-density areas of the
Region besides the central business district of Manhattan,
the site situation for large firms is only slightly improved.
True, the nominal cost of land is no longer so clearly pro-
hibitive. But in some of the high-density areas the problem
of finding a site large enough to house more than 200 or
300 employees is still a bothersome one—both costly and
time-consuming.[7]

For many manufacturers in the Region, however, the
process of location has never involved the choice and assembly of a building site. Small establishments do not typically build their structures from scratch, and the Region's
industrial complexion, even since its earliest days, has been
dominated by small establishments. Indeed, even as late as
1956, about two-thirds of the Region's establishments had
fewer than 20 employees. As a rule, the only course for
such establishments is to occupy industrial space wherever
it is offered for rent by others. Yet such establishments,
too, have been appearing at a faster rate in the outlying
portions of the Region than in the old cities.

The shift of these smaller firms was in one sense an
aftermath of the shift of the larger establishments. Early in
the twentieth century, rental space for small producers
existed principally in the oldest sections of Manhattan and
of other established industrial centers of the Region. Even
today as one wanders through such sections, in narrow
streets and alleyways, he still comes upon the little manufacturing shop set up in a mellow brick structure much
older than its occupants. With the flight of time, however,
the choice of locations for the little shops has broadened.
As factories which had passed their prime were abandoned
by their original owners for newer properties, they were
offered on the rentals market. By World War I, a small
manufacturer could find significant amounts of industrial
space for rent in parts of Brooklyn and the Bronx, in Jersey
City and Newark, and in various other localities. By
World War II, the selection had widened even further.

Today, rental space can be had almost anywhere in the Region's cities. To be sure, Manhattan still harbors the greatest amount of such space, over 180 million square feet, most of it contained in loft buildings designed for manufacturing purposes. Though about half of this space is within special districts pre-empted by various garment and allied industries,* the other half is to be found in miscellaneous loft districts, available for such activities as electronics, chemicals, fabricated metal products, and so on. The space can typically be had on short lease, often only a year or two. But rentable space is also found in considerable quantity outside the crowded borough of Manhattan, located in obsolete factory buildings and sometimes in garage-type structures.

The spreading availability of rental space, therefore, has been a factor adding to the increase of industrial activity outside the old cities. And the tendency has been stimulated not only by availability but also by a difference in the level of rents. Rents in Manhattan are high; they are highest of all in the specialized apparel districts, but even outside the specialized districts, the average rent in a sample of available Manhattan lofts, as Table 4 indicates, is well above rents in other selected counties of the Region (though not much different from that of Queens and of the Nassau-Suffolk area). The existing differences contribute to other forces which we shall explore later, tending to push some manufacturing activities out of Manhattan.

There is nothing on the horizon to suggest any great future changes in the effects that the search for industrial space will have on the location of manufacturing firms. Obsolescence in factory structures is a never-ending process. As the owners find their existing sites outmoded, they will be more likely to look outward toward raw land than inward toward developed areas already encumbered by structures. In their wake will appear some of the renters, attracted by offerings of rentable space. From time to time, encumbered sites in the older industrial areas may be re-

---

* We shall have more to say about these special districts in the next chapter, in connection with our discussion of the so-called special industries of the Region.

assembled, cleared of their existing structures, and rebuilt for new industrial uses. But such "recapture" operations will not occur frequently enough to alter the general pattern.

TABLE 4   Annual Manufacturing Loft Rents in New York Metropolitan Region, 1956

	Number of offerings in sample	Cost per square foot		
		Average	Low	High
Manhattan (excluding "specialized" loft districts)	48	$.98	$.40	$1.50
Brooklyn-Bronx	55	.67	.25	1.00
Queens	39	.97	.50	1.50
Nassau-Suffolk	11	.92	.50	1.15
Bergen-Essex-Hudson	14	.78	.35	1.10
Westchester-Fairfield	11	.73	.40	1.25

Source: "Industrial For Rent" advertisements, taken from the *New York Times* and *New York Herald Tribune* at intervals during 1956, on what appeared to be roughly comparable properties. Indicated ranges were subsequently verified by local real estate experts. The term "loft," as used here, means manufacturing space in buildings with more than one tenant, whether or not the buildings were originally designed to be multi-tenanted.

Of course, the outcome could be very different with major changes in public policy. One such possibility is the launching of extensive subsidized programs in the old cities to facilitate the recapture of sites for industrial use. Such a program is conceivable, for the exodus of manufacturing jobs could eventually stir governments to take vigorous counteracting measures. But such measures could not be expected to shape the locational decisions of many manufacturers unless they involved a subsidy so great as to bring the price of the acquired land to levels much closer to those prevailing in suburban locations. In the New York Metropolitan Region this might mean making city sites available for industrial development at $20,000 or $30,000 an acre even though the cost of acquisition and demolition could be expected to run at many times that figure whenever the land was encumbered by existing structures.

A plan to recapture industrial sites for the building of
new structures for small industrial renters would face
greater difficulties still. In the New York Metropolitan Region, the going rate for industrial rentals is so low that a
developer could not recapture the cost of the structure
alone, even if he received the building site free of cost.
For the going price of industrial space is determined in
part by the availability of a pool of depreciated buildings
outgrown by their original occupants.[8]

Our working assumption is, therefore, that the industrial
redevelopment of old sites will not be a major force in
shaping the future distribution of jobs in the Region.

FROM RIVER TO RAIL TO RUBBER

The search for space, whether in 1860 or 1960, has always been conditioned by the manufacturer's need to assemble his materials and distribute his goods at reasonable
cost. If the railroad and the truck had never been invented,
America's manufacturing centers would have developed
very differently. Great multistoried factories would probably have lined the nation's riverbanks in order to hold down
transport costs.

Indeed, something like this pattern seemed to be emerging in the New York Metropolitan Region some 75 or 100
years ago. At that time, the Manhattan shores of the Hudson River and the East River were lined with shipbuilding,
slaughtering, grease-rendering, and soap-making plants,
with iron works, engine works, and plants of many other
kinds. The Brooklyn shore of the East River and of its
tributary, Newtown Creek, were already beginning to be
crowded with chemical and paint factories, and later with
petroleum refining plants. In Newark, the banks of the old
Morris Canal bore an array of tanneries and leather-
product plants. Yonkers and Poughkeepsie kept their industry alongside the historic Hudson, and Bridgeport's factories clung to Long Island Sound and its inlets.

Up to that time the railroads had not reduced this water
orientation very much. Their routes on the eastern seaboard were laid out to serve the existing nuclei, not to open

new territory. Accordingly, the main lines converged on the New York harbor; among others, the New York Central and the Erie Railroad came in from the north and the west, the Pennsylvania Railroad from the west and the south, and the New York, New Haven & Hartford from the northeast.

But the railroads did not stop with the development of their main lines; soon they pushed spurs in all directions. Rail facilities became available in areas not directly abutting the main lines, and most of the larger plants were supplied with them. Table 5, based on a survey of 476 existing plants in the Region (practically all of them outside New York City), shows that 63 per cent of the plants erected prior to 1920 possessed rail sidings.

TABLE 5   Percentage of Plant Sites Having Railroad Sidings, New York Metropolitan Region, 1956

Year site acquired	Entire Region	New Jersey counties	Rest of Region
Prior to 1920	63	71	50
1920–1945	50	59	39
1946–1956	40	42	36

Source: Questionnaire replies from 476 manufacturing plants, practically all of them outside of New York City. Of the 476, those which acquired their present sites prior to 1920 numbered 120 (76 in N.J. and 44 elsewhere in Region); those which acquired them between 1920 and 1945 numbered 160 (90 in N.J. and 70 elsewhere); and those which acquired them after 1945 numbered 196 (123 in N.J. and 73 elsewhere).

The advent and spread of railroad spurs in the Region had two major effects on the location of plants: plants were freed from waterside locations and were allowed to spread out from the old cities into the surrounding towns; and the New Jersey side of the Region obtained a major transport advantage over the New York side. A glance at Map 4 (map insert) will show why the latter effect developed. The Hudson River lies as a formidable barrier between most of the New York counties of the Region and the nation's markets or materials to the west. Accordingly, nine intercity railroad lines terminate on the New Jersey side but only three can be found on the island of Manhattan and on Long Island.

To be sure, heroic efforts were made to link the islands on the New York side to the mainland. An elaborate car-float system was developed to ferry rail cars between New Jersey and other points in the harbor area. But the carfloat service, ingenious and extensive though it might be, was still time-consuming. A carload originating in Mineola for delivery in the West, for example, would be transferred from point to point, classified and reclassified before it ever reached the New York harbor. Then it would be shunted onto a float with other cars bound for the same rail termi-nal in New Jersey, pushed across the harbor to the termi-nal, removed from the float, and switched about until assembled in a train going west. All this could take two or three days; or it could take longer.

On top of this, there was no getting over the fact that New Jersey was nearer to the rest of the nation than was Long Island. The island stretches a hundred miles eastward from New York harbor, and a manufacturer shipping his goods to a national market had to move them part of that length. The difference did not seem overwhelming in in-dividual products; the rate from Mineola in Nassau County to a Midwest point like St. Louis, for instance, was typi-cally only a few mills higher per pound than the rate paid by a competitor in New Brunswick, New Jersey. But dif-ferences of this sort could constitute a real competitive handicap for bulky goods.

In any case, plants which needed rail connections in the pre-truck era tended to favor New Jersey. Table 5 shows that plants located in New Jersey in the pre-1920 period were more commonly served with rail facilities than those located in the rest of the Region. This advantage must have been one of the main forces which spurred the rapid growth of the New Jersey side of the Region in that era. Between 1899 and 1919, New Jersey's manufacturing em-ployment grew from 20 per cent of the Region's total to 33 per cent.

Then came the truck. Beginning about 1920, as this new mode began to be adopted for haulage inside the large metropolitan areas, additional forces favoring the newer areas were set in motion. Now a quicker and more flexible means existed for moving bulky goods for short distances, reducing the disadvantage of settling away from the railroad lines and harbor piers. In this period, one began to see the erection of factories without rail connections, a trend which accelerated abruptly as intercity truck haulage took hold. For plants acquiring sites in the Region from 1920 on, as Table 5 shows, rail connections declined sharply in relative importance.

Motor transport had a double-barreled impact in pushing industry out of the cities of the Region. Not only did it offer a new freedom to the manufacturer in selecting a site but it accentuated the disadvantages of the obsolescent street layout of the cities by aggravating the problems of traffic congestion. To be sure, as early as the Civil War period, the crossing of Broadway at Fulton Street had been considered a risky enterprise. And fifty or sixty years ago, as contemporary photographs attest, the streets of downtown New York and downtown Brooklyn were sometimes strangled with drays, carts, trolleys, and rigs. But the automobile added new dimensions to the problem. It diverted traffic from buses and trolleys to smaller vehicles occupying much more space per passenger; and it brought some of the subway traffic onto the surface. As a result, traffic congestion spread beyond the old bottleneck points and became more general, especially in Manhattan's central business district. Between 1924 and 1956, the number of automobiles entering the district on a typical day tripled in number, though truck traffic rose only 50 per cent in the same period.[9] It does not strain the credulity too much to assume that the influx of automobiles crowded the central business district to the point of forcing the trucks to avoid this area if they could.

At the same time, motor transport began to redress the imbalance between New Jersey and New York which the railroad had induced. To be sure, it could not change the fact that New Brunswick's distance from St. Louis was less than Mineola's. But manufacturers serving national markets by truck were far less concerned at having to cross the

Hudson River than if they had been reliant on rail. Accordingly, New Jersey's early transport advantage was reduced. From 1919 to 1956, manufacturing employment on the New York side of the Region displayed a rate of growth which almost matched that of New Jersey. Excluding the two already-developed Core counties of Manhattan and Hudson, the New York counties had a growth rate of 55 per cent in manufacturing employment, compared with 56 in the New Jersey counties.

In the latest portion of that period, from 1947 to 1956, it is possible to trace the record of different segments of industry in some detail. Accordingly, one can isolate and examine the distribution pattern of a group of industries especially sensitive to transportation considerations—those that ship a low-value product extensively to markets outside the Region. In 1947 the New Jersey counties had about 48 per cent of the Region's employment in this group of industries, but by 1956 this percentage had declined to 45. On the other hand, Nassau and Suffolk Counties managed to increase their share of such industries in the Region from 2.0 per cent to 5.0 per cent during the same period, as if to underline the point that their transportation handicap may be less significant than it once was. Table 6 shows the distribution of these industries in the Region on the later date.

There are some industries in the New York Metropolitan Region, however, whose major transportation problem is not that of shipping to far-flung national markets but simply that of distributing their output to local consumers. The modern transport revolution has had rather a different impact on this group of manufacturers than upon those shipping to national markets.

The industries which ship to local consumers are a familiar group; they include such establishments as newspapers, bakeries, breweries, bottling works, and milk plants. Their distribution problem typically has two aspects: deliveries must be closely timed at the peril of missing sales; and the cost of transport must be held to a minimum because of the comparatively low value of the delivered product.

As a consequence, these industries have sought out comparatively central locations in the Region. The main newspaper plants are found well down in the city centers. The plant of the *New York Daily News*, which has the largest circulation in the Region, sits at 42nd Street and Second Avenue in midtown Manhattan; the *New York Times* is found on 43rd Street near Times Square; the *New York Herald Tribune* on 41st Street near Eighth Avenue; and the *Newark News* on Market Street in downtown Newark.

The principal bakeries, breweries, and bottling works of the Region, though influenced by locational forces not unlike those of the newspapers, have developed on a somewhat different pattern. The market for bread, beer, or soft drinks is less highly concentrated at the center of the Region than the newsstands and rail stations to which newspapers need access. Accordingly, these plants are not quite so tightly tied to the Core of the Region, though their search for a least-cost point of distribution still makes the Core a relatively attractive location.

As Table 6 shows, about 63 per cent of the Region's employment in these industries serving local consumers was located in New York City in 1956, a concentration significantly higher than that for manufacturing as a whole.

Because the distribution problem of these industries is so different from that of the national-market industries, their response to the advent of the motor vehicle has differed in some respects. For one thing, they have not been so free to escape the Region's center, for the obvious reasons that the center of an area, generally speaking, is the least-cost point from which distribution can be made. Nonetheless, even these industries, though seemingly locked to a central point, have shown a tendency to move outward in recent years. New York City's share of the Region's total, 63 per cent in 1956, had been even higher—70 per cent—nine years earlier. One reason for the outward shift is that consumers are gradually spreading out from the center of the Region. Another reason, it is now becoming evident, is that, after all, the center of the Region is not always the least-cost point for distribution, because the center is more highly congested than the surrounding market areas.

TABLE 6 Distribution of National-Market and Local-Market Manufacturing Industries[a] in New York Metropolitan Region, 1956

		Percentage shares of Region's employment (NYMR = 100)				
	Number of employees (thousands)	New York City	Nassau and Suffolk	Other New York counties	New Jersey counties	Fairfield County, Conn.
National-market industries, total[b]	830	33.8	8.9	6.8	41.3	9.2
Those manufacturing products of:						
Low value[c]	104	39.9	5.0	6.0	44.8	4.3
Medium value[c] .	449	29.4	2.6	9.7	47.3	11.0
High value[c]	277	38.8	20.5	2.5	30.3	7.9
Local-market industries, total[b]	261	50.6	2.0	4.7	39.8	2.9
Those manufacturing products for:						
Consumers	109	62.7	2.2	4.2	27.9	3.0
Other producers .	152	41.9	1.8	5.1	48.3	2.9

[a] Excludes industries in certain special categories to be discussed in Chapter 3. Also omits many other industries for lack of sufficient information, but the aggregate employment of these was relatively small.
[b] National-market industries ship one-half or more of their products (by weight) outside the Region; local-market industries less than half.
[c] Low-value products are those valued at less than $0.50 per pound; medium value, $0.50 to $1.99; high value, $2.00 or over.

Source: Our estimates, based on employment data collected by state departments of labor under unemployment insurance programs (further details in Appendix A, Part II), and on a transportation survey conducted by Benjamin Chinitz of the New York Metropolitan Region Study.

Two recent relocations of large bakeries in the Region illustrate the pattern. In one case, the firm determined that its best distribution point was the New Jersey end of the George Washington Bridge and, accordingly, settled within a few miles of that point. In the other, the plant was relocated in eastern Queens. In both cases, the plants were responding to the diffusion of population and to the advantages of escaping the nub of high congestion down in the center of the Region. With a location outside the nub, such plants avoid the need to start each delivery trip from the place of worst congestion, an advantage of considerable importance when serving their markets outside the nub.

So much for local-market industries catering to consumers. Table 6 also gives the distribution of local-market industries which sell all or a considerable part of their product to other manufacturers rather than to final consumers. This group presents a distribution pattern quite different from the newspapers, bakeries, and other plants which make up the consumer-oriented group. In delivering to other producers, speed of delivery measured in fractions of an hour is not usually of the essence. As might be expected, therefore, these producers do not have as much affinity for a central location in the Region as those who cater to final consumers. They are found throughout the Region, concentrating more in New Jersey—and less in New York City—than the consumer group.

To generalize about the effects of the transportation revolution upon the New York Metropolitan Region's manufacturing industries is to blur important distinctions and to sacrifice critical detail. Yet one may say that, after the first stage of railroad-building in the Region, the impact of later developments of rail and rubber has been little by little to reduce the advantages which one locality in the Region enjoyed over another. For various reasons, these advantages are likely to decline further in the decades ahead. The introduction of circumferential high-speed highways, which are a feature of the long-run federal highway program, will contribute to this result. So will the growth of piggy-back rail freight—the movement of truck trailers on rail cars, to carry goods from one city to another—which will extend some of the advantages of rail traffic to any point that a truck can reach. The growth of air freight, which is about equally available in most parts of the Region, should also tend to reduce transportation differences in the Region. Developments of this sort can never entirely overcome the disadvantages which handicap the eastern side of the Region in serving national markets, but they are bound to reduce those disadvantages somewhat.

All told, these transportation developments should continue to favor growth in the outer portions of the Region, as industry is pushed by congestion at the center and pulled by the search for added space. This does not mean that congestion is expected to increase very considerably at the Region's center. If jobs should decline in such areas as New York City and Newark in the future—a possibility not to be ruled out—this might tend to hold down the added congestion which the continued spread in car ownership would otherwise bring. But during some decades to come a differential in congestion still will exist between the old areas and the new—between Jersey City and Somerset County, for instance, and between Bridgeport and its Connecticut hinterland. As the search for space continues, the search will inevitably move outward to exploit the new locational freedom which the truck, the airplane, and piggy-back freight have afforded.

THE ROLE OF LABOR

Labor considerations once played a sizable role in the shifting of industry within the New York Metropolitan Region. For it was not long ago that marked differences existed both in the supply and price of labor in different parts of the Region.

Sixty or seventy years ago, rapid transit facilities were not well developed; automobiles were not yet in use; women—the "secondary labor force"—were not accustomed to travel very far from home for their job opportunities. With job opportunities centered at the Region's Core at the time, there is not much doubt that wages were substantially higher in New York City than in the other counties, particularly those at the edges of the Region. Table 7 shows, for instance, that in 1899, production workers in the Outer Ring received, on the average, only 84 per cent of the annual pay of workers in Manhattan, and that the figure was progressively higher for points closer to Manhattan. Differences of this sort, of course, were not due purely to differences in wage rates for comparable jobs; perhaps as important in creating the differences was the fact that the industry "mix" at the center of the Region was so much different from that at the periphery. Yet wage levels must also have played a part.

At one time, therefore, many industries in the Core probably had a real wage incentive for shifting outward toward the Rings. Even in 1947, such wage differences lingered in some industries. But 1947 saw the beginning of the end; between that date and 1955, the remaining differences were sharply reduced. Hourly earnings in breweries, which had been 12 per cent lower in the Rings than in the Core in 1947, were only 2 per cent lower in 1955; in commercial printing the difference narrowed from 5 per cent to 1 per cent; in handbags and purses, from 33 to 18; in women's dresses, from 16 to 7; in women's underwear and nightwear, from 19 to 9; and so on. To be sure, the narrowing was not perfectly uniform; but it is clear that the dominant tendency in the period was to reduce wage differentials that might favor the Rings.

TABLE 7   Average Annual Earnings of Manufacturing Production Workers in Zones of New York Metropolitan Region as a Percentage of Wages in Manhattan, Selected Years, 1899–1954

(Manhattan = 100)

	1899	1919	1929	1939	1947	1954
Core (excluding Manhattan)	93.0	93.2	88.0	96.1	91.7	105.2
Inner Ring	88.7	90.4	83.2	96.3	96.8	120.9
Outer Ring	83.5	87.0	78.0	89.2	92.4	117.5

Source: Calculated from U.S. *Census of Manufactures* for each year shown.

Yet, for all the recent narrowing, the differentials that remain in some industries are fairly significant. The figures in Table 8 compare New York City's hourly earnings with those of the rest of the Region in a number of industries in 1955. Though there is no clear pattern of large or persistent differentials in favor of one area over the other, these figures show the outlying counties well under New York City in several of the apparel industries.

It is conceivable that this seeming differential might still attract some plants from New York City locations to the periphery, but the assumption may be a trifle dangerous. For, if the figures in Table 8 suggest anything about earnings and location in the New York Metropolitan Region, they indicate that earnings in an industry tend to be higher where that industry is concentrated and lower where the industry is sparse. Thus, if one investigates the location of the fourteen industries in Table 8 which had higher wages in New York City than in the rest of the Region, he finds that New York City contained 69 per cent of their employment in the Region. By contrast, in the nine industries with comparatively low wages in New York City, only 43 per cent of their employment was found there. Wage levels, therefore, seem to be a consequence rather than a cause of location in the Region.

But this is not the whole story as regards the impact of labor costs on the Region's development. What the figures in Table 8 do not show is that certain types of labor are to

TABLE 8   Hourly Earnings in New York Metropolitan Region Outside New York City as a Percentage of Earnings in New York City, Selected Manufacturing Industries, 1955

(New York City = 100)

Handbags and purses	82.2	Malt liquors	98.2
Women's suits and coats[a]	84.9	Shipbuilding and repairing	98.3
Blouses and waists	89.0	Commercial printing	99.2
Knit outerwear	89.3	Metal stampings	100.0
Men's dress shirts and nightwear	90.8	Machinery, except electrical[a]	100.5
Women's underwear and nightwear	91.2	Machine tool accessories[a]	101.2
		Paperboard boxes	105.7
Children's dresses	92.7	Confectionery	106.6
Women's dresses[a]	93.0	Toilet preparations	108.9
Radios and related products	94.9	Paints and varnishes	109.5
Corsets and allied garments	97.4	Pharmaceutical preparations	112.3
Bread and other bakery products	97.5	Tin cans and other tinware	116.3
		Lighting fixtures	117.1

[a] These figures are based upon wage rates for selected occupations in New York City and in labor markets of the Region outside New York City for which such rates are available; in these cases, the weights ascribed to each occupation were the same for New York City and the other markets. For other industries, the figures shown are average hourly earnings.

Source: Published and unpublished data of U.S. Bureau of Labor Statistics and N.Y. State Dept. of Labor.

be had only in certain limited areas of the Region. There are some industries in the Region which employ unskilled labor at wages somewhat below those prevailing in other industries and which accept the consequences of high turn-over and absenteeism. Most plants of this sort are found in the low-priced apparel and accessory lines, in inexpensive toy production, or in the least exacting electronic lines; but now and then they are found in other industries as well.

Plants of this sort are attracted, on the whole, to the Core counties. This is the case partly because the people on whom they draw for their labor force tend to settle in the Core, crowding the run-down brownstones and tenements which are available there. Though some plants of this sort are found from time to time in the Inner and Outer Rings, the penalty of locating there is the constant need to recruit a work force as the former recruits drift off in pursuit of higher-paying jobs. It is only at the outermost fringes of the Outer Ring—for example in portions of Orange and Dutchess Counties and in Monmouth County—that the labor force is somewhat isolated; here, it is possible for small plants, paying wages somewhat lower than those in the Core and Inner Ring, to live in comparative isolation with a work force which for the time being is tied to the plant. But by and large the plants which pay wages below the prevailing norms of the New York Metropolitan Region are held by that fact to the congested low-income portions of the Region.

Another problem of labor supply which has an influence on plant location relates to installations with a considerable research complement. Research establishments cannot easily be identified in the available census statistics, but, apart from testing laboratories and other establishments which provide "research" service on short notice, it is evident that research facilities exhibit a heavy preference for suburban locations. In some 1100 industrial research laboratories in the New York Metropolitan Region that were covered in a nation-wide survey by the National Academy of Sciences in 1955, about 84 per cent of the employment was located outside New York City. This preference has various nonlabor causes, such as the desire to

avoid impure air, but it is also due to the locational proclivities of the scientists who constitute the key personnel.
For reasons which the sociologist may one day illuminate,
such personnel tend to shun plants located in the center of
the Region. And this is one of the reasons why the principal research laboratories of the Region are found in the
Inner and Outer Rings—in suburban places like Nutley,
Bound Brook, Summit, White Plains, New Rochelle, Mineola, and Hicksville.

Labor considerations operate in still another dimension
to influence the Region's industrial development. We have
already seen that certain industries are pulled to one portion or another of the Region by compelling needs which
have nothing to do with labor, like needs for adequate
transportation or for space. The result is that some parts of
the Region have come to specialize in industries of a given
type, and, where this is the case, the wage patterns of
these dominant industries color the wages of the other
plants in the vicinity. The heavily industrialized area which
surrounds the waters of Newark Bay and Raritan Bay and
their connecting waterways, for instance, contains a large
number of chemical and petroleum refining plants while
the Nassau-Suffolk complex is dominated by a few aircraft
plants. Since these industries, on the whole, tend to pay
high wages, other plants in these areas are under heavy
pressure to pay high wages as well. Firms which cannot
afford to be as insensitive to their wage bills as the dominant industries in these high-wage areas, therefore, are
disposed to pass these areas by.

The strength of this force was already suggested as we
examined the figures in Table 7, showing the average wage
paid to production workers in different zones of the Region
without adjustment for differences in industry type. The
1954 figures reflect the impact of the high-wage aircraft
industry in Nassau, Suffolk, and Bergen, which sets a high
pattern of earnings for those counties, while Hudson, Middlesex, Union, and Richmond, where chemical and petroleum industries dominate, show similarly high over-all
earnings. On the other hand, the more diversified industry
in Manhattan, Brooklyn, Queens, and the Bronx produces a

lower average earnings level for those parts of the Region.

All in all, however, it is doubtful that wage differences will play much of a role in the future shift of industry within the New York Metropolitan Region. Here and there, individual manufacturers may find some isolated community in Orange or Somerset County where a reserve of wives and daughters can be brought into the labor market at comparatively low wages. A plant may cling to the central city for similar reasons—because of the availability in some neighborhoods of a group of Puerto Rican or Negro women who have not yet acquired the mobility or skills to command a higher wage. At some points, too, industrial location may continue to be influenced by the industry mix—by the fact that the establishments in the neighborhood consist primarily of high-wage industries like chemical plants or refineries which pay a prevailing wage so high as to affect the pay scales of other plants nearby. But these forces are not likely to be of much importance in the total locational pattern.

THE SPREAD OF EXTERNAL ECONOMIES

Once or twice in our discussion so far we have felt impelled to make a distinction between the needs of small establishments and those of larger ones. Small plants, we noted, were sometimes obliged to share buildings with others and to confine their search for a location to areas where fractional space was being offered for rent. The same distinction could have been made in other contexts. Time and again we find that small plants are held in the more crowded portions of the Region in order to share in some essential product or service—that they depend, in short, upon the "external economies" of these crowded portions, the economies that a firm can obtain through the use of facilities or services "external" to itself.

As a result, industries whose plants are typically small tend to have a higher proportion of their employment in the Core than do industries whose establishments are typically large. Table 9 shows, for instance, that the Core has more than half of the Region's employment in industries with 60 employees per plant or less. On the other hand, in industries with plants averaging 240 or more employees, less than 8 per cent of the Region's employment is in the Core.

Another point, a point to be distinguished carefully from the first, is that *within* any given industry the smaller establishments tend to be pulled toward the crowded areas much more strongly than their larger competitors. This is not to say that small establishments are wholly absent in suburban or rural locations in the New York Metropolitan Region. A great many small establishments exist everywhere in the Region. But, by and large, size is closely related to the affinity for the central areas.

The extent of this second tendency may be illustrated in various ways. If we look at the 101 industry groups in the Region for which comparisons can be made in 1956,*

TABLE 9   Distribution of Manufacturing Jobs in Zones of New York Metropolitan Region by Size of Plants, 1956

| | | Percentage shares of Region's employment (NYMR = 100) | | |
	Number of employees (thousands)	Core[a]	Inner Ring[a]	Outer Ring
All industries covered by table[b]	1,310.4	49.6	32.0	18.4
Industries with average establishments of:				
60 or less employees	734.6	61.2	24.7	14.1
61 to 240 employees	435.3	43.3	37.2	19.5
More than 240 employees	140.5	7.7	54.1	38.2

[a] In this case Richmond is included in Core instead of Inner Ring.
[b] Excludes industries in certain special categories to be discussed in Chapter 3. Also excludes establishments with less than 4 employees.

Source: Our estimates, based on data collected by state departments of labor under unemployment insurance programs. Further details in Appendix A.

* Again, we exclude the special categories to be discussed in the next chapter. In all, there were about 140 industry groups in the Region in 1954. These are so-called "three-digit" industries, broader in scope than the 400-odd industries ("four-digits") mentioned at the outset of this chapter.

we find that in 83 of them, the average plant in New York City was considerably smaller than the average plant outside the city.[10] Even if the same kind of industry existed in equal proportions both in New York City and in the outside counties, the tendency for smaller plants to locate in the former would still persist.[11]

The tie between small plants and central locations arises partly from pull, partly from push—the pull of small plants to high-density areas and the push of large plants from them.[12] The pull of small plants, as we have already indicated, stems mainly from the wisdom of sharing certain facilities with others. One reason why small plants often follow this course is that they cannot take on certain costs —such as the salary of a full-time electrician, the purchase and operation of a delivery truck, or the purchase of a heavy-duty lathe—because they are unable to utilize these production factors at a high enough rate of capacity. If the small firm assumed the burden of such factors, therefore, its unit production costs would be higher than that of its larger competitors and might force it out of business.

Many small plants in the New York Metropolitan Region pursue an obvious alternative, an alternative much more readily available in the denser areas of the Region than at its far-flung periphery. Such plants commonly find outside establishments which specialize in one phase or another of the contemplated production process and which are in a position to act as processors or suppliers. In the end, the price paid by the small firm for such subcontracting operations and supply operations may not differ very much from the cost of the same process borne by its larger competitors who make the products or provide the services for themselves.

One must not assume from this discussion that small businessmen are always successful in matching the cost structure of their larger competitors by these means. The process, as we see it, is one in which persons aspiring to go into production on a small scale have found themselves less obviously barred by a high cost structure at the center of the urban area than at the periphery.[13] In the end, of course, the smaller entrants may not quite achieve a competitive position. Despite the efficiencies of their subcontractors, they may still have to bear a higher cost structure than their larger competitors and may soon be pushed to the wall. In fact, a few scraps of data suggest that something like this process may continually be going on. For instance, calculations made for the late 1920's and the 1930's showed that new firms were springing up and being wiped out in the principal cities of 33 industrial areas at about twice the rate at which they were appearing and disappearing in the periphery of these areas.[14] But, at any given point of time, these new firms—whether or not they are destined to survive—constitute a significant proportion of the plants located in the Region's denser areas.

The problem of sharing certain pieces of capital or labor would not pull small firms so strongly toward the center of the Region, were it not for the second critical feature of the small establishment—its exposure to greater uncertainties in sales and production than those confronting its larger competitor in the same line.[15] Of course all producers, large and small, are faced with certain planning problems which involve uncertainties. On the selling side, they must forecast the volume of orders they are likely to receive; on the production side, they must consider a number of things —such as the time when their scheduled materials are likely to arrive, the rate of labor absenteeism they are likely to face, the rate of "down-time" their machinery is likely to register, the rate of spoilage in production. If the large producer has 100 customers and the small producer has 10, the large producer is likely to be more accurate in his sales forecast; if the large producer has 100 workers instead of 10, he will make a better forecast on absenteeism; if he has ten machines instead of two, he will probably predict his down-time rate more accurately.

Small plants have done their best to meet this inherent competitive handicap by locating in areas where sudden needs could be easily met from sources outside the plant. To avoid stockpiling their materials in disproportionately large amounts, they have clung close to the center of the urban cluster, where they can get materials on short notice; to meet the problems of labor force variation or machine breakdowns, they have chosen locations where they can recruit workers for brief periods or on short notice. They have chosen loft space, short-run in commitment and flexible in size, in preference to the separate factory building away from the urban center. In sum, the denser areas of the New York Metropolitan Region are acting as a common pool for space, materials, and labor, meeting the inherent uncertainties of the small plants which occupy those areas.

Considerations of this sort, of course, bind industries with small plants to the congested parts of the Region more strongly than they bind industries with large plants. One finds, as a consequence, that the small-plant industries have been tending to shift out of New York City more slowly than the large-plant industries. Table 10 shows, for instance, that between 1900 and 1922, New York City's share of small-plant industries declined by 9.3 per cent, while the corresponding drop for large-plant industries was 14.8 per cent.[16] The same trend is even more clearly evident in the 1947–1956 period.

Only during the depression interval, 1929 to 1939, does a different pattern appear. But the underlying data show that if industries with shrinking employment in the Region had been omitted from the table, the dispersion pattern would have been the same as in the other periods. In the expanding group, New York City's share of both large-plant and small-plant industries was declining, and its share of large-plant industries was declining faster than its share of small-plant industries.

Yet, one cannot overlook the fact that small-plant industries have shared in the outward shift. Indeed, in the years 1947–1954, Manhattan suffered an absolute decline in the number of its small plants; in this period, the number of manufacturing establishments in Manhattan with less than 20 employees fell from about 19,300 to 18,500.[17] Every other county in the Region meanwhile increased the number of its small establishments, with Bergen County and Nassau County showing especially large increases.

What lies behind this exodus? The answer is found in the spread of the Region's external economies from the old

cities to the smaller towns, the suburbs, and the open land
of the Region. Rentable manufacturing space, we pointed
out earlier, is being offered to smaller plants over a growing area. Repairmen and subcontractors, for a considerable
range of services, are now found almost anywhere in the
Region. Sewage, fire protection, police protection, adequate
power, and adequate trucking services also are penetrating
the undeveloped open spaces between the old cities. The
early city monopolies—their ability uniquely to provide an
environment in which small plants may settle—are being

TABLE 10   New York City's Percentage Share of
New York Metropolitan Region's Employment in
Small-Plant and Large-Plant Manufacturing
Industries,[a] Selected Periods

	Small-plant industries[b]		Large-plant industries[b]	
	City's share	Per cent change in share	City's share	Per cent change in share
1900	75.6		40.5	
1922	68.6	} −9.3	34.5	} −14.8
1929[c]	66.3		34.3	
1939[c]	63.0	} −5.0	36.8	} +7.3
1947	58.4		31.6	
1956	55.4	} −5.1	25.9	} −18.0

a Excludes industries in certain special categories to be discussed in
Chapter 3. This table, for the 1947–1956 period, covers the same group
of industries as Tables 3 and 9, having 1,310,000 employees in the Region
in 1956. For the earlier periods, we approximated these same industries,
though they were classified differently.

b For 1900–1922, small-plant industries are those averaging less than
35 employees per establishment, and large-plant industries 35 or over.
For 1929–1939 and 1947–1956 the dividing line is 60 employees. For 1947–
1956, establishments with less than 4 employees are not included in the
averages.

c 1929 and 1939 figures show the City's ratio to the 12-county New
York Industrial Area (defined in Table 3) rather than the 22-county
Region.

Source: Our estimates, based on the following: For 1900–
1922, Committee on Regional Plan of New York and Its Environs,
Regional Survey of New York and Its Environs, Vols. 1A and
1B (New York, 1928). For 1929 and 1939, U.S. *Census of Manufactures*. For 1947 and 1956, data collected by state departments
of labor under unemployment insurance programs. See Appendix
A for exceptions and further details.

broken. And in time small plants will have almost as wide a geographical choice as their larger competitors in selecting a site for their activities in the Region.

THE FLIGHT FROM TAXES

We come at last to the final factor in our roster of major locational forces, namely, local and state taxes. This is a subject steeped in pure emotion and impure data, one whose importance is not measured by the statistician's yardsticks or the economist's models.

To begin with, any appraisal of the locational implications of differences in local and state tax levels has to be done in recognition of the fact that the businessman commonly reacts somewhat differently to the subject of taxes than he does to other business costs. For one thing, it is not only the *level* of taxes with which the businessman is concerned, but also their *form*. Taxes conjure up ideological and political images of the community involved. Accordingly the businessman may regard the structure and level of state and local taxes as an index of the balance of political power—as a measure of the community's responsiveness or hostility to business.

For example, most businessmen would apparently prefer to pay their taxes in the form of levies on real property, that is, on land and buildings, rather than in the form of a corporate income tax. This is the case partly because an increase in a corporate income tax is more difficult to resist than an increase in a property tax; a proposed rise in corporate taxes would have to be fought primarily by business interests, while a proposed rise in a tax on real property might also meet with resistance from other groups in the community. In addition, a corporation tax imposes a tax levy roughly proportionate to the future growth of an enterprise, while a property tax need not rise proportionately with the firm's profits.

Until 1958, when New Jersey introduced a state corporate income tax, business taxes in the nine New Jersey counties of the Region were based predominantly on property—not only land and buildings but also "personal property," including machinery and inventories. In the twelve New York counties, on the other hand, manufacturers pay no tax on personal property but do pay a corporate income tax to the state. In New York City they also pay a tax on gross receipts, thus giving the city a corporate tax structure that has no counterpart elsewhere in the Region. Finally, in the one Connecticut county, Fairfield, the taxing system is different still, combining elements found in New Jersey and New York.

It is clear from extensive field interviews that, until the 1958 change, businessmen commonly viewed the absence of a corporate income tax in New Jersey as an indication of a more benign business climate than that in New York State—this quite apart from the relative level of taxes in the two states. On the other hand, there was also a clear aversion for the arbitrariness with which local authorities could and did assess personal property—a problem especially acute in New Jersey.[18] Finally, there was a widespread distaste for the paper work associated with New York City's gross receipts tax—this quite apart from the cost. All told, then, New York City emerged as one of the less attractive areas in the Region in these terms, though some New Jersey localities whose history is associated with tax corruption shared its position. Those localities aside, the rest of the New Jersey portion of the Region tended on the whole to appear more attractive to the businessman who was concerned with the form of his taxes than did the rest of the New York State portion.

So much for tax *form*. What about tax *level?* It is out of the question to attempt to reconstruct the trends in tax levels for different parts of the Region over any long time span. For reasons which Appendix F makes apparent, any such effort would likely be spurious. But, with considerable difficulty, some reasonably reliable indicators of the levels of state and local taxes at various points in the New York Metropolitan Region have been developed as of 1955. These measures are based on a sample of 25 manufacturing firms actually operating in the Region. For each of these firms we calculated what the taxes would have been at each of 64 selected localities in the Region; and from these calculations we constructed an index reflecting the "typical" tax level for manufacturing plants at each of the 64 locations.*

The resulting figures, shown in Table 11, establish the fact that there is little difference in the over-all average level of taxes at the New Jersey locations as compared with those in the New York locations. However, tax levels at the large city locations in the Region tend, on the whole, to be significantly higher than those in other portions of the Region. Taxes in the two leading New Jersey cities are higher than in New York City, although elsewhere in New Jersey they average lower than elsewhere in New York State. Once more, therefore, the old cities are handicapped relative to the rest of the Region.

TABLE 11   Local and State Tax Levels of Manufacturers in Various Parts of New York Metropolitan Region, 1955

(Average for 25 selected firms, placed hypothetically at 64 locations, equals 100 per cent)

Average at 29 New York State locations	103.3%
Manhattan	129.6
Bronx, Brooklyn, Queens	122.3
Other 25 locations	99.9
Average at 31 New Jersey locations	96.2
Newark	140.6
Jersey City	160.1
Other 29 locations	92.5
Average at 4 Connecticut locations	119.5
Bridgeport	133.8
Other 3 locations	114.7

Source: Survey by New York Metropolitan Region Study. See Appendix F for rankings of the 64 locations and other details.

But these averages submerge some important differences which are of relevance to the individual firm. Because of the differences in state and local tax structures among the states—particularly because of the fact that New York State depends heavily on a corporate income tax, while New Jersey still depends largely on property taxes—New

* See Appendix F for a discussion of methods used. The only significant taxes omitted from the calculations were workmen's compensation taxes.

York State tends to be the more attractive location for establishments with low profits relative to their property, while New Jersey tends to be the more attractive for establishments with high profits relative to their property. The strength of this tendency in 1955 is illustrated by the data in Table 12, which classifies the 25 firms in our tax study according to the ratio of net profit to property, and shows their hypothetical tax levels in various geographical areas.

TABLE 12 Local and State Tax Levels of Manufacturers in New York Metropolitan Region as Affected by Differences in Financial Structure, 1955

(Average for 25 selected firms, placed hypothetically at 64 locations, equals 100 per cent)

	Firms with ratio of net profit to real and personal property of:			
	30% and over	20 to 29.9%	10 to 19.9%	0 to 9.9%
New York State locations				
5 boroughs of N.Y. City	152.2%	125.5%	111.3%	104.0%
24 other locations	128.1	102.5	91.7	83.2
New Jersey locations				
4 cities over 100,000[a]	90.0	120.9	137.7	140.7
27 other locations	67.5	89.7	98.2	106.2
Connecticut locations				
Bridgeport	138.7	131.3	138.7	132.5
3 other locations	123.5	113.1	115.2	111.9

[a] Newark, Jersey City, Paterson, and Elizabeth.

Source: Survey by New York Metropolitan Region Study. See Appendix F.

In New York State, as net profit decreases relative to property, tax levels move downward. But in New Jersey, they move upward. The relation of profits to property has less effect on tax levels in Connecticut where the corporate income tax rate is lower than in New York.

To the extent that tax considerations play a role in location decisions—and ignoring other locational factors—it would seem to follow that firms with a high ratio of profit to property would have done well to locate in New Jersey, while those with a low ratio should have preferred to locate in New York State.

As one analyzes the distribution of the principal industries in the Region, he finds that their location follows a pattern seemingly consistent with their tax interests. New Jersey counties, for example, have a larger proportion of the Region's employment in industries with relatively high profit-to-property ratios than in industries with lower ratios. Yet we are strongly inclined to doubt that the relation is really due to businessmen's response to the tax factor. We suspect, rather, that the relation is brought about through the propensity for small-plant industries to settle in New York City for other reasons. Industries that tend to have a lower level of profits relative to their property are the small-plant industries, as it turns out. Plants in these industries have little property but they have even less profits relative to their property. It is this fact, in our judgment—not taxes—which explains why the New York portion of the Region contains plants with a relatively low ratio of profits to property, as compared with the New Jersey side of the Region.

Though it may be difficult to reconstruct the past trends in the tax levels of the Region's various areas, one can project the future with a certain assurance. The scope for variation in the tax levels of different areas contained within a single state is narrowing. More and more of the total tax bill is coming to be represented by state and federal taxes, correspondingly less of it by local taxes; more and more of the funds expended locally are being channeled through state and federal grants-in-aid, less and less from local tax receipts. New Jersey's recent adoption of the corporate income tax is a manifestation of the trend; there is not much doubt that the level of that tax will rise more rapidly than the level of local property and other local taxes in the future. On top of this, the leveling of population densities in the Region in the future[19] may well add to the general equalization of local tax rates. Some communities will manage to hold aloof from the general pattern of density equalization, but many that do are unlikely to welcome industries anxious to avail themselves of the lower tax structure.[20]

Aside from this general pattern within each of the states in the Region, we see little to suggest that the states themselves will draw apart from one another in the tax structure which they impose upon their respective industries. The tax tendencies which New Jersey once manifested, as a state dominated by rural interests, are gradually being suppressed by its continuing urbanization and by the political compulsions generated by population growth. Our projection therefore will proceed upon the assumption that the tax differences among New York, New Jersey, and Connecticut will decline with time. But once more, it is well to note, a change in the present directions of public policy could impair the validity of the assumption.

THE SUM OF THE FACTORS

When all is said, the calculus of location is still something to be done firm by firm, plant by plant. Any synthesis which fails to take into account the myriad of different cost structures of the different plants could easily mislead. Accordingly, any effort at synthesis would be foiled at the outset if it were not for the fact that most of the forces move so clearly in the same direction.

Transcending everything else is the fact that the initial lead of the old cities is rapidly being overcome. Once, these areas were unique in the transportation facilities which they could afford. But revolutions in transportation have been reducing the cost in moving goods and the time in moving people outside the city centers. Distance no longer represents the barrier which it once did. And, as the handicaps of distance have been overcome, the differences between areas—differences in transportation facilities, labor market characteristics, and external economies—have been reduced.

As the cities have come to share their once-unique features with other areas of the Region, they have found themselves handicapped in one respect in comparison with the newer areas. Land in the cities has been encumbered by the existence of obsolete structures and outmoded streets. The cost of recapturing this encumbered space for new uses has been a major handicap, one which contributed heavily to the incipient decline in the absolute levels of the cities' manufacturing employment since the end of World War II. And there is no prospect, short of some new forces of major dimensions, that this incipient decline will be arrested in the decades just ahead.

THE SPECIAL MANUFACTURING INDUSTRIES

There is an element of anticlimax in turning from a general analysis of manufacturing to an analysis of the special needs of a select group of industries. Yet some 600,000 of the 1,900,000 manufacturing jobs in the Region fall in industries whose location is governed by some overriding special need. It must not be assumed too readily, however, that these special industries detract much from the generality of what has already been said. Much of the earlier discussion applies almost as well to the industries treated here as it does to manufacturing industries in general. What sets these special industries apart is the fact that, while being influenced by the considerations of space, transport, labor, external economies, and taxes discussed in Chapter 2, they are nonetheless dominated by some added locational need which, for the industry as a whole, outweighs all the others. Of all these added locational needs, that of facilitating face-to-face contact is one of the most important.

THE COMMUNICATION-ORIENTED INDUSTRIES

THEIR NATURE

About two dozen manufacturing industries in the New York Metropolitan Region stand out from the others as possessing common traits—traits critical in their locational decisions. Each of them is heavily concentrated in the Region's center; each is dominated by comparatively small plants; each is an industry which one associates with the need for speedy communication and transportation and with a high degree of unpredictability as regards the nature of its final products.

Industries of this sort are mainly concentrated in two broad groups. Segments of the industries producing women's outerwear and related trimmings constitute one group; and certain branches of printing and publishing constitute the other. Apart from these broad groups, the industries include models and patterns, signs and advertising displays, and games and toys. (The full list appears in Appendix G.) On the average, plants in these industries are generally half the size of the average plant in the Region, measured by the number of employees per plant. Geographically, the employment in these "communication-oriented" industries is highly concentrated. More than three-quarters of the employees work in New York City. And an added 5 per cent are found in Hudson County just across the river. These industries are concentrated not only in the Core but particularly in the central business district of Manhattan.

A clue to the reasons for the heavy clustering of these industries is to be found in the interrelations of speed, small size, and uncertainty of outlook. To unravel these interrelations, we can begin with the special role that timeliness plays in these activities. Time is of the essence in the output of these industries, and its essentiality introduces a new dimension in the nature of the product or service being offered. Consider the printer of legal briefs or financial prospectuses; his production cycle—the lapse of time between the moment when he receives the manuscript and the time he delivers the finished product—is critical to his existence. Indeed this is generally true of most of the industries which we have called communication-oriented. The firms are not offering, as their stock-in-trade, the products themselves but the products-by-a-time-certain.

If the products of these industries were "standardized" in nature—if they were products the specifications of which could be precisely described and anticipated, and the demand for which justified quantity production—the manufacturer might have the option of producing them when and where he chose, and of warehousing a supply close to the prospective market. But the specifications of these products cannot ordinarily be anticipated; they are "unstandardized" products for the most part, often created by a process of consultation between customer and manufacturer. Accordingly, if the technology does not exist for satisfying the relevant time deadline except by locating in the central city, producers have been obliged to settle there without regard to cost. This fact has accounted for the Core locations of the printing industries and of the manufacturers who serve the women's clothing industries.

The sensitivity of some of these Core-located industries to communication time is heightened by the fact that many of the materials which go into the production process are as unstandardized as the final products. In the making of high-style apparel, these materials consist of the fabrics, designs, and colors which eventually are to be incorporated in the firm's product. For the publisher whose periodical offers a varied output, the "materials" develop from conferences with authors, artists, and reproduction specialists; and from gossip with people who have an ear to the ground. The process of assimilating these essential elements can best be done face-to-face; even if the time element were not pressing, the need for keeping the sheer cost of personal communication in bounds would have the effect of pulling related groups of processors and their customers together.

In some of the industries, the minimizing of the time and cost of personal communication is important in still another context, namely, in the final selling stage. The familiar story of the apparel buyers descending on New York's Garment Center from all quarters of the country has been recounted many times. These buyers must see a great deal in the briefest possible time. As a result, their disposition is to shop where the most concentrated cluster of sellers may be. The sellers, in turn, seek to locate their showrooms at a point convenient to a maximum number of buyers. To a considerable degree the sellers are also the producers, and therefore their selling needs are added to the other compulsions which lead to their clustering. In certain branches of the women's and children's apparel industry, the tendency to cluster is so pronounced that most of their employment in the Region is found in a group of loft buildings packed in an area of 96 acres between West 34th and 40th Streets in Manhattan. Indeed, about 15 per cent of the country's millinery is produced in one building located at 65 West 39th Street. At 500 and 512 Seventh Avenue are key buildings in the women's coat-and-suit industry. Just below, at 463 and 498 Seventh Avenue, are important concentrations of dress manufacturing. In all, probably more than 100,000 apparel workers are employed in the Garment Center. And the demand for space in the heart of the area is so great that the typical rental rate for manufacturing loft space runs about 50 per cent higher than for similar space in other parts of the Region.

If the industries we have so far discussed were dominated by large firms, we might envisage a different locational pattern. If the firms were large enough, dominant brand names might emerge, and superior bargaining power might accrue to a few firms. If so the producer might be able to select his location with more freedom. But the fact that so many of these industries typically are confronted with a continually changing product places a damper on opportunities for the development of large plants and dominant firms. Few firms can afford to accept the rigidities involved in specialization and growth: a specialized piece of equipment, making up in speed what it lacks in versatility; a specialized labor force, more productive at a given operation but not easily trained for alternative operations.[1]

Since the establishments cannot afford to commit themselves to such rigidities, their typical pattern is to rely on subcontractors and other outside sources for services and operations which otherwise they might consider providing from inside the firm. We saw in the preceding chapter that small firms rely on external economies more than large ones do. But the heavy dependence of communication-oriented firms on outside services is a direct result of uncertainty and is over and above the sort of dependence which the small firms in any industry tend to display. Thus, makers of handbags are restrained from setting up their own metal-working facilities as long as the metallic components are continually changing in shape and function. Pamphlet printers avoid the commitment involved in the purchase of one of the many kinds of metal or plastic binding machines. Producers of specialized electronic products generally turn to outside specialists for metal plating and testing; and, where special-purpose tubes must be fabricated in small quantities, specialized glass-blowing facilities are often brought into the picture. Manufacturers of costume jewelry meet their rapidly changing consumer demand by turning to special suppliers of clasps, ear clips, hinges, blanks, joints, pin stems, and other things which can be made to relatively standard specifications with expensive specialized equipment.[2]

Because the subcontractors serve many diverse plants, the aggregate demand for their services tends to be rather more stable than the demand for the products of the typical plant which they serve. Accordingly, the subcontractors are in a better position to mechanize for specialization than their customers are. When one line of dresses is not using a paint-sprayed buckle, another may very well be; and even if no dress lines are using paint-on-metal accessories, perhaps there are other garments which need them. When the women's apparel industry turns away from some type of thread, lining, tape, or binding, the men's and boy's industry may find a use for it. Similarly, when a bookbinding firm encounters a decline in demand from one printing establishment, there is a good chance that this decline may be offset by an increase in demand from another.

One begins to see, therefore, the interrelations which link product uncertainty with small manufacturing establishments, and which link small establishments with a central city location. Uncertainty generates a need for flexibility; the need for flexibility compels a reliance on outside suppliers; and, throughout the process of creation, production, and sale, there is a substantial need for speedy personal communication. On top of this, the common use of facilities by different industries creates ties among the manufacturing clusters which contribute to a high degree of centrality in manufacturing activity. So strong are these needs that many—though not all—of the firms involved take on higher rental payments, taxes, and other costs in the central city in order to fill their locational demands.

THE LOCATIONAL TRENDS

Even so, the refrain is always the same: the communication-oriented industries, like others in the New York Metropolitan Region, have lately begun to show something like the same dispersive tendencies, leaving the Core of the Region for other locations. Again, this is not simply a decline in the Core's share of the Region's jobs but an absolute decline in the number of jobs in the Core. The pattern of movement of these industries, however, has unique elements which deserve a word of comment.

From their infancy to the present, the communication-oriented industries have been an integral part of the Core, their basic locations changing only as the dimensions of the Core itself changed. In the horse-drawn age, some 75 years ago, the Core of the Region was crammed into the area below 14th Street in Manhattan. In this constricted area such industries as the printing and garment trades could satisfy not only their communication needs but their labor needs as well. For the first stopping-off place of the streams of immigrants of the period tended to be in the nearby housing of the same areas; from there, the more skilled hands among the immigrants found ready work in the clothing and printing industries.

By the early 1900's mass transit had become faster and more efficient, the horse-drawn car had given way to the electric trolley, the steam-driven elevated trains had been electrified, and the subways were being dug. These developments opened up new housing possibilities for the Core's working populations. More and more of them moved uptown in Manhattan, to the Bronx, and across the East River to Brooklyn, commuting each day to the southern part of Manhattan where their shops remained. By about 1907, according to a survey conducted at the time, only 29 per cent of the male workers and 40 per cent of the female workers in Manhattan below 14th Street actually lived in that district.[3]

As the residences of the working population spread out, the overriding need for industries to be close to the downtown tenement districts was weakened, and influences which had once been secondary in their locational decisions became more important. One such influence, strong among women's dress firms, was the desire to attract buyers away from competitors. Until the advent of air travel, women's clothing buyers came to town via the railroads, primarily the Pennsylvania Railroad which in 1910 established its terminal at Seventh Avenue near 34th Street. This was a magnet which began to draw the showrooms, one by one, from their locations downtown. Its force was increased by the fact that the growing hotel industry and the theater and nightclub districts were also stringing out northward and beginning to regroup in the railroad terminal area.

But the move to 34th Street by branches of women's wear could not be a sudden jump. The industry was firmly tied to its multitude of suppliers, subcontractors, and services. In the first quarter of this century, therefore, the communication-oriented portion of the industry—principally dresses and coats and suits—inched its way from below 14th Street to its present location in the upper 30's along the west side of Manhattan, taking its suppliers and subcontractors with it. The short moves were spearheaded by the style-setting leaders in the industry as they constantly attempted to shake off the copyists who clustered about them at each new location.

The extent of the present Garment Center, approximately between 34th and 40th Streets and between Sixth and Ninth Avenues, was fixed by another set of considerations which took hold in 1916 when city zoning first was introduced. This regulatory tool gave the Fifth Avenue merchants a means of blocking off the invasion of the migrants from lower Manhattan, whose presence threatened to clog streets and sidewalks throughout the shopping day. By the 1920's the industry had settled in the location that has been its home for the last 35 years.

The movement within the Core of the communication-oriented segments of the printing industry was slightly different. The clustering of these establishments (consisting chiefly of commercial printers and closely related firms, but excluding newspaper plants) had been due only partly to the ties among its many establishments; at least as important had been the link between each printing establishment and the law firms, financial houses, and central offices which dominated lower Manhattan. About 1900, as the central business district expanded northward, the printing industries began to disperse noticeably from the City Hall area which originally had been close by the bulk of their customers. That area remained, and still remains, an important printing center, but other clusters grew up in midtown Manhattan as well.

The shift of the communication-oriented industries was not entirely confined to movement within Manhattan. The development of the subway and the improvement of bridges and highways increased the radius in which a manufacturer could locate his plant and still be in close contact with people and firms in the Core. Manufacturers in some apparel lines sought out the pockets of cheap female labor found in Harlem, in eastern Brooklyn, along the elevated lines of the east Bronx, and in Yonkers. Across the Hudson lay similar pools of womanpower, in Jersey City and Newark, and in more distant Orange, Middlesex, and Monmouth Counties. From such locations, manufacturers who relied on others to do the designing and selling could get to Manhattan offices quickly enough to consult on the details of production. Similarly, large printing plants were set up in the Bronx, Long Island City, and Newark, where they could still maintain their Manhattan contacts by coming and going.

New York City as a whole suffered little relative decline from these developments between 1900 and 1922, for what was Manhattan's loss was often Queens' or Brooklyn's gain. We estimate that the City's share of communication-oriented employment in the Region declined only from 84 per cent to 81 per cent.[4] But the central business district of Manhattan showed a larger relative loss, with a drop in share from about 72 to 60 per cent.

After 1922 the trend continued, embracing a larger area of the Region. River crossings improved; motor trucks became ubiquitous; large portions of the Region's hinterland were drawn closer to the critical contacts of the central city. Between 1929 and 1939, New York City's share of communication-oriented industries declined from 89 to 81 per cent, probably as a net result of Manhattan's losing ground and the other boroughs' gaining; these figures are not strictly comparable with the earlier percentages because in this period we were able to identify a larger group of industries as communication-oriented and the statistics were available only for a smaller number of counties, but the important fact is that the same downward trend continued.[5] And, in the period from 1947 to 1956, when

TABLE 13 Distribution of Communication-Oriented Manufacturing[a] in New York Metropolitan Region, 1947 and 1956

| | Number of employees (thousands) | Percentage shares of Region's employment (NYMR = 100) | | | |
		New York City	Hudson	Essex	Rest of Region
Communication-oriented industries, total					
1947	418.6	82.6	3.9	2.9	10.6
1956	415.0	77.5	4.6	3.5	14.4
Segments of the apparel industries					
1947	259.5	84.2	3.8	2.1	9.9
1956	234.6	80.7	5.0	2.0	12.3
Segments of the printing and publishing industries					
1947	89.5	82.2	3.1	2.0	12.7
1956	101.3	73.8	4.1	2.4	19.7
Others					
1947	69.6	77.2	5.5	7.0	10.3
1956	79.1	72.7	4.1	9.0	14.2

[a] See Appendix G for list of industries included.

Source: Our estimates, based on data collected by state departments of labor under unemployment insurance programs. See Appendix A, Part II, for exceptions and further details.

figures again became available for the entire New York Metropolitan Region, New York City's share of communication-oriented industries was still slipping downward, as shown in Table 13; here, again, fragmentary figures suggest that Manhattan led the decline, while the other boroughs may even have gained.

Despite the long decline from 1900, however, New York City's percentage was still around 78 per cent in 1956, reflecting the basic symbiotic relation between the final producer and his suppliers, subcontractors, and customers.

The locational prognosis for the communication-oriented industries depends perhaps as much on the technology of communication as on any other single factor. Nothing so far quite takes the place of personal examination of the goods, patterns, styles, layouts, formats, and colors which are the ingredients of the industries. Nothing quite substitutes for the higgling, gossiping, luncheoning, and nightclubbing which are a part of the selling process. Closed-circuit television may achieve what the telephone apparently has not, by reducing some of the apparent need for face-to-face contact in these industries. But our disposition is not to make such an assumption for projective purposes.

Even if the need for face-to-face communication does not decline, a further dispersion of employment in these industries may yet occur—an outmovement from the Core to the Rings of the Region and to areas beyond the Region.* Obviously some dispersion already has occurred, and more may follow. But dispersion in the more communication-conscious parts of industry groups like apparel and printing and publishing does not take place readily. The need to cluster is so great that no one plant can readily

---

* In point of fact, major segments of apparel production and of the printing industry have been shifting to other parts of the country, but these have been chiefly the more standardized segments, oriented to labor or transportation rather than to communication. Most of the activities that have shifted have been in industries not listed in Appendix G as communication-oriented. Some of the "migratory" activities were indeed in the industries listed, but they were usually in the more standardized lines of those industries.

make the decision to move without regard to the decisions of the others. A maker of toys or women's high-style dresses too far removed from his competitors may not survive; a printer too far removed from the law office or the advertising agency may be eliminated as well; and so may the magazine publisher too far isolated from his principal sources of information. It is not easy to envisage a dissipation of the Garment Center even if lofts should grow progressively outmoded and if traffic should clog the streets even worse than it does now. From all appearances, nothing short of some major intervention of a new sort—intervention by a government agency or by some new industry organization—could move the nucleus to a different location. Our projections do not assume that such intervention will develop. But, if this intervention did come to pass, it could effect dramatic changes in the economic activities of midtown Manhattan.

The dispersion from the Core in these communication-oriented industries is likely to continue. But it will not usually consist of a simple relocation of existing firms or of the generation of new firms on the periphery very like the old ones in the center. It will consist instead of a much more subtle process—a separation of functions once merged in a single firm and a reshuffling of these functions in establishments of a different sort. Selling will be separated from manufacturing; publishing separated from printing; and so on. This kind of separation has gone on in the past and may well continue in the future.

Our disposition is to assume that the redistribution of communication-oriented manufacturing jobs from the Core to the Rings will continue at a slow pace, with certain manufacturing activities draining out and leaving behind the specialized functions which still demand personal communication. The pace at which this will occur is necessarily problematical, depending on the possibilities of reorganizing the operations to isolate the communication-oriented functions and to operate the rest in an environment whose external economies are not as great as those in the Region's Core. These prospects involve nice questions of judgment. Special studies of the women's apparel industries and the printing and publishing industries, reported in another volume in this series, present some of the materials on which that judgment will be based.[6]

THE OTHER SPECIAL INDUSTRIES

The other industries of the New York Metropolitan Region which we have found it useful to identify as special industries are very different in nature from the communication-oriented group. In some cases the location of these industries is dominated by the need for water transport; in some by the need for comparative isolation, where neighbors will not be at hand to protest against noxious odors, heavy smoke, or peril of explosion; in a few cases, even, by the need to be at the site of some raw material, such as clay or stone.

We do not propose to review in detail the locational pattern of each of these groups. In each case the shift has been roughly similar—an outward trek from the city areas to the spaces beyond, and from the Core to the Rings of the Region.

One of the groups, however, is worth examining with care. Though its employment in the Region seems insignificant, its impact on land use in the Region is great. This is the group which we shall call the "nuisance" industries.*

Any exact classification of nuisance plants is a vulnerable exercise, since it depends so heavily on the subjective reactions of the five senses. But there is not much doubt that the slaughtering, grease-rendering, and soap-making plants which lined the Hudson River shore of Manhattan less than a century ago would have been regarded as a nuisance, at least by today's standards. Newark's tanneries of

* Lists of these industries, applicable to the different periods for which statistics are available, are given in Appendix G. In drawing up the lists, and in discussing the trends, we could not practicably take into account the considerable variations in individual plant characteristics. But the reader will of course understand that there are some individual plants in these industries that are not in the least offensive to their neighbors whether upwind or downwind.

the same vintage would likely have fallen under the same heading, as would the paint and varnish plants, the other chemical plants, and the petroleum and copper refineries, situated on the East River and Newtown Creek.

Even in the nineteenth century the nuisance industries tended to shift away from the built-up sections of the Region, and after 1900 the tendency took on considerable momentum. Between 1900 and 1922, explosives plants virtually completed their exodus from New York City; fertilizer plants disappeared from the City; and employment in oil refineries fell off. Eight large Manhattan plants in the chemicals industry were relocated in New Jersey, and six in Brooklyn were relocated—five in New Jersey and one in Richmond—but no case of a reverse movement was recorded.[7] Of the nuisance categories in which data can be had for those early decades of the century, the slaughtering houses, meat-packing and fish-packing plants, and paint and varnish factories appear to have clung the most strongly to New York City. So far as the meat and fish plants are concerned, they were no doubt pinned down by the need for speedy delivery of their perishable output. The market orientation of kosher slaughtering has always been especially strong.

Various forces pushed nuisance plants from their original locations or encouraged expansion elsewhere. By the 1920's, the facilities of Newtown Creek no longer matched the needs of some of the plants on its banks engaged in the refining of petroleum and copper. The draft of ocean-going vessels, always on the increase, had begun to limit the use of the Creek. At the same time, nearby dumping grounds grew scarce.

The preference of the nuisance group for other areas was also speeded by lawsuits and acts of local government. In 1898 New York City applied its sanitary code to limit slaughtering houses in Manhattan and Brooklyn to narrowly defined areas. In 1916 the City followed this up with its first zoning ordinance, which among other things barred the nuisance industries from many areas. Newark followed suit in 1920.

The direct impact of these zoning requirements was

augmented by the growth of numerous other ordinances and administrative practices in the older cities. Regulations aimed at reducing fire hazards gradually made their way into construction and building-inspection codes. Regulations on waste disposal were inserted in sanitary codes. In short, the external economies of the crowded city areas, on which so much emphasis was laid in the last chapter, were gradually matched or outweighed by external "diseconomies."

Outside the old cities, town and neighborhood attitudes were of critical importance in the locational decisions of the nuisance industries. By the early twentieth century, certain local attitudes toward industry were growing clearly evident. The Westchester and Long Island shores of Long Island Sound, for example, were being pre-empted by expensive residences, yacht clubs, and other uses fiercely antipathetic to nuisance neighbors. The estuary areas of New Jersey, on the other hand, had already begun to show their long-run commitment to heavy industry. Around Newark Bay and the lower reaches of the Raritan River, sometimes at the water's edge, sometimes on isolated bits of firm ground surrounded by tidal marshes, one found ideal sites for plants giving off dense smoke, generating objectionable odors, or constituting a fire hazard. There, too, one found local governments predisposed to accept such plants in their jurisdictions.

We come now to the last thirty years of industrial history, a period for which figures become more plentiful and observation more accurate. Table 14 indicates the trends. From 1929 to 1939, the outward shift of the nuisance industries continued, and the center of gravity of the group continued to move toward New Jersey. In this period New York City's share of the nuisance-industry jobs in the New York Industrial Area (a 12-county area covered by Census data) dropped from 46 to 34 per cent. But at some time after 1939 the outward distribution appears to have been arrested, for we find that, between 1947 and 1956, nuisance-industry jobs in the City were almost unchanged, though considerable change was occurring elsewhere in the 22-county New York Metropolitan Region. It may be that the locational adjustment of these industries—so far as New York City is concerned—has been largely achieved and that the fraction remaining in the City is sufficiently insulated in industrial enclaves, or sufficiently buffered by run-down residential areas, to exist without great difficulty.

TABLE 14   New York City's Percentage Share of Metropolitan Area's Employment in Nuisance Industries and Other Special Manufacturing Categories, 1929–1939 and 1947–1956

	N.Y. Industrial Area[a] (12-county total = 100)			N.Y. Metropolitan Region (22-county total = 100)		
	1929	1939	Change in percentage points	1947	1956	Change in percentage points
Nuisance industries[b]	45.6	34.1	−11.5	22.5	21.4	−1.1
Industries oriented to water transport[b]	63.4	45.0	−19.3	40.2	36.5	−3.7
Industries oriented to raw materials[b]	n.a.	n.a.	n.a.	29.2	30.4	+1.2

n.a. = not available.

[a] New York Industrial Area consists of New York City's five counties plus Westchester, Bergen, Passaic, Essex, Hudson, Union, and Middlesex. Because of the difference in geographical area, the 1929–1939 percentages are not strictly comparable with those for 1947–1956.

[b] Industries are listed in Appendix G. Note that the lists are somewhat different for the two periods because of differences in classification. Some industries are both nuisance and water-transport industries and are included in both categories. The three categories had the following estimated employment in 1956: nuisance, 129,685; water-transport, 45,653; raw-material, 4,327. After duplications are eliminated, the total 1956 employment covered by the table is 152,734.

Source: Our estimates, based on the following: For 1929 and 1939, U.S. *Census of Manufactures.* For 1947 and 1956, data collected by state departments of labor under unemployment insurance programs. See Appendix A for exceptions and further details.

On the other hand, a major shift is obviously taking place between the two Rings of the Region. Once having fled from New York City to the Inner Ring, this group of industries now is shifting from the Inner to the Outer Ring. Once more the desire to avoid close contact with congested areas is making itself felt. This time the growth is particularly noticeable in Middlesex County, New Jersey, adjoining the areas where the earlier growth had been manifest.

A long-run projection of the location of the nuisance industries in the Region must take into account both the changed situation in New York City and the continuing outward shift from the Inner Ring to the Outer Ring. The comparative stability of New York City's employment in these industries in recent years suggests the possibility that the deterioration of residential neighborhoods surrounding the nuisance plants has finally eliminated a source of land-use conflict, and that the opportunity for such plants to expand in these neighborhoods is better than it has been since the nineteenth century. If so, however, the expansion would still be severely limited, and, if this group of industries should grow substantially in the Region during the next quarter century, the probability seems high that a considerable part of the growth will be outside New York City and outside the congested portions of the Region's other principal cities. Indeed, when one adds local attitudes to physical restraints, there are only a few remaining areas in the Region which can conceivably accommodate a large additional expansion of nuisance plants. These are the areas toward which such plants have been tending —the Raritan River estuary and the uninhabited shores of the long, narrow channel between New Jersey and Staten Island.

THE WHITE-COLLAR CORPS

While 28 out of every 100 persons working in the New York Metropolitan Region are occupying themselves in manufacturing establishments, 25 more of the 100 are engaged in financial activities and other office functions in the Region's myriad of office buildings or in wholesaling. At first glance, one is almost at a loss to find common forces determining the locations of these employees and the more than 300 million square feet of floor space which they occupy in the Region. The negotiating, managing, record-keeping, letter-writing, interviewing, researching, advising, and gossiping that go on in office buildings and wholesale establishments seem such a heterogeneous mass of activity as to defy systematic understanding. Yet our analysis suggests that common locational forces have been operating to create the distribution of these jobs, and that most of these are forces already encountered in our analysis of manufacturing.

Like most lines of human endeavor, the present office community is where it is primarily because something else was there before. The advertising offices chose Manhattan's Madison Avenue in preference to Jersey City's Journal Square largely because so many central offices of the nation's major corporations had selected the Grand Central area a generation or so earlier. The great trusts and railroads chose lower Manhattan for their headquarters in the late nineteenth century partly because the nation's financial community was in Wall Street. The financial community was centered on Wall Street in the early nineteenth century partly because commerce was concentrated near the Battery. And commerce was concentrated at Manhattan's tip—rather than in Newark or in Yonkers—partly because lower Manhattan offered a flat terrain washed by two broad navigable rivers, one of which (the East River) hardly ever froze over.

If this was the sequence, it suggests the order in which we should look at the location of the various types of office jobs in the Region.

THE WHOLESALERS

THE EARLY DAYS

There is not much doubt that the origins of the New York Metropolitan Region's role as the nation's principal wholesaler were tied directly to the sea. Histories of New York City recount the lucky incident after the War of 1812 when the British chose New York over Boston as the market in which to dump their surplus woolens, cotton cloth, hardware and cutlery that had been accumulating during the war years; this choice, so the story goes, created national wholesale markets in New York where scarcely any had existed before.

Early in the nineteenth century, the New York Port outstripped all others on the Atlantic seaboard. In that period, a high proportion of the goods offered for sale in New York's wholesale markets came from overseas. Textiles, wines and liquors, hardware and cutlery, coffee and tea, china, glass, earthenware, "fancy goods," and "segars" were among the leading imports. In those days, as today, the location of the wholesale market was determined by problems of communication.

The wholesalers had two main communication problems. First, they had to have the earliest possible news of the prospective arrival of ships. Soon after the ships docked at South Street along the East River, the cargoes were sold at auctions, commonly held on Pearl Street, and the wholesaler who did not know that the ship was in simply was not a part of the market. The other communication problem which bound many wholesalers to the Port arose from the fact that many of their best customers came by sea from the southern states, using New York as a base for the sale of their crops, the financing of their operations, and the provisioning of their plantations and businesses. Thus the wholesalers carved out their districts in the streets just behind the wharves, such as Front, Water, and Pearl Streets.

The coming of the railroads eventually weakened the ties to pierside locations. By the 1850's, good connections with rail terminals were becoming an important consideration. A rising proportion of the goods handled by the wholesaler came overland rather than by sea. At the same time, more and more of his outgoing shipments were carried by the iron horse, supplementing the slower way of the river and the canal.

By this time, too, the expense account had arrived on the American business scene. Out-of-town buyers, coming annually by rail from all points, expected to be wooed by wholesalers. Jacob Knickerbocker, in a passage concerning the 1850's which could as well apply to the 1950's, tells us that each salesman in the wholesale business "had his list of customers from the various sections of the country. When they came to New York to purchase, most of them also expected to have a 'good time' and looked to the salesmen to provide it for them. Sometimes the entertainment graded the extent of the purchases. . . ."[1]

Wholesaling districts, freed from their waterfront anchorage, began increasingly to specialize and to move. Textile wholesalers, for instance, emerged as a separate group and congregated in a new area in Worth Village, not far from the mid-century location of the City's brightest lights and best restaurants. This was the beginning of the Worth Street textile district, which was to dominate the wholesaling of textiles for about a century thereafter.

As the decades went by, locational distinctions began to develop between wholesalers concerned primarily with selling and wholesalers preoccupied with the physical distribution of goods. Wholesalers of the first group, offering such unstandardized products as furniture and apparel, typically did their selling as part of a market to which buyers were wont to come for comparative shopping. Here, adequate communication was the critical locational need:

communication in the sense that the product demanded on-the-scene inspection, and communication in the sense that the necessary higgling was best accomplished face-to-face. Let such a market become established in any area of the Region and there were great restraints on its ability to move. Any single seller left the pack on pain of isolation from the profitable center of the marketplace.

Nevertheless, pressures developed for a northward movement of these merchandising wholesalers on Manhattan Island. As we mentioned earlier in connection with the crawl of certain manufacturing districts, people and jobs were pushing northward along what Henry James called "the long, shrill city." Decisions on the location of the original Grand Central Terminal in 1871 and the Pennsylvania Station in 1910 accelerated the northward crawl. Once these were set down, the midtown location of the newest crop of hotels, theaters, and department stores was pretty well determined, and many of the wholesale selling markets were sure to join them sooner or later, depending on how fast they could organize for the journey.

The fur district—a mixed area of manufacturers and wholesalers—was one of the earliest to move, shifting from a nucleus well below 23rd Street in 1900 to a nucleus above 23rd Street by 1922. The firms in men's clothing, which combine wholesaling with manufacturing, continued gradually northward after the stabilization of the fur district, and by World War II had settled between 14th and 26th Streets. The diamond dealers moved uptown from the Fulton Street area in one big hop, for they were organized around a Diamond Dealers Club and it took only a move of the club in 1940 to draw the individual firms to 47th Street. In the end even the venerable Worth Street district succumbed, as textile firms began to move their sales offices closer to their manufacturing customers in the Garment Center and to textile buyers from out of town.

The location of the fur, diamond, and apparel wholesalers was influenced very little by the problem of physically distributing their goods, but there were other types of wholesalers who had to take into account both selling and the costs of physical distribution. These groups be-

haved in a more complex pattern, pulled as they were between the need for centrality to make an effective market
and the need for dispersion to facilitate distribution.

The fruit and vegetable centers illustrate this conflict of
forces. It must have been about the time of the Civil War
that lower Manhattan began to assume some importance
as a major distribution point for farm produce shipped
from distant areas. The wholesaling was a pier-oriented
trade, reliant on water transportation to a considerable
degree for the receipt of potatoes and other farm products.
Later in the century the rails took the lead in bringing
in fruits and vegetables. Rail cargoes were brought to the
New Jersey side of the Hudson River, then floated across
to the railroad piers on the New York side where they
were auctioned in the pier sheds or carted to nearby wholesaling houses in the Washington Street area. Meanwhile
the smaller cities of the metropolitan area had local fruit
and vegetable centers of their own, each within horse-
and-wagon distance of a clientele of retail stores and restaurants.

With the large-scale advent of trucking in the 1920's
and 1930's, the busy Washington Market district of Manhattan became more accessible to a wider metropolitan
circle of customers. At the same time, ironically, its inadequacies as a food wholesaling center, already fairly apparent, became even more so. The streets of downtown
Manhattan had never been laid out to accommodate over-
the-road truck trailers loaded with onions or lettuce. What
is more, the retail stores and secondary distribution points
which had arisen elsewhere in the New York Metropolitan
Region were now spread over a much larger area. Clearly,
the needs of efficient distribution pulled in the direction
of establishing additional wholesaling depots at points removed from the market center.

What was desirable for efficient distribution, however,
was not necessarily attractive from a marketing viewpoint.
When the horse had been the prime means of delivery,
many retailers had had to content themselves with the
limited offerings of wholesale markets nearby. But once
the retailer had a truck at his disposal, he could search

out a market whose variety and price levels were more favorable. The result was a compromise between conflicting forces. The smaller local markets withered away; a few major centers managed to survive and develop away from the Washington Street area, notably the Bronx and Brooklyn Terminal Markets and Newark; each center of this kind offered considerable quantities of products with enough variety to satisfy discriminating retailers.

So much for the selling-oriented wholesalers and for the seller-distributors, dependent on face-to-face confrontation with buyers, or on giving buyers the opportunity to inspect each lot before buying. The wholesalers who were acting *primarily* as distributors, and were not part of an organized market involving face-to-face communication, followed still another pattern. Successful distribution, for the distributors of beer, wine, and liquor, tobacco products, and groceries, demanded frequent and closely timed deliveries of comparatively small quantities of the product. This method involved extremely high distribution costs, even as late as 1939.[2] The spread of the telephone and the motor vehicle—and the declining importance of the railroad—weakened any incentive which these groups may previously have had to cluster at some given point. Wholesalers tended to cultivate a small area of the Region intensively and to maintain their distribution facilities in the center of that area. Besides, for goods-handling wholesalers of this sort, extensive modern warehousing layouts could sometimes be used to good advantage in the paring of costs. Accordingly, these groups tend to disperse into less congested areas, following the homes and stores in their outward move.

RECENT TRENDS IN WHOLESALING LOCATION

At least since 1929, perhaps for longer, the most prominent aspect of the locational change in all sorts of wholesaling has been their slower growth in Manhattan than in other areas of the New York Metropolitan Region. Table 15 shows the extent to which this tendency has advanced. Between 1929 and 1954, Manhattan's share of the Region's wholesale jobs fell from 76 to 59 per cent; indeed,

in the last six years of that period there was an absolute
decline in Manhattan's wholesale jobs—from 181,000 to
169,000.[3]

Manhattan's loss was the gain of practically every other
area in the Region. All the other boroughs of New York
City and all six of the other major cities of the Region[4]
showed considerable growth in their relative and absolute
wholesaling employment during the 25-year period. The
six cities managed to increase their aggregate share from
6.7 per cent to 9.3 per cent. But the greatest relative

TABLE 15 Distribution of Wholesaling Jobs in New
York Metropolitan Region, 1929–1954

| | | Percentage shares of Region's employment (NYMR = 100) | | | | |
	Number of employees (thousands)	Man-hattan	Rest of New York City	Essex and Hudson	5 Inner Ring counties[a]	Outer Ring
1929	269.4	76.4	11.7	6.1	2.5	3.3
1939	283.4	71.8	13.4	7.5	3.9	3.4
1948	373.2	67.8	14.2	8.3	5.7	4.0
1954	381.5[b]	58.8	16.5	9.0	10.1	5.6

[a] All of Inner Ring except Essex (which is here combined with the
Core county of Hudson) and Richmond (included in "Rest of New York
City").

[b] This figure is not strictly comparable in coverage with the 1948 figure; milk bottlers and some manufacturers' sales branches and agencies
were not included on the later date. The 1954 coverage is also rather
different from that of Table 17, which is based on other sources.

Source: U.S. *Census of Distribution*, 1929, U.S. *Census of
Business*, 1939 and 1954.

growth of all—from 5.2 to 15.4 per cent—occurred in the
Region outside the city areas.

Meanwhile, something like the same experience was observable in other major metropolitan areas in the nation.
In every one of twelve major areas for which we developed
data over the 25-year period, employment in wholesale
trade was growing more slowly in the central cities than
in the suburbs; and for five of these areas there was an
absolute decline in such employment in the central cities
during the last six years of the period.[5]

The outward shift of wholesaling in the postwar years

was typical of each of the major types of wholesalers enumerated in Census figures: of the "merchant wholesalers," who typically buy and store the stocks they sell; of manufacturers' sales offices, both those with stocks of goods and those without; and of the two or three other main Census groups. Of all these kinds of wholesalers, the merchant wholesalers embrace a little more than half of the Region's total employment. Within the merchant wholesaler group, it is possible to trace the locational shifts of different lines over time. As Table 16 shows, some thirteen of the fifteen lines of merchant wholesaling experienced an outward trend from Manhattan in the period from 1947 to 1956.

But by and large the outward movement was not very pronounced in those lines in which selling is a primary function, dry goods–apparel and furniture being notable cases. In lines importantly engaged in the physical distribution of commodities, such as beer, wines, and spirits, and in those of a mixed selling-and-distribution type, the declines in Manhattan's share were generally more marked. But there were also special cases whose behavior could not be understood in these terms alone, such as the handlers of waste products, whose locational problem is one of collection and storage, rather than selling or distribution.

Despite the general outward trend, wholesaling is still quite highly concentrated in the center of the Region, as can be seen in Table 17. Powerful links hold such establishments in locations well down toward the Region's center. For those groups engaged primarily in making a market, clustering is still the compelling need. And for most wholesaling groups, whether organized as part of a market or not, the minuscule size of the individual firms limits them to areas where space can be had on a rental basis, a fact which constitutes another centralizing force.[6]

Nonetheless, the growth of wholesaling will almost surely be slower in the innermost portions of the Region than in the outer areas. Wholesalers covering the whole Region will find advantages in locating their distribution points outside the central nub of congestion, following the pattern of the bakeries and other local-market manufac-

TABLE 16 Distribution of Lines of Merchant Wholesaling in 18 Counties[a] of the New York Metropolitan Region, 1947 and 1956

Wholesaling lines ranked in order of 1956 employment in Region	Number of employees (thousands)		Percentage shares of 18-county employment							
			Manhattan[b]		Rest of N.Y. City[b]		Essex and Hudson		Remaining 11 counties	
	1947	1956	1947	1956	1947	1956	1947	1956	1947	1956
Merchant wholesaling, total	196.5	225.0	65.1	57.7	16.9	19.1	10.5	10.0	7.5	13.2
Dry goods and apparel	33.7	38.0	96.9	93.9	1.5	3.1	0.8	1.4	0.8	1.6
Grocery, confectionery, meat	21.1	21.7	44.8	46.0	28.9	31.2	17.1	10.8	9.2	12.0
Machinery, equipment, supplies	17.1	20.6	65.5	50.4	15.9	19.2	10.7	12.9	7.9	17.5
Drugs, chemicals, allied products	16.0	15.0	70.3	58.8	14.1	18.7	10.4	9.8	5.2	12.7
Farm products (edible)	14.4	15.0	45.4	41.8	29.2	28.4	12.2	12.0	13.2	17.8
Electrical, electronic items	10.3	13.2	64.1	46.3	13.3	20.9	17.1	17.5	5.5	15.3
Paper and allied products	9.1	11.6	76.1	62.8	14.9	20.5	5.5	6.9	3.5	9.8
Furniture and home furnishings	7.8	10.6	82.2	75.2	8.8	11.9	5.1	5.9	3.9	7.0
Hardware, plumbing, heating	8.2	10.2	45.1	37.6	27.7	25.8	13.3	13.3	13.9	23.3
Beer, wine, distilled spirits	8.7	9.5	39.6	28.1	33.5	35.8	16.7	15.5	10.2	20.6
Metals, metalwork (except scrap)	7.5	9.2	57.5	45.3	17.9	20.6	14.7	14.1	9.9	20.0
Automobiles and equipment	6.0	7.3	26.9	27.1	34.4	31.6	15.3	14.6	23.4	26.7
Scrap, waste materials	6.7	6.9	28.7	26.6	34.9	32.7	19.7	21.8	16.7	18.9
Tobacco and its products	2.3	2.9	39.8	35.9	30.1	30.5	13.0	12.7	17.1	20.9
Farm products (raw materials)	2.0	1.9	95.2	90.0	1.7	5.6	1.9	3.0	1.2	1.4
Other merchant wholesalers	25.7	31.6	73.3	67.2	10.2	10.0	10.7	8.9	5.8	13.9

Note: Because of rounding, columns may not add exactly to totals. For other notes, see page 83.

turers discussed in Chapter 2. Wholesalers with more limited areas of distribution in the Region will continue to follow the population and retail stores outward. Some of the space in the one-time factory structures of the old suburban cities is likely to be taken up by added wholesaling operations. Areas like the New Jersey meadowlands and such acreage as remains on the outer edges of New York City's boroughs are also likely to benefit moderately from these trends.

For the few lines of wholesaling that combine a central-market function with the physical distribution of goods in the Region—for the fruit and vegetable centers, for instance—the outward movement may not be so smoothly achieved. More likely, it will take place on a much more irregular and erratic basis, as the institutional means appear for organizing scores of independent businesses to move in concert to some other location. Elaborate plans for the relocation of Manhattan's Washington Market have been proposed sporadically for at least 20 years, perhaps longer; one very much in favor at this writing is to relocate the market in the Bronx. The gains to be made from relocation have grown with time. Data developed by the U.S. Department of Agriculture suggest that, in 1956, distribution costs at a location outside Manhattan—this one in Queens—would have been about 31 per cent lower than at the Washington Market. Eventually, almost certainly within the next 25 years and perhaps much sooner, relocation will occur, telescoping into a brief period the shifts in employment which have been occurring more

---

NOTES FOR TABLE 16

a The other four counties, Orange, Dutchess, Putnam, and Fairfield, were omitted because the detailed data for 1947 were not available. These four counties had only about 7,000 jobs in merchant wholesaling in 1956.

b The distribution of New York City's employment between Manhattan and the rest of New York City for 1947 and 1956 is based on borough data for the individual wholesale lines obtained from the U.S. *Census of Business* for 1948 and 1954.

Source: Based on data collected by state departments of labor of New York and New Jersey under unemployment programs, except as described in footnote b. Further details in Appendix A, Part II.

TABLE 17 Distribution of Principal Types of Wholesaling, New York Metropolitan Region, 1956

	Number of employees (thousands)	Percentage shares of Region's employment (NYMR = 100)				
		Manhattan	Rest of New York City	Essex and Hudson	5 Inner Ring counties[a]	Outer Ring
Wholesaling, total	444.7	62.4	17.6	7.4	8.0	4.6
Merchant wholesaling[b] ..	232.2	55.9	18.5	9.7	9.8	6.1
Manufacturers' sales branches, offices	154.4	72.1	14.4	5.7	5.9	1.9
Merchandise agents, brokers	37.0	91.9	4.0	1.4	2.0	0.7
Petroleum bulk stations	18.4	1.4	62.9	6.8	15.7	13.2
Assemblers of farm products .	2.6	37.1	27.5	7.0	7.0	21.4

Note: Because of rounding, columns may not add exactly to totals.
[a] All of Inner Ring except Essex (which is here combined with the Core county of Hudson) and Richmond (included in "Rest of New York City").

[b] See Table 16 for distribution of the various lines of merchant wholesaling in an 18-county area of the Region.

Source: Based on data collected by state departments of labor under unemployment insurance programs, except for New York City. Further details in Appendix A, Part II. For definitions of types of wholesaling, see U.S. *1954 Census of Business.*

gradually in other lines. If the shift does not occur, economic activity in lower Manhattan may prove considerably different from the pattern which we envisage.

THE FINANCIAL COMMUNITY

Since the era when Wall Street's principal landmark was a buttonwood tree, a century and a half ago, lower Manhattan has been associated with an interrelated mass of enterprises and institutions which collectively make up the financial community. Like its counterpart in London, the community—much of it—is cramped into a few narrow and cavernous streets, held together by seemingly potent forces. Yet, on first blush, the community seems to be made up of a fairly diverse and loosely related group of operations: commercial banks, securities and commodity brokers, insurance companies, and a variety of other financial enterprises. What is the magnetism that keeps them together?

THE COMMON PREOCCUPATION

The strongest centralizing force, the thing that attracts most of the pieces of the New York financial community toward one another, is a common preoccupation with the operations of the nation's money market.

The phrase "money market," however, is deceptively simple. This "market" consists of a variety of institutions and firms, all devoted to the common purpose of providing a market for the purchase and sale of negotiable instruments. In one of its segments, banks are engaged with one another in trading their deposits with the Federal Reserve banks. In another segment, dealers are engaged in buying and selling the short-term notes of the nation's corporations. In still another, United States Government bonds are being bought and sold. Then again a heavy traffic is taking place in the sale of thousands of other securities, sometimes through the mechanism of the organized securities exchanges and sometimes through a network of private wires and interoffice teletypes which collectively comprise the "over-the-counter" markets of the nation.

The actual consummation of most of these transactions does not require that the principals should face each other across a luncheon or conference table; the telephone or teletype will usually serve. But the professionals who participate heavily and continuously in any of these segments of the money market all have their ears and minds attuned to a common background of facts and surmises against which commitments are made and avoided. The course of inflation or disinflation, the fiscal and monetary policy of government, the strength of industry, the temper of public buying—all these factors are critical. They affect the attitudes taken, and the decisions made, at the trading desks of securities dealers, the offices of commercial paper houses, and the investment and lending departments of banks and insurance companies.

To the money-market participant, therefore, the phrase "what's new?" is much more than a conversational opener. It bespeaks the essence of his business. There is a perpetual exploring—to develop new sources of information, to ferret out the results of other people's analyses, to draw upon the wisdom of colleagues and competitors. The participants in it inevitably gravitate toward one another, feeling a certain safety in pooled information and common apprehensions.

It is doubtful, however, that these factors alone would have created the tight cluster of 130,000 financial jobs in Manhattan below Chambers Street. The men at the core of the money market—the leading commercial paper dealers and traders in government bonds and corporate securities —represent only a tiny fraction of this total. But these dealers and traders are typically elite members of firms engaged in other financial activities. Traders in government bonds, for instance, are commonly members of large commercial banks, which are engaged in a variety of other financial functions such as the negotiation of loans with firms or individuals and the management of trusts and estates. Traders in corporate securities are often officers in firms which handle customers' accounts as well.

But this is still not the whole story of the extraordinary clustering of financial jobs. Part of the explanation—but only a minor part—lies in the need for the speedy movement of various important pieces of paper, such as stock certificates and checks, between the establishments of the financial district. Part of the answer, as we shall see, lies in history, going back to the period when the assembly of a large number of literate clerks was practicable at only a few congested points in the Region. But much of the current explanation is found in the schizoid role played by the partners and officers of the banks, dealer firms, and insurance underwriters. In many cases, they are not only negotiators with persons outside the firm but are also supervisors of the firm's routine operations. For each such supervisor, there are perhaps four or five clerks, stenographers, and messengers engaged in routine operations.

Such partners and officers see disadvantages in being physically separated from the subordinates who are accountable to them. Accordingly their instinct is to draw the repetitive functions close to them.

Like everything else in the New York Metropolitan Region, however, the location of its financial community is not fixed for all time. Major movements are going on inside the Region. To trace these movements and the forces behind them, we must go back to the days of the buttonwood tree.

THE MOVING FORCES

At the outset of the nineteenth century, the banking, insurance, and securities-trading functions which the financial community of the Region performs today were barely separable from the general wholesaling and shipping activities of the Port of New York. The chief financing problem was the financing of the movement of goods, and the major insurable risks were the risks of the sea—of piracy, barratry, mutiny, and shipwreck. Besides, the Port was a gateway for news of war and politics, a fact of some consequence to traders in securities. Accordingly, the Region's financial community, to the extent that it existed, was closely anchored to the Port area.

Early in that century, the financing function began to be drawn out of the counting houses of the merchants into formal banking institutions, and, by 1815, New York had eight commercial banks. Insurance companies appeared at about the same time, specializing in sea risks and other property insurance. By mid-century these nonlife companies had been supplemented by life insurance companies, many of which peddled wild schemes for the insurance of lives and invested the premiums of their clients just as wildly. And the rise of these financial entities was accompanied by the rise of institutions for the sale of securities, such as the New York Stock Exchange. This nucleus of the financial community in lower Manhattan had an extraordinary growth during the nineteenth century. As it grew, it experienced some movement northward on Manhattan Island, but not much.

Each of the emerging segments, as it took on a distinguishable identity, settled close to the site of activities out of which it had sprung and tended to stay there. The reasons we now know—among them the urgent need for personal communication in the process of testing the market and negotiating transactions. Also, near the end of the century the lower tip of the island managed to accumulate some unusual advantages, unrelated to the sea. The invention of the elevator stimulated the invention of the steel-framed skyscraper. The skyscraper, in turn, made it possible to cram several hundred thousand people in a square mile or so of land space, each able to reach any other within ten or fifteen minutes. Manhattanites were quick to plant the new invention on the solid rock of their island, and, as a result, the communication requirements of brokers and bankers there were better met than anywhere else on the face of the earth. Accordingly, though the financial community grew enormously, it was slow to spread its facilities.

Yet, as time went on and the city and the metropolitan area expanded over the countryside, major locational shifts did take place, and others were foretokened. The nature and the causes of the shifts can be seen by tracing the patterns of two large segments of the financial community —the commercial banks and the life insurance companies.

The commercial banks. When the twentieth century opened, the commercial banks still had fewer than ten branches between Chambers Street and 59th Street in Manhattan. They retained most of their employees in the older district for reasons already given; and their disposition to cling to Manhattan's tip was strengthened for a time by still another factor. The new network of mass transit facilities, then being developed to carry the hordes of bookkeepers, clerks, and other workers to their jobs, was at first designed to converge on lower Manhattan.

As the century progressed, however, the midtown area became the focal point for rapid transit, what with the Grand Central and Pennsylvania terminal facilities, the Hudson & Manhattan tubes under the Hudson River (serving both downtown and midtown), and the steady enlargement of the subway system. The shift in the benefits of transit service was a large factor in the growth of the midtown business-office district—a development to which we shall presently turn. And it was the growth of the midtown office district that finally began to alter the early pattern of commercial bank location. The business offices, developing later than the banks, showed considerable midtown orientation in the first few decades of the century and even more after World War II. The commercial banks, whose major clients were the business offices, spread themselves accordingly. Torn between a need for close contact with the financial community at the tip of Manhattan and a need for contact with business clients, the banks greatly expanded their branches. By 1926 the area between Chambers Street and 59th Street had 124 branches; and by 1947 it had 152 of Manhattan's 228 commercial branch banking offices. Between 1947 and 1956, this middle section was the only section in Manhattan which experienced a net increase in commercial bank branches, though the gain was not more than 22.

Apart from the question of bank branches, there were also indications of the movement of certain operating functions, such as check-sorting and accounting, to midtown by banks which retain a central office downtown. The First National City Bank has gone very far in that direction; it has moved many of its operating personnel out of lower Manhattan and now seems bent on locating the bulk of its clerical operations in a new midtown structure on Park Avenue.

Yet, for all the midtown activity of the commercial banks, the ties of their headquarters offices to the downtown complex of financial activity remained powerful. In the late 1950's the Chase Manhattan Bank went forward with the construction of a new 60-story building adjacent to its existing downtown location. This decision spurred other major banks to initiate important construction programs to improve or expand their existing headquarters in the same general area. Indeed, the downtown expansion of the banks in the postwar period, measured in deposits and employment, was greater than that in midtown.

Today, the commercial banks stand poised uneasily between a midtown and a downtown headquarters location. Three factors will influence the directions of their development in the decades ahead. One is the question whether daily travel to a downtown headquarters location for executives and staff becomes significantly more difficult than travel to a midtown location. If the rail and ferry facilities which serve the downtown area from suburban points deteriorate by comparison with the passenger facilities converging on the midtown area, this could tip the scales to midtown; this is a question whose answer lies today more in the hands of government than of business. A second consideration is ease of circulation between midtown and downtown within the central business district; if this circulation should grow more difficult or time-consuming the need to cater to the requirements of the midtown business client may override the desirability of being close to the rest of the downtown financial community. And a third is the direction of future growth of the nonfinancial activities in Manhattan's central business district. We shall touch on some of these issues again as our story develops.

But, in all the discussion of the choice between downtown and midtown Manhattan, we must not overlook the fact that the distribution of commercial bank facilities in the Region has been changing in still another way during recent decades. Deposits and employment in commercial banks have been growing far faster in the predominantly suburban areas of the Region than they have in the old cities. From 1947 to 1956, for instance, commercial bank employment grew by 19 per cent in New York City and by 9 per cent in Essex and Hudson Counties, which contain the old New Jersey cities.[7] In sharp contrast, the growth in Nassau and Suffolk Counties was 132 per cent, and that of the rest of the Region 53 per cent.[8]

Behind these facts is a revolution in the nature of commercial banking activity. Whereas the customers of commercial banks were once primarily business enterprises, today they consist in good part of individuals—individual depositors making their household payments through checking accounts, and individual borrowers financing the purchase of homes or automobiles. In fact, about half the personnel of commercial banks today are associated with the servicing of consumer loans.

Individuals rarely have an overwhelming preference for one bank over another. Therefore, commercial banks must now give much greater attention to the public accessibility of their facilities. And this has tended to shift bank employment to the areas in the Region where jobs and residences are increasing most rapidly. The resulting pattern can be seen in Table 18, which shows the 1956 distribution of employment in various segments of the financial community. By that year, over 20 per cent of the Region's commercial bank employment was found outside of New York City and Hudson and Essex Counties.

TABLE 18   Distribution of Financial Community, New York Metropolitan Region, 1956

	Number of employees (thousands)	Percentage shares of Region's employment (NYMR = 100)			
		Manhattan central business district[a]	Rest of New York City	Essex and Hudson	Rest of Region
Financial community, total	311.7	66.7	10.5	10.5	12.3
Commercial banks ...	82.3	63.7	9.9	6.1	20.3
Life and health insurance	83.2	62.1	10.3	18.5	9.1
Property insurance ..	72.6	69.6	5.0	12.6	12.8
Securities industries .	38.1	94.9	3.0	1.3	0.8
Miscellaneous finance	35.5	48.1	31.4	7.5	13.0

[a] As mapped in our Map 3. The district consists approximately of Manhattan south of Central Park.

Sources: Estimates based on 3rd-quarter data collected by state departments of labor under unemployment insurance programs; U.S. Census Bureau, *County Business Patterns, First Quarter 1956;* and Dept. of City Planning, N.Y. City.

The life insurance companies. The locational adjustment and change which the life insurance companies have experienced in the New York Metropolitan Region have had some marked similarities to those of the commercial banks; yet there have been critical differences. On the whole, the insurance companies appeared later than banks; among the earliest of them, New York Life was organized in 1845, Equitable in 1859, and Metropolitan Life in 1868. By that time, the downtown financial district of Manhattan had been clearly delineated and there were compelling advantages in being close by. For, in the earliest days of the life insurance business, neither the insurance policies nor the investment practices of the companies were anything like as standardized and conservative as they were later to become.

As time went on, new forces emerged to affect the location of the insurance companies. By the twentieth century the industry had grown much more staid. Its investments were no longer the speculative sort, sensitive to the daily gyrations of the securities markets. Its insurance contracts became more and more standardized, both in coverage and in cost, as mortality tables became reliable and experience with claims grew. The need to be current, to be close to other companies and close to the securities markets, gradually declined. And, when state regulation of their activities developed and grew after 1905, the personal communication needs of the life insurance companies were reduced even further.

What is more, the growing volume of business had turned life insurance companies from shoestring operations to some of the largest employers of clerical help in the New York area. The staff of Metropolitan Life, which could be accommodated in two and one-half rooms at 243 Broadway in 1868, required a seven-story building only eight years later. The firm now has about 15,000 employees in its home office.

The main locational needs of life insurance offices in the twentieth century, therefore, settled down to these: First, the offices had to be where replacements for a large work staff could be readily recruited; proximity to the financial district was useful but not essential. Second, they needed exposure, that is, some outstanding location which would associate the company with permanence and solidity in the public mind. These were the considerations which placed Metropolitan Life and New York Life at Madison

Square in its heyday, and Prudential and Mutual Benefit on Broad Street in downtown Newark.

Though it is unlikely that any of these large institutions will make spectacular moves in the next few decades, such as shifting their home offices to suburban locations, it is not at all unlikely that the relative attractiveness of Manhattan's central business district and Newark's downtown area will be reduced. As we shall point out in Chapter 8, the changing distribution of populations in the Region, the impairment of mass transit facilities, and the ubiquity of the automobile are all reducing the relative strength of the old central points of the Region as gathering places for workers. Though Metropolitan Life, for instance, drew 41 per cent of its office force from Manhattan homes in 1910, the proportion had gone down to 15 per cent by 1946 and is probably lower today. An analogous tendency has been evident at Prudential in Newark. The ties of life insurance operations to the environment of a central business district, therefore, now seem more slack.[9] And, though we do not propose to predict much outward movement of these home office operations as a result of such slackness, that conclusion might need re-examining if mass transit facilities were to undergo a much greater decline in efficiency.

Life insurance activities in the Region promise to disperse outward toward the newer areas, however, for quite another reason. In addition to generating home-office employment, these activities generate employment in the field —partly in branch offices which are an integral part of the company structure, and partly in the offices of independent insurance brokers. These field offices are the selling and servicing centers of the insurance companies; hence, unlike the home offices, they must be placed with due regard for holding down the travel time and travel costs of salesmen. The outward spread of people in the Region, therefore, has the effect of pulling these field offices outward as well. This is why, in the period between 1947 and 1956, employment in life insurance field offices grew most rapidly in the areas where population and jobs experienced the highest increases, while areas with slower rates of growth in population and jobs had relatively slow field-office growth. And this tendency, one may predict with assurance, will continue in the decades ahead.

THE OTHER OFFICE WORKERS

All told, the great amorphous body of office workers in the New York Metropolitan Region—apart from those in the financial community—numbers roughly 895,000, spread through scores of activities and occupations. These are office workers in office buildings; that is, they exclude the 685,000 or so clerks, typists, and other office employees tucked away in manufacturing plants, retail stores, transportation terminals, garages, warehouses, and other miscellaneous structures.[10] For our purposes the distinction is important; for these latter 685,000, we must assume, are located according to the locational needs of the enterprises to which they are attached and not with regard to any special locational needs of the office itself.

New York's early lead in wholesaling and in finance broke ground for its ascendancy as the office headquarters of most of the nation's large corporations. Yet, in analyzing the locational aspects of the Region's office work, it would be misleading to equate central offices with office work as a whole, for the Region's office buildings house a diverse group of activities of which central offices are only a fraction. Exactly how big a fraction depends on how one chooses to define a "central office," but in the narrow sense in which we use the term, central office employees of manufacturing, mining, retail, and transportation enterprises make up 15 per cent of the office workers in office buildings.

Another 17 per cent can be thought of as being closely associated with the central offices and also with the financial community and the wholesaling trades; these are the accounting and legal services, the advertising and employment agencies, the architects and engineering services, and a variety of similar activities—groups which look for much of their business to the office community and to one another.

Once removed from these are the offices of the public utilities, including the gas, electricity, and communications services. They, too, cater to the needs of the rest of the office community at large, but they derive most of their business from the homes and factories of the Region. These account for another 10 per cent of the office category we are now considering. Real estate firms, which are sometimes considered a part of the financial community, add another 16 per cent. Government employees in office buildings add still another 14 per cent. And finally the balance of 28 per cent is taken up by a group so heterogeneous that it almost defies any classification, though nonprofit organizations, television and radio offices, and news syndicates can be identified as prominent among them.

WHERE AND WHY

If the activities of all these office groups differ widely, their locational proclivities do not. As Table 19 shows, the preferred location by a very large margin is Manhattan, while Newark represents a much smaller center. After that, the preferred locations trail off, with Westchester, Nassau, and Hudson Counties in the lead.

There is a temptation to think of this clustering of office work as being based on some nebulous preference of executives for the fast tempo and bright lights of the big city. Indeed, the literature on the subject abounds with semi-mystical references of this sort. But the forces that have produced the clustering can be much more objectively defined; and their definition invokes familiar concepts, encountered again and again in our earlier discussions.

Central offices house two kinds of activity. For one thing, they are headquarters for a peripatetic group of executives —the office elite. If there is one trait that the elite group has in common, it is that they cannot say with any measure of certainty what their critical problems are likely to be during any given year. These problems may range from tax questions to television advertising, from Guatemala's economy to California's politics.

The variability of the problems bears important locational implications. Even the largest central office cannot

TABLE 19   Distribution of Office Workers in Office Buildings, Other than Financial Community,[a] New York Metropolitan Region, 1956

	Number of employees (thousands)	Percentage shares of Region's employment (NYMR = 100)				
		New York City	Essex and Hudson	Nassau	West-chester	Rest of Region
Nonfinancial office workers, total	895.6	76.3	6.4	2.5	2.9	11.9
Central offices[b]	133.3	84.5	6.3	0.8	1.7	6.7
Services closely identified with central offices[c]	156.3	79.6	6.6	2.5	2.2	9.1
Public utility offices ..	85.8	63.9	9.1	3.2	5.0	18.8
Real estate offices[d] ...	147.4	81.5	5.9	2.3	2.6	7.7
Government offices ...	127.7	73.1	6.0	3.8	2.5	14.6
Nonprofit organizations[e]	171.0	69.5	6.6	2.7	4.9	16.3
Radio and television offices and news syndicates	20.6	95.7	1.5	0.3	0.1	2.4
Others[f]	53.4	74.0	5.5	3.0	1.8	15.7

Note: Because of rounding, columns may not add exactly to totals.

[a] Excludes not only the financial community (given in Table 18) but also many office workers in establishments such as retail stores and manufacturing plants.

[b] Includes about 35,000 employees who were also counted as wholesale workers (see Table 15) because of the dominant selling function of the central offices involved.

[c] Examples: offices of accountants, advertising and employment agencies, lawyers, engineers, and architects.

[d] Includes law and insurance functions of real estate offices.

[e] Principally the offices of business associations, research institutions, professional societies, labor unions, and political, charitable, religious, civic, and social organizations.

[f] Examples: adjustment, credit, and collection agencies; duplicating services; and certain business and professional services not classified elsewhere in table.

Source: Estimates based on U.S. Census Bureau, *County Business Patterns, First Quarter 1956,* and on data collected by state departments of labor under unemployment insurance programs. Further details in Appendix A.

easily staff itself internally to deal with all the specialized problems that will come up. If a major patent case arises once in every two or three years, the company's house counsel may act as a conduit to outside legal advisers but can hardly be expected to provide the most expert advice in the field. If some esoteric aspect of depreciation policy is involved in an income tax audit by the Bureau of Internal Revenue, the expertise of the company's comptroller or treasurer is likely to need supplementing from outside the firm. If a new cost-accounting system is to be installed, outside experience may have to be tapped. In short, the volume of business done by the central office in many of these specialized fields is neither so large nor so constant as to justify internal staffing to deal with them. On the other hand, the aggregate volume of business provided by the whole office community in any such specialty is quite enough to justify the existence of outside specialists in the field.

This factor alone would not draw the business elite physically toward their outside advisers were it not that face-to-face interchange is the only adequate means of communication for much of the executive's work. Here we have once again the situation encountered in the analysis of communication-oriented manufacturing and of the financial community; delicate negotiations and subtle, complex ideas are not easily entrusted to the telephone or the letter. In this respect, the Manhattan central business district has a clear advantage over any other location in the Region, since its working population is so densely packed in a tiny land space.

One may well ask, however, whether some alternative central-office location in the Region may exist where costs would be lower, albeit the advantages just mentioned were less. In looking for the answer to this question it is important to note that although alternative manufacturing locations can be compared with some measure of precision, alternative office locations cannot. There is no process of accounting that can weigh the enhancement in the quality of executive decision-making in a given location against the added costs of operating in that location. Besides, the central office contains the ultimate authority in the firm. For practical purposes there is no force beyond the management itself which might independently decide that a preferred location—a location which made management's job easier—was not worth the added cost it entailed. Accordingly, management's choice of a location is peculiarly insensitive to the cost considerations typically involved in locating most types of enterprises. As long as the general conviction exists that Manhattan is the only place to locate a central business office, any economic fact to the contrary is likely to be slow in making itself felt.

Thus far, however, we have been discussing only the elite function of the central offices. Much more important in numbers and payroll are the workers who handle the routine aspects of the central-office functions. Fragmentary figures indicate that in the larger firms such office workers outnumber the elite group by 50 to one or even 100 to one.

Though the duties of these workers do not require them to be located in the central business district to the same extent as their superiors, the near-universal practice is to locate them there. One reason, of course, is mass transportation. Repetitive office work has traditionally been the special preserve of young women; nearly two-thirds of office workers in the Region are women and better than half of these are less than 30 years of age. With a work force of this sort, there is some benefit in locating at the apex of a network of mass transit lines. This gives Newark and Manhattan a significant advantage over most other areas in the Region.[11]

Yet too much can be made of the superiority of Newark and Manhattan as points of collection for pools of office labor. In a rapidly increasing proportion of cases, young women have the alternative of commuting by car to a point in the Region outside the central business district. In Westchester County, where a few large office establishments and many small ones exist, automobile commuting by young women is commonplace.

The young women's preference for a job in the central business district today, therefore, is not based quite so solidly as before on the hard compulsions of the transportation net; it is based instead on the increased opportunities for after-hours recreation, lunch-hour shopping (or window-shopping), and the greater opportunities for husband-hunting. This means, as we observed in connection with life insurance companies, that office establishments with a large complement of workers—our field work suggests that the critical level may be 500 or so—would have a considerably easier time recruiting and maintaining a staff of clerical workers in the central business district. For smaller office establishments, however, the advantage is not nearly so great.

Manhattan's status as an office center depends on other factors as well. Its dominance as a site for mass repetitive office operations might be somewhat imperiled, for instance, if the cost of office space in that borough were clearly higher than elsewhere. But this is not the case. To be sure, "prestige" buildings in Manhattan command a premium rental, but the run-of-the-mill modern office structure in Manhattan rents at rates very little different from those located elsewhere in the Region. The annual rental for such buildings in Manhattan is $4.75 to $5.50 per square foot. In downtown Newark, roughly the same range prevails, while in downtown Brooklyn slightly lower rates are typical.

A comparison of rentals does not tell the whole story, however, for an institution which is sufficiently large can envisage constructing and owning a suburban office facility. But if it does, according to calculations presented in Appendix H, the space cost per employee is likely to exceed those of the run-of-the-mill Manhattan location and to be roughly equal to a prestige location in Manhattan. Suburban office construction is usually burdened by the need for devoting space to various amenities for employees, such as snack bars and beauty parlors. As a result, the amount of space per employee in such buildings runs about one-third higher than in Manhattan office buildings. And zoning laws and parking demands add still further to the cost of land and buildings. Thus the margin which otherwise might favor suburban construction is wiped out.

The prevailing pattern for central offices in the Region, then, is to favor a Manhattan location. And their decision largely determines the location of the accountants, lawyers, advertising agencies, and similar specialists who contribute to the operations of the office elite.

Of course, there are other reasons why advertising agencies, lawyers, and other such groups tend to congregate in a compact urban area. Like the suppliers to the garment trade, they are influenced in their locational tendencies not only by the need to be near their market but also by the need to be near the services on which they in turn draw. The illustrations are legion: the advertising agencies' dealings with free-lance artists and lithographers, as well as their dealings with publishing firms, radio and television networks; the lawyers' dealings with printers and with one another; the accountants' dealings with the lawyers; and so on. In each of these cases, there is no practicable way of assimilating the outside service into the firm. And in each case, face-to-face contact is an almost indispensable prerequisite of effective communication.

Though 80 per cent of the Region's employment in these business services is concentrated in New York City, such services are not nearly so concentrated as the central offices themselves. The other 20 per cent of their employment is distributed in the 17 counties outside New York City and is particularly noticeable in Essex, Nassau, and Fairfield—where it is somewhat out of proportion to the total employment of the counties. The reason why such activity is more diffused than central offices is that the clients of lawyers, accountants, architects, engineers, and so on, are not exclusively the central offices. Other clients exist in the retail stores, warehouses, manufacturing plants, and even in the residences distributed about the Region. Hence, a locational compromise ensues. While seeking a large measure of centrality by congregating in the most populous counties, these groups nevertheless spread out among the clients from whom they expect to receive a portion of their business.

Similar forces determine the location of other identifiable groups of office workers. In general, establishments with functions of Region-wide or national scope are very heavily concentrated in New York City—indeed, in the central business district of Manhattan. Among the major government agencies which fit this description are the Port of New York Authority and the field offices of federal agencies like the Customs Service, Department of Commerce, and Securities and Exchange Commission. The pattern is the same for real estate firms. The organizations whose interests extend throughout the Region or beyond it are almost always found in New York City. Webb and Knapp, James Felt & Co., Pease and Elliman, Bing and Bing, and William A. White & Sons, among others, are in the central business district. Once again with utilities: the Bell System's national offices are in Manhattan and so are the national offices of those public utility holding companies that are located in the Region. And finally, the nonprofit institutions with wide interests once again congregate in Manhattan—the national trade associations, the welfare and charitable organizations, the unions. (But since every rule must have its occasional exceptions, the Boy Scouts of America are located at the southern edge of the Region in New Brunswick, New Jersey.)

Almost always, what pulls these groups to Manhattan, rather than to Newark, to White Plains, or to Bridgeport, is one variant or another of the motivations that influence the central-office elite. In many cases, too, no inexorable economic force would operate to wreck the organization if it erred in its locational decision. Thus, one could readily envisage many of these organizations remaining in New York City well beyond the time the City had ceased to be their optimum location in some objective sense; or, alternatively, leaving the City for other locations despite the fact that the move might reduce the organization's efficiency. The Darwinian principle, which operates to destroy manufacturing plants or sales offices which have chosen an egregiously unsuitable site, plays a very dilute role here.

The spread of some office establishments beyond New York City into the other counties is largely a reflection of the fact that they have less-than-Region-wide scope for their activities. Their narrower scope, with the need for communication, has placed many of these entities at the approximate center of their respective "markets." This pattern is illustrated by local government offices and, once again, by labor unions, charitable organizations, and operating public utilities. The main offices of the electric and

gas companies, for example, are located in the denser portions of the territories they serve. Public Service Electric &
Gas Co., serving Hudson County and most of Bergen, Passaic, Essex, Union, Somerset, and Middlesex Counties, is
centered in Newark; the Long Island Lighting Co. has its
principal office in Mineola; the Brooklyn Gas Co. in downtown Brooklyn; and so on.

The hierarchy of markets descends continuously from
major portions of the Region to counties and neighborhoods. At the neighborhood level, one finds the smaller
real estate establishments, the local lawyers, the local accountants and architects, and offices of the smaller town-
ships and municipalities. At each level, the prime locational force is the need to minimize the time and cost of
the communication process.

PAST AND FUTURE

Still, there are changes afoot. It is not easy to measure
how far these changes have progressed, since any effort to
trace the changing locations of office workers in the New
York Metropolitan Region over significant stretches of time
bogs down in a morass of incomplete and unreliable statistics. Yet something can be said about the past and prospective location of such office activities which is more than
pure surmise.

The great mushrooming of office activity did not really
get under way until late in the nineteenth century. Prior
to that time even the largest business enterprises operated
with a tiny office force. In 1856 one textile firm with annual sales of $1.3 million had only four clerks. Not until
the last three decades of the century did the maintenance
of detailed accounting records become general. The first
planned national advertising campaign was not launched
till 1898. Management advisory or consulting organizations
did not assume much importance until the 1920's, and
most of their growth has taken place since World War II.

The location of each new increment of office activity was
governed by the location of the pre-existing mass and by
the ties of communication to the mass. For the elite group
in central offices in the 1880's, for instance, much of the

preoccupation was with arranging finances, negotiating mergers, and manipulating securities; this focus of interest tied the group closely to the financial community. For the advertising agencies which came into existence later, two lines of communication were critical: one led to the central offices, from which business flowed and with which ideas and budgets were developed; the other led to the newspapers, periodicals, and broadcasting network offices —media for the dissemination of the advertising agencies' output. In a rough and ready way, one sees each layer of office growth settling in on the edge of the central business district, its center of gravity a little further north from the last.

Yet the pattern was not that smooth. There were hops and skips in Manhattan, from the nucleus below Chambers Street to the nucleus above 34th Street, and there were streamers of growth north from 42nd Street, concentrating on some avenues but overlooking others. We ascribe some of these seemingly capricious locational choices to the influence of the location of mass transit facilities, such as the importance to the elite group of the location of Grand Central Station. Another factor is the greater ease of amassing an adequate site for an office structure in some portions of the business district than in others. One reason why office developers chose Park Avenue in preference to some of the other main avenues for the intensive development of new office structures was the fact that sites on Park Avenue could be accumulated so much more readily. For Park Avenue was lined with huge apartment houses, one or two to the block, while the other streets typically were covered by seven or eight small structures to the block. The multiplicity of structures meant a longer planning span for anyone concerned with amassing a building site; the increased span represented an impediment to any corporation anxious to get on with the business of creating a new home for its central office, and it represented a major risk to any developer anxious to take advantage of a current demand for office space. Considerations of this sort outweighed questions of site costs.

In the future development of the central business district of Manhattan, however, one factor still stands out as the critical locational determinant, namely, the location of mass transit facilities. Despite the trend to automobiles and buses for commuting purposes, the proportion of jobholders in Manhattan's central business district using subway and suburban trains is still overwhelming. One study shows that two-thirds of the persons entering Manhattan south of 61st Street on a typical business day in 1956 used rapid transit or railroad;[12] for persons en route to work the proportion would be considerably higher. An increase in the proportion using rubber instead of rails in the decades ahead seems inevitable, for reasons which are explored in Chapter 8. But the increase will be restricted by the capacities of the streets, tunnels, and bridges which provide ingress to the central business district and by the facilities for daytime parking; these appear to offer severe limitations on the rate of automobile traffic growth in Manhattan, though they are less important in curbing the use of automobiles to downtown Newark. Accordingly, the complex of transit lines and connections at the Grand Central area offers an anchor point to which the central business district still remains firmly attached. To the extent that future office growth requires it, therefore, there is a presumption that developers will tend to favor sites near the Grand Central area, sites that have been bypassed in the first postwar rash of building.

The distribution of office activity in the New York Metropolitan Region, however, is not solely a question involving the central business district. Though 76 per cent of office workers in office buildings were found in New York City and though all but a small fraction of these were in Manhattan's central business district, the future pattern could conceivably be quite different.

One possibility is that some central offices and some of the business services related to them may prefer a location in a secondary office center like Newark or in a suburban setting. Many national or regional organizations have considered the possibility of settling in a suburban location. A few large companies, notably General Foods and Standard-Vacuum, have actually made such moves, and so have a considerable number of smaller ones. Westchester County has been a preferred area, but a few companies have chosen locations in the New Jersey and Connecticut suburbs.

The motive for such moves, as we indicated earlier, was probably not the cost of space. Neither could labor-market considerations have figured very heavily in the calculation. In fact, the problem of labor recruitment—in a quantitative if not in a qualitative sense—may have been exacerbated. Besides, communication with the rest of the business world was somewhat handicapped by the move to the suburbs. Indeed, the one clear strength of a suburban office over a Manhattan setting was the possibility of reducing the journey to work on the part of executives.

Yet the choice was made. Some of the smaller firms felt, no doubt, that they could afford to choose the suburbs because their work-force replacement problem did not loom very large. Others made the choice because the activities of the office were of such a nature as to require few personal contacts in Manhattan's business district. Illustrative of the latter type of office were numerous regional sales centers.

The position of the business district of Manhattan, therefore, is not invulnerable. And its vulnerability increases in measure as its relative advantage declines as a collecting point for large office complements. As already seen, this advantage is clearly declining because of the outward dispersion of the work-force and the increased use of the automobile by young women. As for Newark's position as an office center, that city could conceivably benefit from the decline in Manhattan's relative position while at the same time losing some of its own office activities to the New Jersey suburbs—in a modified game of musical chairs. It is more likely, however, that in the competition between Manhattan and the rest of the Region, Newark will be bypassed and suburban locations will benefit.

In the end, the office population of Manhattan's business district may be held down without the overt transfer of many central business offices to other locations. This could happen in two ways: either by a peeling-off of specialized self-contained functions to other locations, functions with few communication ties to the rest of Manhattan; or by a marked increase in the productivity of office workers brought on by office mechanization. Nor are these mutually exclusive possibilities; both could occur.

Finally, there is one other force at work which may tend to shift the distribution of the office populations of the New York Metropolitan Region outward from the long-established business districts. Some of the offices of the Region are quite local in the scope of their interests and are bound to follow the population drift. Probably this drift was primarily responsible for the outward shift evident in real estate offices from 1947 to 1956; during this period, the Core's share of such employment in the Region dropped from 89 per cent to 84 per cent. For a miscellaneous group of business services, the comparable ratio dropped from 87 per cent to 81 per cent, while for non-profit organizations the ratio fell from 82 to 76 per cent. For each such group, the Core's relative decline was taken up by expansion in both Rings of the Region. The outward move of the Region's populations and total employment in the future will lay the groundwork for a further outward shift of these office jobs.

THE BOOM IN SKYSCRAPERS

In one sector after another of the office community, we see the same general picture: a high concentration of activity in Manhattan and one or two other districts but a tendency for the most rapid growth to occur in the newer suburban areas. Yet, for all the unanimity of the figures, the eyes tell a story with a somewhat different emphasis. Millions of feet of new skyscraper space have been created in Manhattan since the end of World War II. In a Park Avenue setting where the elegant office building is replacing the elegant apartment house, up and down Third and Sixth Avenues where the "el" no longer is heard, and on 42nd Street east of Grand Central, metal-and-glass buildings of about 30 floors, more or less, have been altering the Manhattan skyline. An impressive group of postwar office structures has also risen in downtown Newark. And the drafting boards are crowded with plans for more office buildings in both cities. How does one reconcile the two seemingly diverse impressions?

Here, we must emphasize the point that "percentage shares" are a tricky measure. Manhattan's *share* of the Region's employment in accounting offices or commercial banks may decline but still the absolute number of employees in Manhattan's offices may rise—albeit at a slower *rate* than in the rest of the Region. This is exactly what has happened in many lines of office employment. Taking the financial community and other office building employment together, crude estimates suggest that Manhattan's employment may have grown by about 10 per cent between 1947 and 1956, from 753,000 to 830,000 persons.

So far, the growth in Manhattan's office space in the postwar period has been somewhat greater than the growth in its office population, and this disparity will continue for the next few years. There was something like 120 million square feet of space in Manhattan's office buildings in 1947 and by the end of 1956 the total was up to 138 million, an increase of 13.9 per cent. By 1960 another 25 million feet will have been added.

The postwar expansion in office space, therefore, has been due to more than the growth in office employment. It has also been due to an upgrading in the kind of space many enterprises have demanded. Salesrooms, for instance, occupy no insignificant part of the office buildings of Manhattan. When times were poor in the 1930's, many lines economized on rental costs by doing their selling out of loft buildings—buildings designed for light manufacture. When business boomed in the early postwar period, such lines were obliged for a time to cling to their old loft quarters because of the acute shortage of space. But, as new office buildings opened up, many salesrooms eagerly switched from the aging loft structures they had long inhabited to more elaborate—and more expensive—space in office buildings.

A reflection of the shift is found in recent changes in the quantity and use of space in Manhattan's loft buildings. Total space in loft buildings has been declining in Manhattan in recent years, largely because of demolitions and conversions.[13] At the same time, the proportion of space in loft buildings used for nonmanufacturing activities —activities such as sales and office work—has also been shrinking perceptibly.[14] Quite clearly, some of the shrinkage is accounted for by the fact that erstwhile loft inhabitants have been moving into such office structures as the Union Dime, the Empire State, and other buildings in the midtown area.

Something else has probably been going on to expand the amount of office space in Manhattan. Though documentation of the trend is hard to come by, it is fairly clear that the amount of square feet of office space allotted to the average member of the office elite and his immediate entourage has gone up in the postwar period.[15] The potency of this factor as a source of present and future demand for space should not be minimized. The average office dweller uses about 150 square feet of space in Manhattan, and a comparatively small addition to this average could greatly expand the total amount of space in use. An addition of only 10 feet per person—an addition which could be had for about $65 per year per person—would absorb half of the postwar growth in office space in Manhattan through 1956.

One important inference may be drawn from this sort of speculation. Whether the skyscraper community continues to grow does not depend alone on the number of office workers in Manhattan. It depends also on who those office workers are and what they do. Manhattan's position as an office location, we have suggested, is weakest for repetitive, standardized office work, strongest for the elite activities of the office. Therefore, if standardized office activities peel off from Manhattan locations in the next decade or two, the space demands of the average office worker in Manhattan will almost certainly increase—and this will happen whether or not the office elite continue to expand the amount of space per person that they occupy. In the decade or two just ahead, no requiem will be sung for the skyscraper. But it must never be forgotten that the future growth of the skyscraper community is tied to the mass transit web which serves it.

5

THE PURSUIT OF CONSUMERS

In any analysis of the location of jobs in a metropolitan area, a discussion of the jobs which serve the consumer usually brings up the rear. The reason is simple. Such jobs, common observation tells us, are likely to be distributed on a pattern which accords closely with the distribution of population.

Common observation is right, of course. But it is right with major *caveats*. The figures in Table 20 show that a quarter of the Region's one million proprietors and full-time employees who serve consumers fall in the glamor-and-glitter categories of consumer trades and services—in theaters, nightclubs, eating places, bars, and hotels. Another 18 per cent are found in department stores, jewelry shops, apparel stores, and furniture outlets. All these consumer facilities show a pronounced affinity for the three central shopping areas of the Region—the big one in Manhattan* and the smaller ones in downtown Newark and downtown Brooklyn. Some of these activities are on the move. Accordingly, major questions arise about the future distribution of employment in consumer trades and services in the Region.

CRAWL OF THE CENTRAL SHOPPING AREA

The forces which determine where a retail merchant is to settle have not changed a great deal in the modern his-

* Manhattan's "central shopping area," as used in this chapter, means the area located approximately between Third and Tenth Avenues and between Central Park and Canal Street, as contrasted with the much larger "central business district" shown in Map 3.

tory of urban areas. Whether retail buyers have traveled on foot, by horsecar, or by auto, one element in their choice of an outlet has been the desire to conserve the time and cost of transportation. Ideally, buyers would wish all outlets to be at their doorsteps. And, indeed, whenever the demand for a product or service in any small neighborhood has become stable enough that a retailer could readily predict it, an outlet handling the product or service has generally had a way of appearing there.

In the New York of the early nineteenth century, this was the principle which created outlets for flour, sugar, and kerosene in every neighborhood, but it was a principle hardly applicable to the sale of fine fabrics or pianos. Given the uncertainty of demand in matters of taste, no neighborhood store could predict the demand for any fine fabric it might carry. And, given the infrequency of piano purchases, no purveyor of pianos could afford to rely on the erratic demand generated in any small area. So, even in

TABLE 20   Employment in Consumer Trades and Services, New York Metropolitan Region, 1954

(in thousands)

Grand total	1,019	Drugstores	20
Consumer trades, total	747	Other consumer trades[b]	129
Eating, drinking places	183	Consumer services, total	272
Food stores	138	Laundries, cleaning, shoe	
Apparel and accessories	89	repair[c]	88
Department stores	51	Hotels, motels	49
Automotive group[a]	42	Amusement, recreation	
Furniture, furnishings,		(including 13 thousand	
appliances	41	in movie theaters)	38
Gasoline service stations	27	Barber, beauty shops	36
Lumber, building		Auto repair, garages,	
materials, hardware,		parking	24
farm equipment	27	Other consumer services[d]	37

[a] About nine-tenths passenger car dealers.
[b] Examples: variety stores (19 thousand), liquor stores (10 thousand), fuel dealers (15 thousand), jewelry stores (7 thousand).
[c] Includes Census categories "laundries, laundry services," "cleaning, pressing, dyeing, garment repair," and "shoe repair shops, shoeshine parlors, hat cleaning shops."
[d] Includes "miscellaneous repair services," plus all "personal services" except laundries, cleaning, shoe repair, and barber, beauty shops.

Source: U.S. *1954 Census of Business*, plus our estimates for certain counties. Figures include proprietors and full-time employees.

those early times, certain kinds of goods were being sold at central locations: style goods, at some common point where many purveyors of rival products were clustered; goods great in value but thin in demand, at central points which could most readily tap a larger market.

The cluster of shopping outlets for style goods in the Manhattan of the early nineteenth century was supplemented, as it is today, by the outlets which catered to the once-in-a-while demands of a large local market. The opera, the theater, and the fine eating places were all located in the middle of the area from which they drew their trade. In the 1830's these facilities were grouped in the City Hall Park area. Their centrality, however, was also due to the fact that they served not only a local market but also a market of out-of-towners brought to the metropolis by business or pleasure.

As the years went on, the consumer facilities of Manhattan crawled northward like almost everything else. By 1850, "the" shopping district stood at about Canal Street and Broadway, just south of the then finest residential section of the City. It continued to travel in the wake of the better residences and was centered at 14th Street in 1880. In this area familiar names like Macy, Tiffany, Altman, and W. & J. Sloane were to be found. But even busy 14th Street lost out to locations farther uptown. Twenty-third Street became the center for a while, only to yield to 34th Street, which became the heart of the department store area just after the turn of the century. Once more the decisions on the location of the Grand Central Station and the Pennsylvania Station were important in determining the rate of northward crawl. Once more a strategic element was the pattern of the subways—themselves induced by the distribution of the shopping centers, yet inducing more change in their turn.

Today, the main retail "nucleus" of Manhattan is more diffused than ever before, being strung along miles of streets and avenues in the midtown area. On the whole, however, it is far closer to Central Park than to the tip of the island. Some signs of added northward crawl are still in evidence. The spectacular Lincoln Square redevelopment project in the West 60's will draw the opera, concerts, and theater productions farther northward than they have so far been. Yet the forces that have pulled the nub of consumer activity northward in Manhattan during the last century or more seem to be waning. Because of trends to be discussed in this and later chapters, our expectations are that the consumer trades and services of Manhattan's central shopping area will not grow in employment during the next few decades, and may well shrink. The search for new space, therefore, will not be strong. In addition, the convergence of mass transit facilities will probably remain south of 57th Street—at Grand Central and Pennsylvania Stations, at the Port Authority Terminal, and at Times Square. Besides, as we suggested earlier, there is some reason to anticipate that the office building district will not expand much farther from the Grand Central area; instead it will fill spaces which it had bypassed in previous surges of expansion. These factors will tend to arrest the northward move of consumer trades and services.

But significant changes are likely to take place in the *composition* of these trades and services in the central shopping area. To estimate what these changes will be, we must examine the shifting pattern of consumer trades and services in the New York Metropolitan Region as a whole.

THE OUTWARD MOVEMENT

While the main shopping nucleus was crawling northward, retail trade was being redistributed through the Region on a much grander scale. As we have already seen, the impact of the motor truck and the search for space were propelling some other types of jobs outward from the central business district; witness the jobs in manufacturing and wholesaling. And as Chapter 8 will show, the automobile was spurring residents to join the outward movement. What is more, the new pattern of residential settlement was much less dense than the old; in travel time, therefore, the new residential areas were more remote from the central business district than they would have been if they had crowded in at the old densities.

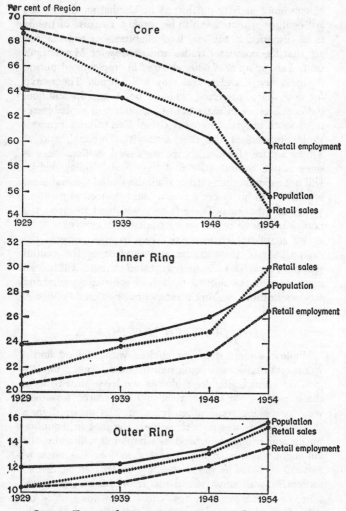

CHART 4

Trends in Retail Employment, Retail Sales, and Population
in Main Zones of New York Metropolitan Region,
1929, 1939, 1948, 1954 (Region = 100 per cent)

Source: For population estimates see Appendix B. Other data
based on U.S. *Census of Business* for years shown.

A reflection of these developments is to be seen in Chart 4, which shows how the Region's Core, Inner Ring, and Outer Ring changed in relation to one another from 1929 to 1954 in both population and retail trade. Here we see the gradual decline of the Core counties and the gradual relative growth of the Rings, with the trends in retail employment going hand in hand with the trends in population.

Between 1948 and 1954, the relative decline of retail employment in the Core was also an absolute decline. The same is true of consumer services, omitted from the chart for lack of data in the earlier years. In consumer trades and services combined, the number of jobs in the Core dropped from 685,000 to 632,000 during the six-year period. And in the years since 1954—the year when the last federal Census of Business was taken—there is evidence that the Core's relative and absolute declines continued.[1]

The same general trends seen in retail employment are also apparent in retail sales; in the 1929–1954 period the Core's share of such sales declined and the shares of both Rings increased. Yet there was a significant difference: retail sales shifted outward even more rapidly than retail employment. One reason for this is clear. In almost every line of trade, as Census data show, outlets in the suburbs have found ways of holding down their labor force while increasing their sales, and they have done this far more effectively than their city competitors. No doubt this difference is partly due to the freedom of suburban retailers to conserve manpower by means of more efficient layouts. But it probably is due also to more subtle factors. In some lines, consumer outlets remaining in the central business district may be concentrating more and more in product lines which are unstandardized in nature and demand comparative shopping or which have so thin a demand that no outlet in a suburban neighborhood could count on enough business to support it.

The outward movement of retail trade shows up vividly in the recent performance of the central shopping areas. As seen in Table 21, Manhattan's central shopping area, which in 1948 had accounted for 17 per cent of the Re-

TABLE 21 Geographical Distribution of Sales in Consumer Trade and Hotels, Motels, and Movie Theaters in Selected Parts of New York Metropolitan Region, 1948 and 1954

	1948	1954
Sales of entire Region	100.0%	100.0%
Manhattan, total	28.9	24.6
Central shopping area[a]	17.0	14.1
Rest of Manhattan	11.9	10.5
Essex County, total	6.8	6.7
Newark central shopping area[b]	2.0	1.7
Rest of Newark	2.1	2.1
Essex outside Newark	2.7	2.9
Brooklyn, total	14.6	12.7
Central shopping area[b]	2.1	1.5
Rest of Brooklyn	12.5	11.2
Region's other 19 counties	49.7	56.0

[a] This is the area defined by the U.S. Census Bureau as the "central business district," but it is much smaller than the central business district as used in this book and shown in Map 3. The smaller Census area falls approximately between Third and Tenth Avenues and between Central Park and Canal Street.

[b] "Central business district" as defined by Census Bureau.

Source: U.S. *1954 Census of Business,* series on "Retail Trade," "Selected Services," and "Central Business District Statistics," supplemented by our estimates.

gion's sales in consumer trade, hotels, motels, and movie theaters combined, accounted for only 14 per cent in 1954. Similarly, the share of Newark's central shopping area declined from 2.0 to 1.7 per cent in the same period, and the share of Brooklyn's from 2.1 to 1.5. One slight reason for these drops has been the decline in the resident populations of these shopping areas—the people to whom the central district is simply a local shopping neighborhood. But a much more important factor accounting for the decline of the central shopping areas of Manhattan, Newark, and Brooklyn has been the relative drop in the total populations of New York City and Newark. The phenomenon has not been an isolated one. In large American cities generally, population has been growing at a slower rate than in their suburbs. As a result, the dollar sales in the central shopping districts of these cities have failed to grow in the period 1948–1954, and there has been a noticeable shrink-

TABLE 22   Sales in the Central Shopping Areas[a] of Manhattan, Newark, and Brooklyn as a Percentage of Sales in New York Metropolitan Region, by Selected Consumer Trades and Services, 1948 and 1954

(NYMR = 100)

	1948	1954
All consumer trades, plus hotels, motels, movie theaters	21.1%	17.4%
Consumer trades		
Department stores	71.5	61.9
Furniture, furnishings, appliances	19.3	18.4
Jewelry stores	47.1	44.8
Apparel and accessories	38.6	36.9
Eating, drinking places	25.8	24.8
All other consumer trades[b]	8.2	6.3
Consumer services		
Hotels and motels	65.0	63.9
Movie theaters	26.6	29.2

[a] "Central business districts" as defined by U.S. Census Bureau. See Table 21, footnotes a and b.
[b] For example, food stores, auto dealers, gasoline stations, and liquor stores.

Source: U.S. *1954 Census of Business*, series on "Retail Trade," "Selected Services," and "Central Business District Statistics," supplemented by our estimates.

age in the shopping districts' share of the sales of their respective metropolitan areas.[2]

Yet, as Table 22 shows, different activities have reacted in different ways to the outward move of populations. The most spectacular response has been that of the department stores, whose changing location pattern reflects several kinds of "moves." Some of the old downtown department stores simply went out of business after the downtown populations thinned out. Others kept going but opened branch stores; Macy's, for example, opened a branch store in the Bronx before World War II and then expanded in the suburbs after the war. Wanamaker's represents yet another pattern; this firm, which for decades had been a downtown fixture at Broadway and 9th Street, opened up shop in the suburbs and then closed its doors downtown.

The effect of all such moves can be summarized by a single measure. Department store sales in the central shopping areas of Manhattan, Newark, and Brooklyn fell from 71.5 per cent to 61.9 per cent of the Region's total in the six years from 1948 to 1954.

In our view, however, it would be a mistake to assume that the relative increase in department store sales outside the three central shopping areas will continue at anything like the postwar rate. The outward movement of department stores, which is clearly a reflection of the dispersion of homes and the growing use of automobiles, has proceeded much faster than these factors would justify. The explanation, we suspect, is that such a movement occurs in fits and starts, not as a gradual and continuous process. Department stores are few in number and large in scale, and the locational shift of any one of them has a substantial impact. Among other things, their postwar moves have represented a catching-up operation, a massive adjustment to a shift in population which had been going on for some time. What is more, Macy's moves have spurred Gimbel's, and vice versa, in a way which is to be expected in a market consisting of a few large institutions rather than of many small ones.

The contrast between the behavior of department stores and that of other center-oriented retail activities is worth a word of comment. We saw in Table 22 that furniture, jewelry, and apparel stores, eating and drinking places, and hotels showed less tendency to disperse out of the central shopping areas toward the periphery of the Region. In receipts of motion picture theaters, the central shopping areas even managed to increase their share from 26.6 per cent to 29.2 per cent, probably because television was making inroads on the neighborhood theater without affecting the first-run movie houses quite so much. All these lines are buoyed in downtown locations by their capacity to draw the consumer from considerable distances and also by the presence of out-of-town visitors in the central city.[3]

On balance, therefore, the pattern seems to add up to this: the lines of retail activity which are tied closely to neighborhood populations—food stores, for instance, and laundries—are already well scattered throughout the Region and can be expected to keep moving outward as residences shift. At the other extreme, those which demand extensive comparative shopping or which rely on out-of-towners for a considerable portion of their sales will resist the continuing dispersion of populations and will cling much more tenaciously to the central shopping areas. In between these extremes are the department stores and other activities that can satisfy comparative shopping needs with clusters smaller than those in the central shopping areas. These may create—indeed, already have created —new retail nuclei from time to time at shopping centers spaced through the Region. But the development of the new centers will proceed in fits and starts, not in a regular growth pacing that of the population movement itself.

NEIGHBORHOOD SHOPPING PATTERNS

Though consumer trades and services in the three counties containing large central shopping areas carry the distinctive stamp imposed by those areas, the distribution of such activities in the other 19 counties of the Region follows a regularity calculated to gladden the heart of the statistician. In many lines, the number of proprietors and full-time employees varies from one county to the next in a strikingly close relation to the total number of residents of each county. In each consumer line of this type, a simple formula is capable of expressing with a fairly high degree of precision the relation between the population of the county and the number of employees in the particular line.[4] The extreme case is that of food stores; in 1954 one could closely estimate the food-store employment in any of the 19 counties simply by assuming about 96 employees for every 10,000 residents.[5]

If county populations offer a fairly close guide to county employment in many lines of consumer trade and service, there are even more lines in which a better guide is the aggregate number of jobs of all types in the county. Apparently enough buying is done away from home in some of these lines, such as liquor stores and drug stores, to tip the scales in favor of aggregate employment as a guide.

The slightly different character of the two groups of consumer activity may be seen in the following lists.

Lines in which county employment in the line is related most closely to county population:

> Food stores
> Eating and drinking places
> Apparel stores
> Cleaning, laundry, and clothing repair establishments
> Miscellaneous repair services
> Parking facilities
> Motion picture theaters

Lines in which county employment in the line is related most closely to county employment of all types:

> Jewelry stores
> Furniture and furnishings stores
> Drugstores
> Liquor stores
> Variety stores
> Department and dry goods stores
> Auto and accessory sales stores
> Gasoline service stations
> Auto repair facilities
> Retail stores not elsewhere classified

Not too much should be made of the differences, since county population and total county employment are so closely parallel from one county to the next. The controlling point is that, with a few minor exceptions, the distribution of jobs serving the consumer in the 19 counties offers no real obscurities and is readily explained by obvious features of the counties. Outside the three central shopping areas of the Region, therefore, the common observation holds: once we know where the population and the other jobs are likely to be, we can predict with a certain assurance the likely locations of the consumer-serving jobs.

PART III

THE PEOPLE

6

SPACIOUS LIVING VS. EASY ACCESS

We turn now from the location of jobs to the location of residences. The two questions are related, of course, one throwing light on the other. We saw in the last chapter that a good many important types of retail stores and consumer services systematically locate as near the customer's home as they can and are consequently spread over the Region in a pattern closely matching that of population. Certain other kinds of employment are located primarily to tap at close range the supply of special categories of labor, like that of recent immigrants in Manhattan. But these are exceptions. By and large, the distribution of jobs in the Region influences the distribution of population far more than the other way round.

If the location of jobs were the only factor determining where people live, the earlier chapters would have gone a long way toward providing an answer to our present question. But the answer is not that simple.

One pervasive and controlling fact is that the vast majority of choices of housing are made from the already existing supply, comprising houses and neighborhoods built some time in the past for other people with other needs and incomes, and under conditions differing from those of today.

Our search for an explanation of existing patterns of population will, then, necessarily lead us to inquire into the historical processes by which the metropolis has spread and its residential neighborhoods have been created and transformed. Chapter 8 will take up those processes in some detail. At the present juncture, however, we can best focus our attention on the present pattern of settlement and the insight it provides about the basic determining forces.

Both in the choice of housing from the existing supply and in the gradual evolution of that supply, we shall see evidences of a basic "balancing" process in operation. On the one hand, the incentive to live near jobs and other urban attractions tends to concentrate population and build up densities. Opposing this is a complex of resistances to concentration and high density based largely, though not wholly, upon the desire for spacious living. As we shall see, this balancing between access considerations and the opposing limitations on density has worked out very differently in the automobile era than in the horsecar days of the past, and it has worked differently for different types of people in the Region.

THE PRESENT DISTRIBUTION OF HOUSING

POPULATION DENSITY AND LAND DEVELOPMENT

We saw in Chapter 1 that population is very unevenly spread over the Region's area, and that density per square mile tends to be lower in the counties more distant from Manhattan.

In part, these differences in density reflect differences in the extent to which land has been developed. The Region's developed area has expanded largely by outward sprawl from a number of original urban centers. The need for daily access to such centers has provided a strong incentive to build up first the nearest available land, and to push urban settlement continuously outward along the routes of easiest travel. But the settlement pattern is patchy. Here and there are sparsely settled areas that residential expansion seems to have bypassed.

Some of those gaps are easily explained. The Jersey Meadows, for instance, were found unpleasant, mosquito-ridden, and costly to build on, and remain largely open to this day. All told, there are in the Region about 137 square miles of land—about 2 per cent of the total—which are rated too swampy to develop.[1] Rough topography has been another barrier to the uniform spread of population. Though the Ramapos lie within sight of the Manhattan skyline in an arc spreading through parts of Rockland and Bergen Counties, their forbidding terrain has kept them bucolic. There and elsewhere in the Region is a total of more than 1000 square miles—14 per cent of the Region's total land—on which residential development is made much more costly and in many instances prohibitively costly by excessive slope.[2]

Extensive public or private reservations, institutions, and other rival uses also interrupt the residence pattern. For instance, sections of middle Westchester County in a belt stretching from the Hudson River to Connecticut are pre-empted by parks and watershed reservations. Similar patterns of pre-emption are found in western Essex County on the New Jersey side of the Region. "Low intensity" uses such as these account for another 8 per cent of the Region's area.

Moreover, as the Region's populations have grown, so has the area claimed by intensive nonresidential uses. In major business and industrial districts, residence has been almost crowded out—for example, along Manhattan's main thoroughfares, and in the waterfronts and rail yards of the Region. The importance of nonresidential encroachment, however, should not be exaggerated. The areas of actual depopulation have been tiny in relation to the total developed area. Manhattan, focus of the Region's and much of the nation's business, still has by far the highest number of people per square mile of all the counties in the Region. Even in its central business district south of Central Park, very few tracts are actually depopulated; about three-quarters of the 126 Census tracts in that area still have 1000 inhabitants or more.[3]

By and large, the proportion of land developed diminishes as we go outward from the Region's center. We pointed out in Chapter 1 that there is little vacant land left in the Core, while in the Inner Ring a substantial proportion of the land still awaits residential development, and in the Outer Ring a larger proportion still. A detailed

close-up of the relation between the centrality of an area
and the extent of its land development is drawn in Table
23. Here we present the results of a detailed land-use
analysis for one portion of the Region—a portion in which
our interest is particularly high. This "Land-Use Survey
Area," as we shall call it, is depicted in Map 5. It is a belt
comprising five whole counties and parts of two others and
including 200-odd municipalities, predominantly suburban
in character and predominantly in the Inner Ring, where
the greater part of the Region's recent population growth
has been taking place. In the Land-Use Survey Area we
have a testing ground where the past's dead hand is a little
less controlling than in the Core, and where one comes
closer to discerning the current tastes of the Region's populations in the selection of their homes.

As Table 23 shows, we find that "centrality," as meas-

TABLE 23   Residential Land Development in Land-Use
Survey Area,[a] in Relation to Travel Time to
Manhattan, 1954–1955

Municipalities classified by access zones[b] (zone 1 is closest to Manhattan)	Number of municipalities in zone	Total acres of residential land available	Acres developed[c]	Acres vacant but suitable for development[d]	Percentage of available residential land developed
1	11	14,390	11,368	3,022	79.0
2	66	70,021	51,626	18,395	73.7
3	73	136,942	91,431	45,511	66.8
4	52	140,047	50,403	89,644	36.0
5	28	51,734	8,126	43,608	15.7

[a] See Map 5.

[b] Access zones were derived from a map based on an analysis of commuter timetables prepared by the Metropolitan Rapid Transit Survey.
Places in each successive access zone have about 15 minutes longer commuting time to midtown Manhattan than those in the preceding zone—
except that the city of Newark has been assigned in our tabulations to
zone 1, in view of its importance as an alternative destination, particularly for New Jersey commuters. In this table the four places in zone 6
have been combined with the twenty-four in zone 5, partly because of
their fewness and partly because of technical classification problems.

[c] Residentially "developed" land includes land primarily devoted to
residences, including abutting streets, where there is at least one dwelling unit per two acres.

[d] "Vacant" land includes land with residences at a density lower than
one dwelling unit per two acres. Land "suitable for development" excludes swamps and areas with slopes exceeding 10 per cent.

Source: See Appendix J.

MAP 5
Land-Use Survey Area

For exact boundaries in Westchester and Passaic Counties
see Table 24, notes b and c.

ured by access to Manhattan,[4] is closely related to the degree of residential development. In the innermost parts of the area covered by the land-use survey, the build-up of available residential land is almost four-fifths complete; that fraction falls consistently to less than 16 per cent for the remotest group of communities. A somewhat lower ratio still would prevail farther out, in the Outer Ring.

Yet the very fact that so much land remains vacant in communities well in toward the center of the Region shows that crude population density (population per square mile of land of all types) is an inadequate guide to an understanding of how and where people live. To gain some useful notions of the character of residential communities and their evolution, we must look at "net" densities—densities, that is, on the residentially developed land alone, apart from the vacant or nonresidential tracts between.[5]

THE DENSITY OF SETTLEMENT

The density of a block of new housing—and related style and quality features as well—generally first sees tangible expression in a developer's plat. But the process neither begins nor ends there. In the New York Metropolitan Region, the odds are very high that the developer will be working under zoning ordinances, since nearly 500 of the Region's 550 municipalities now apply such restraints. What is more, even where zoning does not narrow the developer's choice, his subdivision may be so closely bordered by earlier ones that the developer has little leeway for departing from the general community pattern.

The influence of the general community pattern—zoning or no zoning—is imposed on the developer in a variety of other ways. Street and utility layouts are closely related to the density and distribution of existing dwellings. More important still, a dwelling is likely to be more readily financed, sold, or rented when it is not markedly out of line with its neighbors. Accordingly, neighborhood density patterns, once set, have been rather stubbornly resistant to change.

Where zoning has had an appreciable impact, it has generally been a conservative influence, producing density patterns that are more stable over time and more uniform from one block to another within communities than would otherwise be the case. One important rationale of zoning based on land-use planning is, indeed, that it can produce patterns better adapted to future conditions and therefore subject to slower obsolescence and less need for change. At the same time, residential zoning controls—to the extent that they have had an effect—have generally exerted a downward pressure on the densities of new developments. Characteristically, zoning ordinances impose some minimum lot size, thus putting a ceiling on density. In another volume in this series, it will be seen that communities in the New York Metropolitan Region, when concerned about the tax effects of some new development, typically aim for somewhat lower densities than those that the developers find the most profitable.[6] The fiscal criterion is of course only one of the many reflected in the wide gamut of actual zoning patterns, but it does have some importance.

The fact that initial residential development in a neighborhood tends to set the subsequent pattern, and the further fact that zoning tends to hold down densities, would be enough in themselves to bring about higher densities in the old urban centers and lower ones in the newer suburbs. The older areas of the Region were laid out under the spatial restraints imposed by the slow horsecar and shank's mare. On top of this, zoning did not come into the picture in the Region in any significant way until the 1920's, thus affecting only the more recent developments. And, finally, the wants of people for more spacious sites grew over time; whereas a homesite of about one-sixth of an acre was representative of "middle-income" suburban developments in the Region a generation ago, buyers in the corresponding category today are generally demanding one-third of an acre. The impact of the change is seen by comparing the genteel homes of Pelham, Long Beach, and Teaneck, built in the era of the 1920's, with those built more recently in, say, Millburn or Westbury or the newer parts of Scarsdale.

But these are not the only reasons for the higher densities of the inlying areas. Further factors come into play subsequent to the first development of an area and press for upward revisions in neighborhood densities nearer the center—revisions which occur despite the restraining effects of the early patterns of development. How do these revisions come about?

The first wave of new development in any suburban zone, as we pointed out, is likely to be spotty, leaving extensive empty spaces. The land bypassed in this first wave commonly has some developmental handicap. In the pre-automobile era, a site very far from a railroad commuting station was at a disadvantage, often a decisive one. In all periods, leapfrogging has arisen from other difficulties, such as problems of clearing title or negotiating purchase of a properly rounded tract for development, or remoteness of utilities, or uncomfortable proximity to industry, or, of course, topographical conditions. Thus in practice, as Table 23 showed, fragments or sizable tracts of land that are highly attractive in terms of accessibility may be left vacant while they are progressively surrounded and development proceeds to much more remote areas. When finally the handicaps retarding development of these relatively accessible sites are overcome, their location is no longer on the outer suburban fringe; the developer's interest now may well lie in exploiting their enhanced access advantages by developing at higher net densities than would have been profitable when the area was on the fringe.

Closely akin to this process are two others—subdividing large old single-family houses to accommodate several households each, or replacing single houses with higher-density apartment buildings. Developments involving one or both of these processes are found all around the fringes of the Core and portions of the Inner Ring. The Forest Hills area of Queens—an area of one-family homes before the subway arrived in the 1920's—began subsequently to fill its vacant lots and rocky outcroppings with apartment houses. The Grand Concourse in the Bronx is a similar case. Farther out, as access advantages were enhanced by urban spread and highway development, portions of Mount Vernon, Yonkers, and the rocky slopes of Riverdale also blossomed with apartment houses. Similar developments occurred throughout suburban New Jersey, especially after World War II; towns like Irvington and Englewood saw the proliferation of apartment structures in areas where one-family dwellings had once predominated.

Some reflection of all these processes in terms of net density levels in the Region is seen in Table 24, where a crude approximation to net density is presented. Manhat-

TABLE 24   Population per Square Mile of Intensively Developed Land[a] in Counties of New York Metropolitan Region

(Counties are listed in order of increasing straight-line distance from mid-Manhattan, as in Table 1)

	Thousands per square mile		Thousands per square mile
Entire Region	13.9	Westchester	9.0
		Inner part[c]	11.3
Core counties	44.7	Remainder	4.6
Manhattan	108.0	Union	10.1
Hudson	30.8	Nassau	7.6
Brooklyn	50.5	Outer Ring counties	5.2
Queens	24.8	Middlesex	6.6
Bronx	54.8	Rockland	7.2
		Morris	4.2
Inner Ring counties	9.9	Monmouth	7.1
Richmond	10.9	Somerset	4.9
Essex	16.5	Fairfield	6.5
Bergen	9.2	Suffolk	3.5
Passaic	11.0	Orange	7.4
Inner part[b]	14.0	Putnam	1.9
Remainder	2.0	Dutchess	4.2

[a] "Intensively developed land" includes, with abutting streets, (1) land devoted primarily to residences and having at least one dwelling unit per 2 acres; and (2) land occupied by nonresidential buildings which cover more than 10 per cent of the site. Where the latter category of land is relatively important, as in Manhattan, the figures shown in the table substantially understate net density on residentially developed land alone.

[b] This refers to the part of Passaic County (about ⅓ of its total land area, containing about ¾ of its intensively developed land) extending from the southeast end of the county out to and including the borough of Pompton Lakes in the narrow waist of the county. This much of Passaic County is included in the Land-Use Survey Area (compare Table 23 and Appendix J).

[c] This refers to the part of Westchester County (about 29 per cent of its total land area, containing about ⅔ of its intensively developed land) extending from the south end of the county out to and including North Tarrytown, Greenburgh, White Plains, and Harrison. Thus the dividing line crosses the county approximately at its narrow waist. This much of Westchester County is included in the Land-Use Survey Area (compare Table 23 and Appendix J).

Source: See Appendix J. As noted there, the data for various counties refer to various years between 1953 and 1956.

tan's density towers above that of the other counties, and the figures tend in a general way to fall off with increasing distance from Manhattan. But the progression is highly irregular, and, by the time the Outer Ring counties are being compared with one another, the relation between net density and distance has faded out almost entirely. This is not surprising, for the outermost parts of the Region are comparatively independent of the need for quick daily access to Manhattan.

The relation of net density to access to the Region's center comes back into focus, however, when we use more detailed and appropriate measures of density and access. In the Land-Use Survey Area to which we earlier referred —the inlying suburban area where a major part of the Region's recent growth has occurred—the relation of the net density of any municipality to its Manhattan access is well marked. Table 25 shows the number of dwelling units per acre of residentially developed land in those municipalities, demonstrating how sharply the net density falls off as remoteness from Manhattan increases. Here again, as in Table 24, we can see that the relation between net density and access to Manhattan fades out as we get to the outer

TABLE 25 Net Residential Density of Municipalities in Land-Use Survey Area, in Relation to Travel Time to Manhattan, 1954–1955

Municipalities classified by access zones[a] (zone 1 is closest to Manhattan)	Dwelling units per acre of residentially developed land[b]
1	25.7
2	7.1
3	5.4
4	3.7
5[c]	3.2
All municipalities in Land-Use Survey Area	6.4

[a] For explanation of access zones see Table 23, note b.
[b] Residentially developed land includes land primarily devoted to residences, including abutting streets, where there is at least one dwelling unit per two acres.
[c] For technical reasons no meaningful density ratio could be calculated for the four communities in access zone 6.

Source: See Appendix J.

suburbs. Net densities in the still more remote Outer Ring communities would probably not run much lower than the average shown for that part of access zone 5 that lies within the Land-Use Survey Area.

This impression of declining densities would be incomplete, even misleading, if the special impact of multifamily dwellings upon the figures were not recognized. Density per acre of ground assumes a quite different significance when we begin to pile dwelling units on top of one another and give up the amenity of the individual yard. We have already mentioned the appearance of multifamily dwelling at a certain stage in development of the Region's communities as a major factor in upward revision of initial population densities. The tie between high densities and the incidence of multifamily structures begins to be evident in Table 26. Here we see that Manhattan's housing is nearly all apartments, and that apartments predominate, though less exclusively, in the other Core counties. In the Inner Ring, the single-family structure takes over, and in the Outer Ring its dominance is even more pronounced.[7]

The ties between multifamily development, land saturation, and high residential densities are illustrated even more effectively by an examination of the municipalities in the

TABLE 26   Types of Housing in New York Metropolitan Region, 1950

| | All types of structures | Percentage of dwelling units in: | | |
		Single-family structures[a]	Two-family structures[b]	Multifamily structures[c]
Region	100	32.2	15.0	52.8
Core	100	14.6	13.1	72.2
Manhattan	100	1.8	0.8	97.4
Rest of Core	100	18.9	17.2	63.9
Inner Ring	100	51.7	19.2	29.0
Outer Ring	100	69.8	15.2	14.7

Note: Rows do not total 100 in every case, partly because of rounding and partly because trailers are included in totals but not under any structure type.

[a] Includes semidetached two-unit structures as well as all one-family structures.

[b] Two-unit structures other than semidetached.

[c] Structures with three or more dwelling units.

Source: U.S. *1950 Census of Housing*.

Land-Use Survey Area, presented in Table 27. Where multifamily dwellings predominate, the land is close to being fully occupied. Also, the number of dwelling units per acre is comparatively high, and the access to Manhattan is good. Multifamily dwellings are of small importance in communities where density is lower, more land is free for development, and trips to Manhattan take longer. This relation between the access and density features of available housing is shown in Table 28 for the municipalities of the Land-Use Survey Area.

TABLE 27 Characteristics of Municipalities in Land-Use Survey Area, 1954–1955, in Relation to Extent of Multifamily Housing in 1950

Municipalities grouped on basis of percentage of total dwelling units in multifamily structures, 1950	Number of municipalities	Net density, 1954–55[a]	Percentage of total residential land developed, 1954–55	Average access-zone ratings of municipalities[b]
50% or more	11	18.7	84.0	1.73
30–49%	29	8.4	78.4	2.31
10–29%	49	5.7	68.2	3.01
5– 9%	15	3.7	59.7	3.13
0– 4%[c]	126	4.0	39.0	3.46

[a] Net density here means dwelling units per developed residential acre.
[b] Unweighted arithmetic average of the access-zone ratings of the municipalities in each group.
[c] Includes some municipalities for which no data are available on proportion of multifamily units. It seemed reasonable to include these in the 0–4 per cent group since they are relatively remote, small, and low-density communities, in which apartment development can be presumed insignificant.

Source: U.S. *1950 Census of Housing* on type of housing in 1950; on 1954–55 development status and access-zone ratings, see Appendix J and Table 23, note b.

Table 28 covers only part of the Region. If we were to try to add comparable information for New York City, there would be some very large new figures extending to the left and above the table (that is, at still closer access and higher densities). If we could add comparable data for the parts of the Region lying farther out than the Land-Use Survey Area, most of those additional figures would lie to the right of the lower portion of the table. Thus the

TABLE 28   Distribution of Dwelling Units in
Land-Use Survey Area, by Access and
Density Classes, 1954–1955

Density (dwelling units per acre of residentially developed land)	Thousands of dwelling units in:					
	All zones, total	Access zone				
		1	2	3	4	5–6
All densities, total	1,364	293	366	493	186	26
20.00 or more[a]	288	284	4	0	0	0
10.00–19.99	219	0	115	101	3	0
5.00–9.99	410	9	196	161	43	1
3.34–4.99	310	0	41	192	72	5
2.50–3.33	104	0	3	33	60	8
0–2.49	23	0	7	6	7	2
Unknown[b]	10	0	0	0	1	10

Note: Because of rounding, figures will not necessarily add to totals.
[a] When density is expressed in the conventional way (dwelling units per acre), the distribution of the resulting averages is extremely skewed. In presenting the figures as a frequency series, progressively diminishing class intervals have been used for lower densities. The scheme of class intervals used in the table above is based on the quite meaningful concept of the *reciprocal* of density, i.e., the amount of space per dwelling unit. Stated in those terms the intervals would read (in fractions of an acre): 0.05 or less, 0.06–0.10, 0.11–0.20, 0.21–0.30, 0.31–0.40, 0.41 or more.
[b] Places with "unknown" density either have no estimates available on number of dwelling units, or have a high proportion of land in large estates which is thus classed as "vacant" land, making a meaningful net density figure unavailable. These municipalities are characteristically rather remote, small, and quasi-rural. It therefore seems appropriate to place this group at the low end of the density scale.

Source: See Appendix J and Table 23, note b.

basic concentration along a broad diagonal band from low-density-poor-access to high-density-good-access would show up even more prominently in a complete cross-tabulation for the Region than it does in the truncated presentation provided by the table.

But it would be wrong to think of all remote communities as devoted to spacious housing and all inlying communities as tightly packed. The density-access relation is a loose one. Table 28 shows that a considerable range of space possibilities is offered in every access zone.[8]

One group of communities, we find, seems to enjoy the best of two possible worlds, combining spacious (low-density) development with good access to Manhattan. In Table 28 these appear on the lower or left flank of the

generally diagonal mass of numbers. Communities like
Scarsdale and Pelham in Westchester, and Great Neck Estates and Kensington in Nassau, fall in this category. These
communities and others like them seem to conform in many
cases to a common pattern; namely, that of settled communities which developed at a time when their access was
not nearly as attractive, relatively speaking, as it is today.
By and large, this group has managed to resist successfully
the process of upward revision in densities to which other
communities of their vintage and quality of access have
since succumbed.

Another group of municipalities appears, on the surface,
to lack the advantages of either convenient access or low
density; given their extended distances from Manhattan,
their densities appear unusually high. In Table 28 these
appear on the upper or right flank of the generally diagonal
mass of numbers. Rochelle Park and Woodcliff Lake, in
Bergen County, illustrate this group. But once again, these
seemingly deviant cases remind us of the complexity of
the phenomena with which we are dealing. Some of these
communities are found on examination to have developed
initially as remote summer-cottage colonies, reflecting the
economies of land and construction which often go with
such developments. Others prove to be homesites of workers to whom Manhattan access is as irrelevant as Chicago
access; for them, the relevant jobs market is in nearby industrial New Jersey.

Special features such as these abound in the Region,
coloring and qualifying all the results which simple density-
access considerations may suggest. Monmouth County's
summer seaside developments create a stamp of high "net
residential densities" which may prove indelible; Staten
Island's western flank basks in the lee of the Region's highest concentration of unsavory industry, discouraging residential use; middle Long Island offers a terrain which is
flat, virtually all usable, and easy to develop for light
structures, in contrast with the rocky, irregular terrain of
much of Westchester, Putnam, Fairfield, Rockland, and
the northern and middle Jersey suburban counties; and so
on. Yet despite these aberrations, the strength of the sim-

ple density-access relation as we have defined it shines through, offering some meaningful way of generalizing the forces at work in distributing the populations of the Region.

PRESENT ACCESS CONSIDERATIONS

The present supply and density of housing in the Region, then, show the influence of a general desire to live near the main concentrations of jobs in the Region. But most of the decisions on the location of this housing were made at various times past, when the location of jobs and the commuting facilities were quite different from what they are now. We have yet to learn what role access considerations may be playing today in influencing current choices of housing from the existing stock and in determining the location of new homes.

That the need for access is still a critical force in the selection of a home scarcely needs documenting. Since a high proportion of the waking hours of residents of any metropolitan area is spent away from home, we may take it that access to places of employment, schools, shops, and other away-from-home points of contact is something that practically all households in the Region take into account in weighing the advantages of alternative places to live.

Occasionally a developer places a specific money value on access. The *New York Times* of July 13, 1958, reports that a group of developers offered identical homes for sale at different prices in four different Long Island locations. A Hicksville house, 31 miles from Columbus Circle, sold at $14,000; the same house in Babylon, 9 miles farther out, was $800 lower in price; one 6 miles farther still was reduced another $500; and 4 miles beyond that, the price was $750 lower still. Nonetheless, demand was heaviest for the houses closest to Manhattan.

The importance of access to the *work-place* is underlined by the fact that nearly all metropolitan households include at least one away-from-home worker,[9] and about half of the individual journeys within large United States metropolitan areas are accounted for by travel between

home and work—that is, by trips which we shall hence-
forth refer to simply as "commuting." Next in frequency,
but less than half as numerous, are "social-recreational"
trips. Shopping, school, and miscellaneous trips make up
the remainder.[10]

Actually, the journey to work is probably even more
dominant among access considerations than its relative frequency would imply. Local trips like those to the corner
drugstore or the community shopping center can be left
out of account altogether in considering the impact of the
access factor in residence choice. Such facilities, as the
previous chapter has shown, quickly and half-automati-
cally follow the spread of population and are available in
any community, so that we may presume that people do
not consider access to them in choosing a community
within the Region. Even the big new suburban shopping
centers appear to draw the bulk of their trade from places
within less than 20 minutes' drive.[11]

To be sure, some account does need to be taken of the
special pull exerted by the concentrations of highly specialized and diverse shopping, cultural, and recreational
facilities, as well as employment opportunities, existing at
two or three main focal points in the Region—primarily
midtown Manhattan, downtown Brooklyn, and downtown
Newark. Though their pull appears to be weakening, as
we saw in the preceding chapter, it seems probable that
access to such major centers does play some minor role in
determining the desirability of residence, over and above
what could be measured simply in terms of the relative
number of jobs.

Of course we cannot expect access to appear all by itself as a determinant of location. If access to work were
the sole factor operating, everyone would live where he
worked and commuting time would be zero. Since this
does not happen in reality, it is clear that other factors are
always present to limit the degree to which people can
live close to their work. Our earlier discussion of residential densities suggested that the desire for a spacious
homesite, for instance, might be one such factor. How im-

portant is the access factor, then, among the various conflicting forces?

The first piece of evidence to consider is the county-by-county distribution of jobs and population in the Region, as depicted in Charts 1 and 2 in Chapter 1. The patterns show a strong similarity, with densities of both jobs and population per square mile mounting systematically and in parallel fashion as we approach Manhattan. The main difference between the patterns is that jobs are much more heavily concentrated in the lower half of Manhattan itself than population is, while in the remainder of New York City the ratio of jobs to population is less than in most other counties of the Region. More detailed data would, of course, show secondary peakings of job and population density at each urban or industrial concentration point.

This basic similarity of patterns strongly suggests that access to work-places is a major factor determining where people live in the Region—that they swarm round each concentration of jobs, getting as close as possible even at the cost of crowding.

However, on the basis of this evidence, we cannot really measure the extent to which individual households locate near their respective work-places. A simple calculation will make this point clear. Suppose we were to try to estimate what proportion of the Region's work force commutes to a different county to work, just on the basis of the observed distribution of people and jobs among the counties. Suppose, at one extreme, we were to assume that nobody commutes out of his own county if a job exists within it; then, according to our calculations, only about 26 per cent of all the workers would have to leave their home counties to work, under the existing distributions of people and jobs. At the other extreme, if we were to assume that closeness to work is a matter of no consequence in residence choice, something like 86 per cent of all workers would be traveling outside their home counties to work.[12]

A direct estimate of the proportion of the Region's workers who actually do commute to a different county was derived in a recent sample survey of commuting patterns.[*] The proportion turns out to be 56 per cent,[13] or midway between the extreme limits staked out above. This suggests that there is a strong tendency to reduce commuting distance, but also that the commuter flow pattern includes a great deal of "cross-hauling."

Table 29 and Chart 5 present estimates of commuter flow within and between the three major zones of the Region: Core, Inner Ring, and Outer Ring. (Further detail, by individual counties, appears in Appendix K, Table K-1.) The Core, with about 66 per cent of the employment and 55 per cent of the employed residents, is obviously the recipient of a large net inflow, while the Outer Ring and to an even greater extent the Inner Ring show a net outflow. But each of the three zones participates in a two-way interchange of commuters with each of the other zones. If we choose to regard commutation from Core to either Ring, and from Inner Ring to Outer Ring, as "reverse" commuting, it appears that 4 to 5 per cent of the

TABLE 29 Distribution of Workers in New York Metropolitan Region by Zones of Residence and Zones of Employment,[a] 1956

	Total working in Region	Working in Core	Working in Inner Ring	Working in Outer Ring
Total working and living in Region	100.0%	65.5%	23.1%	11.4%
Living in Core	54.6	51.4	2.9	0.3
Living in Inner Ring	32.2	12.3	18.7	1.2
Living in Outer Ring	13.2	1.8	1.5	9.9

[a] This tabulation covers only those who both live and work within the Region. The survey furnishing these estimates found an additional one per cent or so working in the Region but living outside. It may be conjectured that the number living in the Region and working outside is similarly small.

Source: Unpublished tabulations of 1956 journey-to-work survey made for Regional Plan Association. See Appendix K.

[*] See Appendix K for a description of this journey-to-work survey. As the appendix indicates, there were numerous limitations in the methodology and results of the survey which impair its usefulness. But as rough orders of magnitude, the results presented here are not misleading.

CHART 5

Commuter Flow Within and Between Zones of
New York Metropolitan Region, 1956

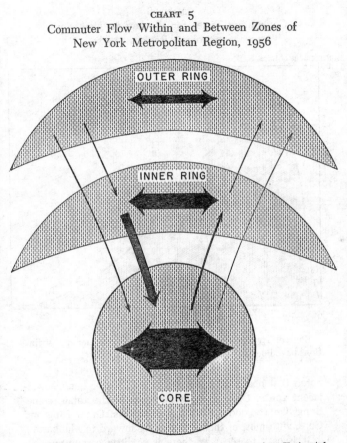

Thickness of arrows is proportional to number of commuters. Horizontal
arrows show commuting from one place to another in the same zone.

Source: Table 29.

total journeys fall within that category. Over 80 per cent
work in the zone where they live, while the remaining 15
per cent or so commute to a more central zone than that
in which they live. As an indication of the extent to which
jobs and residences attract one another, it may also be

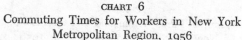

CHART 6

Commuting Times for Workers in New York
Metropolitan Region, 1956

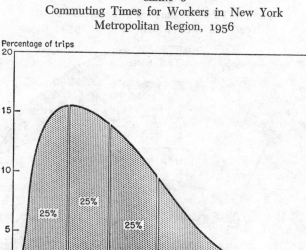

Source: 1956 journey-to-work survey. The frequency distributions have been smoothed. See note 14, chapter 6.

noted that nearly all commuting is within or between adjacent zones. Only about 2 per cent of the total (something like 120,000 a day) travel between Outer Ring and Core, with most of them commuting inward to Manhattan.

It is easy to see why there is so little commuting between relatively distant parts of the Region, except for the flow from distant points into Manhattan. The Region is so vast that anyone living near one edge and working near the opposite edge might well find himself spending more time commuting than working. As it is, commuters in the Region have to devote considerably more time and expense to the journey to and from work than do those of lesser metropolises. In Chart 6 we have a distribution of

New York Metropolitan Region

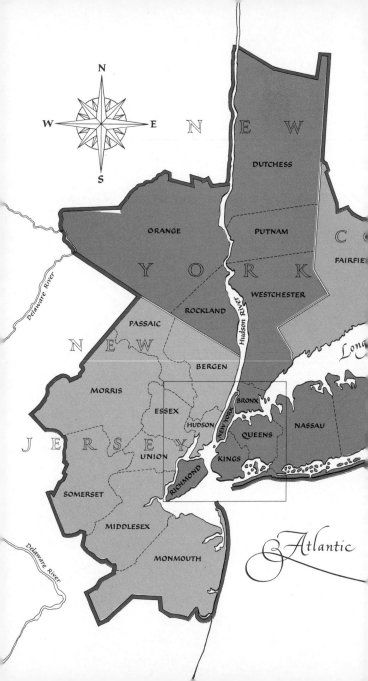

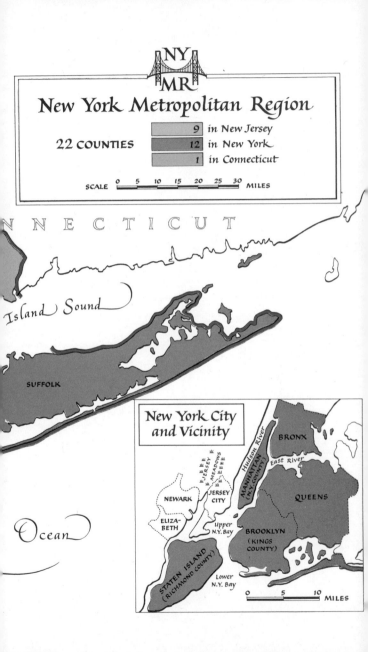

New York Metropolitan Region

22 COUNTIES

9	in New Jersey
12	in New York
1	in Connecticut

SCALE 0 5 10 15 20 25 30 MILES

CONNECTICUT

Island Sound

SUFFOLK

Ocean

New York City and Vicinity

JERSEY MEADOWS

Hudson River

BRONX

East River

NEWARK

JERSEY CITY

MANHATTAN (N.Y. COUNTY)

QUEENS

ELIZA- BETH

Upper N.Y. Bay

BROOKLYN (KINGS COUNTY)

STATEN ISLAND (RICHMOND COUNTY)

Lower N.Y. Bay

0 5 10 MILES

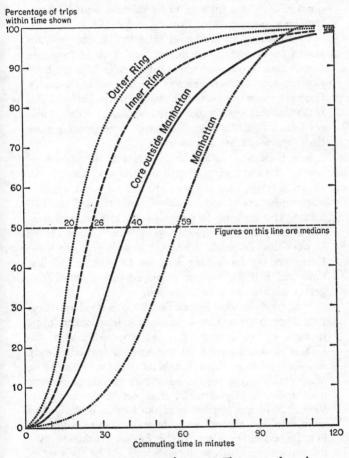

CHART 7

Cumulative Distribution of Commuting Times by
Zones of Employment, 1956

Source: 1956 journey-to-work survey. The curves have been
smoothed. See note 14, chapter 7.

the duration of commuter trips, derived from the same sample survey that underlies Table 29. Only a quarter of the commuters require 24 minutes or less each way; another quarter, anywhere from 24 to 42 minutes; another quarter, anywhere from 42 to 63 minutes; and the hardy remaining quarter, more than 63 minutes.[14]

So far, then, we have said little that is not generally known: most commuting in the New York Metropolitan Region ends in the zone where it begins, and the predominant movement between zones is inward toward the center. Our next major observation, however, is less obvious. This is the fact that jobs located at the center draw their workers from longer distances, measured in commuting time, than jobs which are less centralized.

Jobs in Manhattan are far in excess of the number of people who can find room to live there; and, also, as was shown in earlier chapters, a good many important types of employment are almost exclusively concentrated in Manhattan. This explains, in part, why workers in Manhattan (as Chart 7 shows) typically spend much longer getting to work than do people who work elsewhere in the Core. Commuters to Inner Ring jobs get to work in still less time; and half the workers employed in the Outer Ring get to work in 20 minutes or less.

This generalization is modified by one small qualification. Though jobholders in Manhattan take longer to get to work, on the average, than do other commuters, the longest commuting trips—on the order of two hours each way—are relatively rare for Manhattan workers. Here, Manhattan's unique access advantage of central position and highly developed radial transport comes into play. Very little of the population of the Region lives in areas more than 100 minutes away from Manhattan terminals; but, for any other place in the Region considered as a destination point, this would definitely not be the case.

Table 30, comparing times required to travel to jobs in the various counties, simply elaborates the pattern already shown in Chart 7.[15] The relatively high figure for Essex among the Inner Ring counties is noteworthy, showing the

TABLE 30   Median Number of Minutes Spent in Getting to Work, According to County of Employment, 1956

Manhattan	59	Passaic	23
		Westchester	22
Other Core counties	40		
Brooklyn	46	Outer Ring	20
Queens	41	Orange	26
Hudson	38	Morris	23
Bronx	33	Dutchess	22
		Middlesex	21
Inner Ring	26	Somerset	21
Essex	32	Suffolk	21
Richmond	29	Fairfield	20
Nassau	25	Monmouth	20
Union	25	Rockland	17
Bergen	24	Putnam	12

Source: 1956 journey-to-work survey.

pull which Newark exerts as a secondary job center in the Region.

To say that the more centrally located jobs in the Region exert the longest pull on commuters is to present only one side of the story. To complete the picture, one needs to analyze the length of journeys according to where the commuter *lives*. Table 31 presents this side of the analysis.

Far and away the largest stream of commuter traffic in the Region is Manhattan-bound. Roughly equal to this stream is the aggregate of all intracounty commuting trips, that is, trips which end in the county where they begin. Together, these two categories account for about four-fifths of all the commuting journeys.[16]

Let us consider first the intracounty commuting. Paradoxically, the longest intracounty commuting appears in the highly urbanized Core counties, where both jobs and residences are heavily concentrated. But on reflection the paradox is not so difficult to understand. For in these congested areas considerable specialization in land use has developed; the office employment in each of the City's boroughs is concentrated in a few areas in each borough; the factory districts, though they are spotted through many areas, nonetheless also show a certain measure of concentration. As a result, the factory hand who lives in St. Albans travels a considerable distance to his plant in Long Island

City, though all of his journey is in the borough of Queens. By the same token, the margin clerk who lives in Washington Heights consumes considerable time on his daily trip to Wall Street, even though he never leaves Manhattan.[17]

As we go out to the less urbanized parts of the Region, however, we find intracounty commuting time diminishing despite the fact that the outer counties are large in area. Here we see an attraction of the outer counties which the Core does not seem able to match: commuters who live within the county where they work have shorter trips in the more sparsely settled counties than in the Core.

When we turn from intracounty commuting to Manhattan-bound commuting the picture changes. Not sur-

TABLE 31   Median Number of Minutes Spent in Getting to Work, According to County of Residence, 1956

County of residence	All commuters living in specified county	Commuters to Manhattan	Commuters to jobs in county of residence
Manhattan	35	34	34
Other Core counties			
Queens	50	59	32
Bronx	49	61	30
Brooklyn	48	55	34
Hudson	34	58	23
Inner Ring			
Richmond	63	81	25
Nassau	45	83	22
Bergen	41	72	19
Westchester	33	69	20
Essex	30	74	26
Union	29	83	21
Passaic	22	87	20
Outer Ring			
Putnam	32	91	11
Morris	30	91	18
Suffolk	26	96	17
Monmouth	23	97	18
Somerset	22	92	17
Orange	21	a	20
Middlesex	19	84	17
Fairfield	18	89	18
Rockland	18	94	13
Dutchess	17	97	19
Outside the Region	39	86	a

a Data not available from sample survey responses.

Source: 1956 journey-to-work survey.

prisingly, commutation *to Manhattan* is progressively more time-consuming the farther out one lives—as shown in the middle column of Table 31.

It is a fairly safe assumption on the basis of this evidence that access to Manhattan is still a major factor in explaining the existing structure of the Region. Though the concept is naïvely simple and though it needs to be qualified by such minor observations as the special pulling power of Newark, nevertheless the concentration of excess jobs in Manhattan and the unique importance of Manhattan-bound commuting trips from all points in the Region bolster the basic assumption.[18]

At the same time, it is clear that only a limited contribution to our understanding of the Region's population pattern can be had in terms of the "access" factor as reflected in the relation of the pattern of population-in-general to jobs-in-general. The direction in which any particular worker's residence choice is influenced by access consideration depends in part on what kind of work he does—whether he is in an occupation that is concentrated in Manhattan, concentrated outside Manhattan, or widely dispersed over the Region. We shall, then, have to consider separately the residence choices of people having differently located types of work.

It is clear too that the balancing of access convenience against the desire for space and other amenities works out differently for individuals who have different tastes and housing needs—and different levels of income to satisfy them.

The way in which different kinds of people fit into the over-all pattern of population is the subject of our next chapter.

WHO LIVES WHERE AND WHY

Variety is rampant among the individual households and the communities of the Region. But a large part of the variation can be expressed in terms of just three basic characteristics: job type, income level, and age composition of the household. Each of these has a powerful effect upon choice of residence, an effect that will be traced at some length in this chapter.

Each of them, too, plays a part in the development of relatively homogeneous and distinctively typed communities and neighborhoods. Most people prefer to be able to keep up with the local Joneses and tend therefore to seek more or less their own level in incomes. A family with children will show a strong preference for neighbors who have children of similar ages; childless families, on the other hand, tend to feel out of their element in a child-oriented suburb. Job type, even apart from its association with income levels, also is a basis for neighborhood homogeneity. Thus, "lower white-collar" people often find more in common with one another than with "upper blue-collar" people of equal income and family structure, even if neither talks shop very much at home or on the way to work.

Neighborhood homogeneity as such is still further fostered by zoning and by the economics of construction. As a result, communities—especially small communities—acquire rather stable and marked "type" characteristics and can often be recognizably typed as "upper-crust," "industrial-worker," "nursery," "small-household," and so on. This fact lends some legitimacy to a device we shall have to use a good deal in the analysis that follows, namely, the comparison of groups of *communities* of certain characteristics rather than of groups of *people* with those characteristics.

OCCUPATION AND RESIDENCE CHOICE

The residents of the New York Metropolitan Region, we have asserted, choose their homes with some regard to job access. The occupations of the working members of a household have a direct influence on residence preference because different types of jobs are differently located or concentrated in the Region. For an investment broker, an executive of a national corporation, or a high-style garment manufacturer or operative, "work-access" usually means access to the Manhattan central business district. By contrast, the jobs of barbers, undertakers, retail clerks, and drugstore proprietors are scattered all over the populated areas of the Region.

To some extent, then, we should be able to account for the residence patterns of various types of workers on the basis of the locations of the respective types of jobs in the Region.

The location of jobs was discussed in earlier chapters in terms of the various types of *industry* in the Region. But the workers within an industry group may have little in common in their residence choices, because such a group is likely to include a wide variety of white-collar, manual, and service jobs over the whole range of the income scale. The workers of a specific *occupational* type, such as clerical workers or unskilled manual laborers, are much more alike in the various factors that determine their residence preference.[1] In this context, therefore, it is more meaningful to think of jobs not as wholesale, retail, manufacturing, or office jobs but rather in terms of occupational types.

Since the most recent information indicating where people *live* in the Region by occupational types refers to 1950, our first step was to determine where people *worked* in the Region in that year by the same occupational breakdown.[2] Appendix L describes the method by which this was done. As a result, we were able to examine each job type with the question: where are the work-places and where are the homes of this job type concentrated in the Region?

Table 32 presents the results, using a measure which we may call an "index of specialization." Consider any part of the Region, say the Inner Ring. If the total number of jobs in the Inner Ring represents 21 per cent of the total jobs in the Region, this furnishes a standard against which to compare the Inner Ring's share of each job type. Thus if a given job type, say sales jobs, had the same 21 per cent of its Region total located in the Inner Ring, then its index of specialization in the Inner Ring would be 100. If the Inner Ring had twice that share of sales jobs (that is,

TABLE 32 Specialization of Jobs and Residents in Major Zones of New York Metropolitan Region, 1950

Occupation category	Man-hattan	Core outside Manhattan	Inner Ring	Outer Ring
Professional, technical, and kindred workers				
Job specialization index	98	100	105	101
Residence specialization index	128	82	113	106
Managers, officials, and proprietors, except farm				
Job specialization index	106	96	93	94
Residence specialization index	93	93	122	84
Clerical and kindred workers				
Job specialization index	114	90	88	85
Residence specialization index	95	115	90	72
Sales workers				
Job specialization index	106	96	95	93
Residence specialization index	93	104	102	88
Craftsmen, foremen, and kindred workers				
Job specialization index	86	108	114	115
Residence specialization index	57	102	107	127
Operatives and kindred workers				
Job specialization index	87	110	110	114
Residence specialization index	94	104	92	109
Laborers, except farm and mine				
Job specialization index	88	101	121	108
Residence specialization index	92	94	99	133
Service workers				
Job specialization index	116	91	82	85
Residence specialization index	190	84	81	93

Source: See Appendix L.

42 per cent of the Region's total), the index for sales jobs in the Inner Ring would be 200; or, if it had half that share (that is, 10.5 per cent), the index would be 50. Specialization of residences of workers of the various job types can be measured by the same kind of index.[3]

Table 32, dividing the Region into just four main zones, indicates that professional jobs figure a little more prominently in the employment mix in the Inner Ring than elsewhere, but that they are distributed among the four zones in fairly close conformity to the over-all distribution of jobs. But professional workers' *residences* show a strong concentration in Manhattan, and a less strong one in the Inner Ring, relative to residence in general. Managerial jobs are more highly centralized in Manhattan than jobs in general, but the residences are relatively concentrated in the Inner Ring. In the lower white-collar groups a similar concentration of jobs in Manhattan goes with a concentration of residence in the Core counties just outside Manhattan.

The manual-worker groups are more prominently represented outside Manhattan than in it, with respect to both jobs and residence. The skilled craftsmen and foremen, especially, show a remarkable tendency not to live in Manhattan. Finally, the service group—a mixture of occupations, including such callings as barbers, domestics, watchmen, and elevator operators—is strongly over-represented in Manhattan jobs and spectacularly over-represented in Manhattan residence.

The general impression which Table 32 conveys, therefore, is that each group tends to live in the zone where its jobs are particularly concentrated, or in the next zone outward. In other words, different job distributions are reflected to some observable extent in the corresponding residence patterns.

The two top white-collar groups, however, appear to depart from this general rule. Professional workers show a residence concentration in Manhattan and the Rings, and tend to shun the Bronx, Brooklyn, Queens, and Hudson County. The managerial group shows concentration of jobs in Manhattan but concentration of residences in the Inner

Ring, suggesting rather long commuter journeys. The service group also looks like a special case, being even more concentrated in Manhattan in terms of residence than in terms of jobs.

To get a closer view of the relation between concentrations of jobs and of residences for the various occupational groups, however, one has to look at the individual counties. Table 33 affords such a close-up, showing where the highest indices of specialization appeared for each occupational category.

TABLE 33   Specialization of Jobs and Residents by Counties of New York Metropolitan Region, 1950

Job specialization index		Residence specialization index	
Professional, technical, and kindred workers			
Middlesex	110	*Rockland	144
Hudson	110	*Westchester	143
Passaic	110	*Morris	134
Somerset	110	Manhattan	128
Union	110	Nassau	120
Suffolk	108	Bergen	118
Managers, officials, and proprietors (except farm)			
Monmouth	111	*Nassau	221
Manhattan	106	Westchester	123
Bronx	105	Bergen	119
Suffolk	104	Monmouth	101
Richmond	103		
Nassau	103		
Orange	103		
Clerical and kindred workers			
Manhattan	114	*Queens	125
		Richmond	121
		*Bronx	117
		Hudson	110
		Brooklyn	110
Sales workers			
Monmouth	117	Bronx	113
*Richmond	110	Westchester	112
Bronx	107	Nassau	111
*Orange	107	Queens	107
Manhattan	106	Brooklyn	107
Queens	104	Bergen	105
Craftsmen, foremen, and kindred workers			
Somerset	131	Suffolk	152
Bergen	129	Middlesex	133
Middlesex	128	Somerset	129
Union	121	Morris	128
Morris	120	*Union	123
Passaic	119	*Fairfield	123

Job specialization index	Residence specialization index

Operatives and kindred workers

*Middlesex	142	*Passaic	162
*Passaic	137	Middlesex	138
*Hudson	136	Orange	128
Somerset	134	Hudson	126
*Union	132	Fairfield	122
*Rockland	122	*Brooklyn	115

Laborers, except farm and mine

*Bergen	137	*Middlesex	168
Middlesex	135	*Hudson	167
*Somerset	135	*Suffolk	162
*Morris	129	*Richmond	155
Hudson	128	*Monmouth	138
Union	126	Morris	132

Service workers

*Suffolk	158	*Manhattan	190
*Westchester	126	*Dutchess and Putnam	128
*Dutchess and Putnam	121	Suffolk	123
*Nassau	120	Rockland	120
*Manhattan	116	Westchester	109
*Bronx	116	Orange	106

Note: The highest six county indices in each category are shown in the table, except that (1) no indices below 100 are shown, and (2) seven counties are shown in the managerial job-specialization ranking because the sixth and seventh were tied.

* This symbol indicates that the county so designated had a higher index in this specialization category than it did in any other.

Source: See Appendix L.

A wide disparity between work-places and residences in the professional and managerial groups is apparent here. There is very little appearance of "matching" between the lists of counties on the left and right sides of the table for these two groups. It is also noteworthy that professional and managerial people, though having rather different patterns of *work-place* concentration, choose very nearly the same list of counties for *residence* concentration. This suggests that the people concerned were not simply choosing their residences on the basis of job location, but were looking for other features as well.

A more straightforward relation between job concentration and residence concentration appears when we look at the lower white-collar groups, that is, the clerical and sales workers. Both groups, especially the clerical, show a considerable concentration of jobs in New York City.[4] Indeed, Manhattan is the only county in the Region where clerical jobs are "over-represented." Residentially, however, the clerical and sales groups are "over-represented" in a rather tight ring surrounding Manhattan rather than in Manhattan itself. As a result, this group of workers is put in fairly close proximity to its jobs.*

The craftsmen-foremen group and the operatives group, as we observed earlier, tend both to live and to work outside Manhattan to a greater extent than other groups. It is also apparent that these concentrations are predominantly west of the Hudson River. Much the same list of counties recurs on both the job and residence sides of Table 33 for these groups. Here, as in the case of the clerical and sales workers, the residence pattern appears to "make sense" in terms of proximity to job concentrations.[5]

The unskilled manual jobs—what the Census calls "laborers"—appear strongly concentrated in the industrial areas in New Jersey, and the concentration of residences of this type of worker matches job locations fairly closely.[6]

In the case of the service workers, a much higher proportion are provided with lodging in connection with their jobs than is the case with any other group, and this factor doubtless contributes to the matching of concentrations in most of the counties shown. But service workers appear to be much more concentrated in Manhattan than the distribution of their jobs alone would justify. This suggests that, although proximity to their jobs no doubt has something to do with the location of their homes, other forces also are at work, holding these people in the center of the Region. We shall shortly have more to say about these other factors.

To sum up our findings to this point, it appears that differences in the location of jobs play some part in explaining the differences in residence patterns of the various occupational groups; but, also, that a great deal is left unexplained. In particular, the job-access factor seems inadequate to explain why the top and bottom classes in the occupational hierarchy live where they do.

There is other evidence, as well, which suggests that

* See note 9, chapter 7.

TABLE 34 Median Commuting Time of Workers in
New York Metropolitan Region, by Job Type and
Sex, 1956

Job type	Median commuting time (minutes)		
	Both sexes	Men	Women
Office and clerical	46	50	44
Executive and professional	44	a	a
Shop or factory	34	a	a
Retail sales	27	34	24

a Not calculated. Respondents in this category were predominantly male.

Source: 1956 journey-to-work survey. See Appendix K.

people at the upper end of the job hierarchy are quite prepared to settle far from their jobs. The evidence is provided by the results of the recent journey-to-work study cited in the preceding chapter. Table 34, based on that survey, shows that people in executive, professional, and office jobs, on the whole, do not live close to work. Jobs of that sort are highly concentrated in major central business districts, particularly in Manhattan, while the residences of the jobholders on the average are well separated from their jobs.

By contrast, the relatively short work journey of the typical retail worker stands out. This is at least partly explainable in terms of access, since retail jobs are available all over the Region in a pattern closely resembling that of population.[7] It is relatively easy, then, for a retail worker to live fairly close to his or her job. Besides, the irregularity of working hours among retail workers probably puts an added premium on being close to the job.

The groups that live close to major job concentrations, of course, give up one amenity—spacious living. And those that live far from their jobs manage thereby to achieve greater living space. This is clearly suggested by Table 35, which shows that there are wide and systematic differences in residential density between communities with different occupational specializations. We see in this table that the upper end of the job hierarchy prefers low-density communities and accepts poor access while the lower end lives in

TABLE 35   Access and Density Characteristics of Urban Places in the Land-Use Survey Area[a] in Relation to Type of Occupational Specialization of Residents

Occupational specialty[b]	Access-zone rating (unweighted average) [c]	Net density (dwelling units per acre of developed residential land)
Professional	3.27	5.50
Managerial	3.09	4.10
Clerical	2.50	5.31
Sales	3.08	6.50
Craftsmen-foremen	2.80	6.77
Operatives	2.50	11.59
Laborers	2.51	21.37
Service	2.43	6.28[d]

[a] This tabulation covers only urban places and is confined to one part of the Region—the "Land-Use Survey Area" referred to in Chapter 6 and Appendix J. Thus it omits New York City, where considerably higher densities prevail than those shown in the table. It also omits rural territory and Outer Ring areas, where generally lower densities prevail. Because of this restricted coverage, the results cannot be regarded in all cases as reflecting Region-wide patterns.

[b] Indices of occupational specialization of residents were calculated for each urban place by methods similar to those used for the county coefficients in Table 33 above, and each place was assigned to a specialization category on the basis of the occupation in which it showed the most specialization. For details, see Appendix L.

[c] The reader will recall that lower access-zone numbers mean shorter commuting time to Manhattan. The access zones are explained in Table 23, note b.

[d] In view of the heavy concentration of service workers' residence in Manhattan (compare Table 32), this fairly low density for service-specialized communities in the Land-Use Survey Area alone is highly unrepresentative of the Region as a whole.

high-density communities with good access; among the different groups, only the services group provides a major exception.

The communities which fall in these different occupational groups have distinctive characteristics apart from density. The "laborers" and "operatives" communities are, typically, rather large and mature industrial cities in New Jersey, like Jersey City, Bayonne, and Newark, and a large fraction of their housing is multifamily. The "craftsmen-foremen" communities are generally smaller, more scattered, and more residential in character, with a preponderance of single-family houses—including such places as Mineola in Nassau County and Roselle Park in Union County. These characteristics appear even more prominently in the white-collar categories.[8] Though some of the communities in the Land-Use Survey Area, particularly the newer and smaller ones, may have changed significantly in the last few years, the data as shown offer a fairly clear indication of the kinds of residential environment in which the different groups tend to concentrate.

INCOME LEVEL AND RESIDENCE CHOICE

Occupation is not the only factor which determines residence choice. The income level of the household determines how far its residence preferences can be indulged. People with higher incomes obviously enjoy wider latitude in choosing where and how to live. They can, if they wish, live more spaciously. They can bid higher for sites especially convenient in terms of access to work or to recreational or cultural facilities. They have the option of buying or building *new* housing either in new suburban subdivisions or in new luxury apartments in more central areas. They can afford the higher site-development and construction costs entailed in distinctive single-family construction in hilly or rocky areas like much of Westchester and Putnam Counties. They can afford two cars and are thus better able to live in sections of the suburbs far from urban centers and public transportation facilities. Like everyone else, they are faced with a general choice between convenient access on the one hand and ample space and privacy on the other, but they are in a position to choose from a wider range of more desirable combinations of those advantages.

The range of choice narrows with lower incomes, and the lowest income groups have very little choice at all. Except as rent controls modify the general pattern, the lowest income groups have to live in the housing least acceptable to anyone else, in terms of the combination of condition, location, spaciousness, and character of neighborhood.

Of course, people with high incomes typically tend to be concentrated in certain kinds of jobs and those with low incomes in others. Table 36, covering the 17 counties of the Region that make up the New York Standard Metropolitan Area, shows the difference in income level associated with type of occupation. The white-collar hierarchy includes the highest income levels; the upper layers of the manual workers overlap substantially the lower-paid white-collar categories; and service workers occupy the lowest rung on the income ladder.[9]

TABLE 36 Median Incomes and Sex Distribution of Workers Resident in New York Metropolitan Region, by Principal Occupation Groups, 1949–1950

| Occupation group | Median income, experienced labor force, 1949 | | | Ratio of male to total employed workers, 1950 |
	Both sexes[a]	Males	Females	
All groups[b]	$2,754	$3,120	$1,965	68.3%
Managerial	4,062	4,221	2,786	88.9
Professional	3,866	4,444	2,724	66.4
Sales	3,017	3,388	1,731	77.6
Clerical	2,529	2,961	2,247	39.5
Craftsmen-foremen ...	3,248	3,290	2,269	95.9
Operatives	2,402	2,812	1,704	63.0
Laborers	2,348	2,409	1,714	96.4
Service	1,942	2,401	1,334	57.0

[a] The "both sexes" medians are approximations, calculated by averaging the "males" and "females" medians weighted by their respective numbers of workers.

[b] In addition to the groups specified in the table, the total includes farm proprietors and farm laborers and persons not reporting occupation. The groups specified in the table, however, account for about 98 per cent of the total.

Source: Calculated from data in U.S. *1950 Census of Population, Detailed Characteristics of Population, New York State,* Tables 76 and 78.

As a result of these differences, the occupational complexion of a community in the Region gives at least a general indication of the community's typical income level.[*] This can be seen in Table 37, where the counties in each of the three main zones of the Region are ranked in order of average personal income per capita. The principal occupational specializations, already presented in Table 33, are put alongside for comparison. As we proceed downward in the income range, occupational specialization tends

[*] For discussion of some supplementary evidence on this relationship, see Appendix M.

to shift from the top white-collar professional and managerial types to middle-income white-collar and manual types, and finally to the lowest-income service and unskilled-labor types.

Table 37 also shows that the New York Metropolitan Region is like most other large American metropolitan regions in its broad pattern of income levels. The highest levels of income are in the Inner Ring, while the Core is lower and the Outer Ring lowest of all.[10]

With all the correspondence between income levels and occupational types, however, there is one area in the Re-

TABLE 37 Personal Income Per Capita (1956) and Principal Occupational Specializations (1950), by Counties of New York Metropolitan Region

	Personal income per capita	Principal occupational specializations of residents
Region	$2,592	
Core	2,539	
Manhattan	2,964	Professional, service
Queens	2,749	Clerical, sales
Bronx	2,318	Clerical, sales
Brooklyn	2,317	Clerical, sales, operatives
Hudson	2,175	Clerical, operatives, laborers
Inner Ring	2,884	
Nassau	3,236	Professional, managerial, sales
Westchester	3,220	Professional, managerial, sales, service
Bergen	2,826	Professional, managerial, sales
Union	2,814	Craftsmen
Essex	2,704	Sales, operatives, laborers[a]
Richmond	2,250	Clerical, laborers
Outer Ring	2,231	
Fairfield	2,963	Craftsmen, operatives
Morris	2,375	Professional, craftsmen, laborers
Somerset	2,296	Craftsmen
Middlesex	2,160	Craftsmen, operatives, laborers
Monmouth	2,113	Managerial, laborers
Suffolk	1,869	Craftsmen, laborers
Rockland	1,803	Professional, service
Orange	1,776	Operatives, service
Dutchess and Putnam	1,614	Service

[a] Essex County did not appear in Table 33, because none of its residents' specialization coefficients rated among the top six in its category. The characterization in the table above is based on coefficients of 104, 108, and 106, respectively.

Sources: Income estimates by New York Metropolitan Region Study; occupational specializations from Table 33, except as noted.

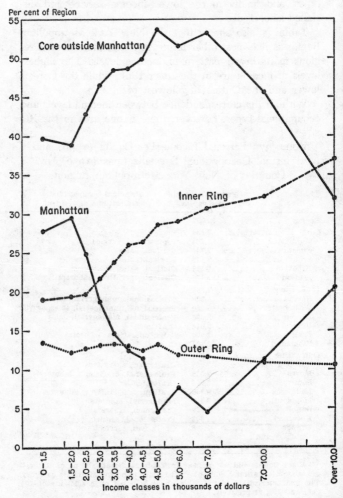

CHART 8

Geographic Distribution of Income Recipients by Income Classes, New York Metropolitan Region, 1949

Per cent of Region

Core outside Manhattan

Manhattan

Inner Ring

Outer Ring

Income classes in thousands of dollars

Note: "Income recipients" means families and unrelated individuals reporting income.

Source: U.S. 1950 *Census of Population*.

gion where income figures must be used with a certain special reserve. This is Manhattan, whose population characteristics are unique in income terms. This is an area whose residents include a disproportionately large number from the very low and the very high income groups; any "average" income figure for the county, therefore, such as Table 37 provides, can easily mislead. The critical facts about Manhattan's income are best shown by Chart 8, which indicates how the middle-income groups are "underrepresented" in the area.[11] This distribution, of course, ties in with the remarkable two-way occupational specialization of Manhattanites already shown in Tables 32 and 33: the high-income professional group and the bottom-income service group are the ones "over-represented" in Manhattan.

Because incomes and job types are so closely interrelated, there are no surprises in Table 38, which shows the types of community chosen by different income groups. Since the picture is confined here to the Land-Use Survey Area, it misses some important extremes—Manhattan, for instance, and most of the latter-day exurbs.[12]

Nevertheless, certain consistent and striking relations of income level to other community characteristics appear at once in Table 38. Higher-income places tend to be smaller in population, as roughly shown by the average number of dwelling units per place in the various income ranges.[13] Net residential density declines consistently with rising income, that is, higher-income people buy more space per household. Associated with this density relation is the fact that the higher-income places have a smaller proportion of their housing in multifamily structures. Commuting time to Manhattan tends to increase with higher income levels, though not at all sharply. For the highest-income fifth of these places, the access rating averages only about half a point more—equivalent to only 7 or 8 minutes' difference in commuting time—than for the lowest-income fifth.

Finally, higher income level appears to be associated with a higher recent rate of population growth and construction activity, as crudely measured by the estimated percentage increase in the number of dwelling units from

TABLE 38 Characteristics of Urban Places in the Land-Use Survey Area in Relation to Median 1949 Income of Families and Unrelated Individuals

Places according to rank in 1949 median income	Median income, 1949[a]	Average number of dwelling units per place, 1954	Dwelling units per acre of residentially developed land, 1954–55	Per cent of dwelling units in multifamily structures, 1950[a]	Average access-zone rating	Per cent increase in dwelling units, 1950–54
All places	$3,929	8,057	8.06	[b]	2.85	10%
Top fifth	5,128	3,510	3.69	12%	2.92	18
2nd fifth	4,288	4,040	4.94	13	3.12	12
3rd fifth	3,925	7,519	7.51	16	2.80	14
4th fifth	3,572	9,016	8.34	23	2.84	8
Bottom fifth	3,235	16,365	14.32	39	2.56	7
Bottom tenth[c]	3,078	24,476	19.10	39	2.23	4

[a] Unweighted median of urban places in each group.
[b] Not calculated.
[c] Hoboken, Newark, Paterson, Orange, Union City, Edgewater, Jersey City, Guttenberg (Hudson), Harrison (Hudson), Passaic, Paramus (Bergen), Glen Cove (Nassau), and Washington township (Bergen).

Source: Income data from U.S. Census of Population; housing data (1950) from U.S. Census of Housing; housing data (1954) estimated by New York Metropolitan Region Study; land-use data, see Appendix J; access-zone ratings, see our Table 23, note b.

1950 to 1954. This reflects the fact that higher-income people tend to live in newer housing than lower-income people, and also the fact that the relatively spacious type of housing that higher-income people choose is more readily available in the kind of suburb in which there is still some space left for new construction.

Table 38 suggests, therefore, that higher-income people use their superior purchasing power to buy lower density, but at the cost of a longer journey to work. The relation is more clearly seen if we sort out the communities by *both* access and income level, as is done in Table 39. Reading up the columns of the table, we can see that for any given degree of access, higher income goes with lower density. Reading across the rows, we can see that for any given level of income, better access goes with higher density. Most of the exceptions are quantitatively insignificant.[14] Finally, reading Table 39 diagonally from lower right to upper left, one can discern a rough tendency for families with higher income to be closer to the center of the Region for any given level of density. Thus, only the two highest income groups get as far in as access zone 2 with densities of fewer than 8 dwelling units to the acre,

TABLE 39 Net Residential Density (Dwelling Units per Acre of Residentially Developed Land) in Urban Places in the Land-Use Survey Area, by Median 1949 Income and Access Zone

(Figures in parentheses indicate what percentage of the 1,015,243 dwelling units is accounted for by places in each access-income category)

Median-income ranking	Access zone				
	1	2	3	4	5
Top fifth	—	3.82	3.86	3.26	—
		(2)	(5)	(2)	
2nd fifth	—	5.69	5.29	4.05	3.21
		(3)	(5)	(2)	(a)
3rd fifth	—	8.90	6.22	6.52	3.28
		(11)	(4)	(3)	(a)
4th fifth	7.80	9.61	8.48	5.39	4.31
	(1)	(9)	(10)	(2)	(a)
Bottom fifth	27.79	7.86	9.29	2.23	3.83
	(26)	(5)	(8)	(a)	(1)

a Less than 0.5 per cent of total dwelling units.

Sources: See source note to Table 38.

settling in such places as Scarsdale, Bronxville, and Pelham Manor; lower-income communities tend to have such space standards only when they are substantially farther out.

Though a good deal has been said in the preceding pages about low-income and high-income families and communities, we have still to get an adequate picture of the process by which the very rich and the very poor have come to settle so heavily in a few restricted areas of the Region, notably in Manhattan. For our purposes, it is indispensable to understand this process; for, on the surface, these two groups seem in constant competition with commerce and industry to pre-empt the scarce space of the most central areas of the Region. Let us then focus upon these extremes.

THE TOP LAYER

Those on the top rung of the income ladder, we have observed, have first choice among existing or new accommodations. What choices, then, are open to a well-to-do household?

Top-income earners are mainly in the executive and professional groups and their jobs are to a very large extent concentrated in Manhattan, with a minor subconcentration in Newark. Their educational level and cultural interests also put a premium on convenient access to the Region's central focus. Though one obvious choice is to live in Manhattan, the day of the Fifth Avenue mansion is past. Those willing to accept apartment life, of course, can choose among a wide range of both old and new types in Manhattan. But once an area becomes as intensively built up as Manhattan has long since become, new construction faces a formidable hurdle of high site-acquisition and clearing costs.[15] Without heavy public subsidy, it has not been possible since World War II to provide new housing in Manhattan except in the luxury bracket. The same is true in most of the rest of the Core, though in lesser degree.

A survey of private rental apartments completed in New York City during the first quarter of 1958 disclosed that "the most typical unit in Manhattan was a three-room apartment with an average rent of $184 a month."[16] New luxury "cooperative" apartments on Manhattan's East Side cost very much the same. The occupant of a three-and-a-half-room unit of this sort is obliged to pay on the order of $15,000 to gain possession of such an apartment; thereafter he pays something like $175 monthly as maintenance charges.

The occupant of new unsubsidized housing in Manhattan thus has to pay high for relatively small quarters. Since not many can afford it and still fewer want to, the outcome is that the top-income neighborhoods which do exist in Manhattan are not buffered, as is generally the case elsewhere, by a gradation of upper-middle to middle-income neighborhoods. Instead, top-income districts are lapped by a sea of dilapidated housing populated primarily by the lowest income groups. Under these circumstances the high-income people who have chosen to live in Manhattan are restricted to a few at the top whose preference for central convenience has been so strong as to outweigh the costs and other disadvantages of the location.

Insofar as unsubsidized private construction still takes place in Manhattan, therefore, it occurs in only a very few neighborhoods—in areas where the access is so superior as to justify the exceedingly high rentals required to meet site acquisition costs. In recent years such construction has been increasingly concentrated in a zone east of Fifth Avenue between 23rd and 96th Streets. In fact, more than two-thirds of all private unsubsidized rental apartment units completed in Manhattan in the years 1952–1956 were in that zone.[17] Once built, these units command the highest rents in the borough.[18]

The attachment to Manhattan of top-income people is apparently strong. In November 1956, when tenants in high-rent apartments in Manhattan subject to rent controls were asked about their preferred next place of residence if they should move, nearly 93 per cent spoke for Manhattan and 68 per cent for the middle East Side zone of Manhattan.[19] A further indication of the strength of attachment of this segment of high-income households to Manhattan living appears in the fact that they devote a much higher proportion of their incomes to housing than do people of similar incomes in most other areas, despite rent controls.[20]

The rest of the Core has far less to offer the wealthy household in terms of residence. Nearly everywhere in the Core outside Manhattan, most of the disadvantages of Manhattan living still apply, but with much less to offset them. Access to the jobs and diverse attractions of the central business district involves an irksome subway ride—cheap, to be sure, but often taking at least as long as a commuter-train journey from the nearer parts of Westchester or Nassau. The highest income groups, therefore, are notably under-represented in the Core counties surrounding Manhattan.[21] Local exceptions occur in a few specially attractive and convenient areas like Riverdale, Brooklyn Heights, and Douglaston.

Where else can the wealthy household settle? A little farther out, mainly in the Inner Ring, are some old, relatively exclusive inner-suburban communities that grew up around rail commuter stations in the days when only the well-to-do commuted from such distances at all: places like White Plains, Scarsdale, Bronxville, Pelham Manor, Montclair, Great Neck, and Garden City. Some of these have, largely by dint of restrictive zoning, managed to retain their upper-income character, and they offer rather quick and comfortable access to Manhattan by rail plus pleasant surroundings and good community facilities. However, these communities do not satisfy the wants of all who could afford them. They are relatively old and close in, and in many there is little desirable vacant land left for new housing. Moreover, all but the most recently subdivided parts were laid out in the pre-automobile era on the assumption that the commuter would walk to the station. Net densities generally average at least 4 dwelling units to the acre, which means a typical lot size of about 8,000 square feet, or one-fifth of an acre. That is not exactly cramped, but is still a far cry from the lots of an acre or larger required by zoning in high-grade developments still farther out.[22] Nor is the existing housing any longer the last word in modernity. Finally, such communities are subject to increasing pressure for higher density and down-grading; and even where a specific community has managed to preserve its character it is likely to have become increasingly hemmed in by more recent lower-income development and a filling-up of the open spaces. Many of the more accessible of these communities have been increasingly pervaded by apartment development—for example, Great Neck Plaza, White Plains, Bronxville, Fort Lee, and South Orange.

If such a suburb is not modern or exclusive or spacious enough for a well-to-do household, the remaining alternative is a flight to virgin territory on the outer fringe where almost unlimited space is available and where lower-income encroachment on privacy and homogeneity can be kept at a distance not just by zoning but by cost and access barriers as well. This calls for a location entailing a long and expensive (but not too uncomfortable) ride to Manhattan; a location that makes two cars in the household almost a necessity; and perhaps a location where the lay of the land makes continuous, standardized housing development prohibitively expensive, so that the semi-isolated luxury single-family house has the field to itself. Pound Ridge, Wilton, and some communities on the North Shore of Long Island are examples. Thus, certain site features of cost and inconvenience become attractive for high-income housing, in the sense that they discourage competition and help to preserve privacy and homogeneity.[23]

The top income group, then, has chosen and is choosing not a single area in the Region nor a single combination of advantages describable in terms of access and density, but essentially three special types of neighborhood: (1) central Manhattan, (2) the older exclusive suburb well preserved by zoning, and (3) the deliberately inaccessible—hence, naturally exclusive—exurb. Which of these is chosen by a specific well-to-do household depends on a wide variety of personal factors. Probably the most important single determinant is the presence or absence of children in the household,[24] which we shall discuss a little further on in this chapter. First, though, we must look at the opposite end of the income scale—the lowest-income households of the Region.

THE BOTTOM LAYER

Building new housing in the Region for bottom-income families is not, and for a long time has not been, economically feasible for the private developer. Such families are housed mainly in old structures, a large proportion of which were originally built for and occupied by middle-income or upper-income people; to a much smaller extent, they are housed in relatively new publicly subsidized low-income redevelopments; and to a still less significant extent in scattered areas, mostly unincorporated, where shanty-building is tolerated. The redevelopment of neighborhoods through the subsidized construction of low-income housing has generally not greatly altered the density or distribution of population. Generally speaking, it has simply provided more tolerable quarters in areas previously occupied by slum dwellers. In essence, then, the lowest income groups live in neighborhoods where there is, or was, housing that middle income groups vacated.

Physical deterioration and obsolescence of style and layout arising just from the passage of time account in large part for the handing-down of such housing to the bottom income groups.[25] Most of Manhattan and Hudson County, major parts of Brooklyn and the Bronx, substantial parts of Queens, and the more central districts of satellite cities like Newark, Paterson, Passaic, Elizabeth, and Bridgeport were fully built up long ago.

It is not only the housing itself which is the victim of obsolescence. Neighborhoods obsolesce too—not only in their objective physical characteristics such as deterioration, traffic congestion, and encroachment of unsightly non-residential uses, but also in the degree to which they satisfy current tastes and demands. Improved transportation, and above all the spread of automobile ownership, have put suburban living within the reach of most of the people rather than just a small minority, a fact which tends to diminish the relative demand for housing in neighborhoods whose main attraction is centrality. Accordingly the oldest and most congested areas of the Region, contained primarily within the Core, have a vast stock of aged housing that middle-income and upper-income people have given up in favor of housing—and neighborhoods—that are newer and more spacious.

Occupationally, the lowest income group is primarily in the unskilled categories of services and manual labor and would thus be led by access considerations to seek housing in and adjacent to Manhattan and in the main heavy-industry belt of the Region from the Amboys to Weehawken, and from Hunts Point and Long Island City to Red Hook. This belt coincides pretty closely with the area where old high-density housing is most prevalent, and in which nearby nonresidential development and street congestion have brought especially great deterioration.

Housing in the oldest and most highly urbanized parts of the Region is accordingly given over mainly to the lowest income groups and to those who, regardless of income, are willing to settle for dilapidated and obsolescent housing. Except for some footholds provided by subsidized middle-income housing, members of the middle income group who insist upon tolerable structures are effectively excluded; this group could not afford to exploit the access advantages of such locations by rebuilding. Such an operation, as we have indicated, is too costly except for the very rich.

Apart from that small luxury market, therefore, the owner of old slum dwellings generally finds profit in capitalizing on the access and cheapness of his property, by providing the maximum allowable number of dwelling units per structure and the minimum (approximately zero) of service and upkeep.

There is, of course, another factor besides income reinforcing the central clustering of bottom-income households in Manhattan. This is the fact that such households consist in large part of recent inmigrant groups, mostly Negroes and Puerto Ricans,[26] who not only find special barriers to settling in the suburbs but also find some advantage in terms of social and economic security by remaining centrally congregated. As long as they are economically insecure, they see advantages in living at the congested center of the labor market; and as long as they are socially insecure, they tend to congregate with others in the group with which they are identified. Traffic studies and other evidence show, indeed, that large numbers of unskilled laborers with jobs in New Jersey industrial centers live in upper Manhattan and the Bronx, giving rise to a large "reverse" commuter flow across the Hudson. There is also a large "reverse" flow across the East River.

Since bottom income groups necessarily have but little choice in where they can live within the Region, we do not find them split into widely separated and radically different areas, as the top income group is split, nor do we find them spread over virtually all the Region as the middle income groups are. To be sure, the outer reaches of the Region do show a marked falling-off in average income level, and Chart 8 above shows that the Outer Ring as a whole has a slight over-representation of lowest-income-bracket families. But only a tiny portion of the substantial area of the Outer Ring can properly be called a slum. To be sure, scattered "rural slums" exist, such as are found in the Ramapos. And every sizable city of the Outer as well as the Inner Ring has its slum district, in a kind of miniature of the pattern for the Region as a whole. But the Region's overwhelmingly predominant concentration of the lowest income groups is in Manhattan and adjacent parts of Brooklyn, the Bronx, and Hudson County.

AGE COMPOSITION AND RESIDENCE CHOICE

Despite the fairly orderly way in which the different occupation and income groups seem to be associated with communities of different characteristics, the locations chosen by particular households within any specific occupational or income group actually run a wide gamut of community types. Only the lowest income group and ethnic "minority" households have a very narrow choice, the rest being able to pick among communities varying in access, density, size, age of housing, and degree of multifamily development.

Actually there is a high degree of predictability in the way in which that latitude of choice will be exercised.

The age structure of the household plays a major role. The higher the proportion of children in the household, the stronger is the incentive for a family of some given income to seek lower-density, single-family housing in communities with agreeable neighborhood conditions and good schools.

One result, as Table 40 shows, is that the proportion of children in the population is comparatively low in Manhattan, while it runs much higher in the rest of the Core, and slightly higher still in the Inner and Outer Rings. This pattern is entirely in keeping with tendencies that have been found characteristic of United States metropolitan areas generally: children are relatively fewer within the highly urbanized central zones of the nation's metropolitan areas than in the suburbs.[27]

TABLE 40   Percentage of Population in Age Groups Below 15 Years, New York Metropolitan Region, 1950

	Age group			
	Total below 15	0–4	5–9	10–14
Region	21.95	8.96	7.21	5.78
Manhattan	16.70	7.09	5.10	4.51
Core outside Manhattan	22.13	8.86	7.31	5.96
Inner Ring	23.69	9.82	7.88	5.99
Outer Ring	23.37	9.51	7.78	6.08

Source: Calculated from data in U.S. *1950 Census of Population.*

Underlying the differences in age structure is a characteristic life-cycle pattern of migration into and within the Region. As new families are created or as families move into the Region, they select their first residence partly on the basis of family structure. Families with children are more likely to locate in the suburbs than single workers or childless couples, who more often gravitate to central areas. When children arrive, the family preference for work access becomes less important relative to that for space and for such other factors as quality of neighborhood, schools, and the like (especially if the mother gives up her job at this point), and some families move to the suburbs. But once the children have finished school and have left home, there is a reverse shift in preference values. If the parents change communities at all at this stage, they may move inward again. Correspondingly, families newly arrived in the Region at this stage in their careers are somewhat more likely to settle centrally than those who come in with young children.

These patterns of movement are drastically altered and circumscribed in the case of very low-income households, especially nonwhite ones. There are special factors which have, in the past at least, drawn the bulk of these types of newcomers into Manhattan and kept them there.[28] Nonetheless, the general picture as sketched above has been documented by various studies of the over-all age and family structure of migrants to central cities and suburban fringe areas. The most comprehensive of those studies, covering the decade 1940–1950,[29] showed that the only age groups with net migration into central cities of metropolitan areas were those from 15 to 29 years; all other age groups showed a net outward movement. By contrast, every age group showed net migration into the suburban "rings" of metropolitan areas in the 1940's. Net migration into the suburbs was heaviest in the age groups corresponding to young married couples and their children (25–34 and 0–9 years).

Families with *young* children, and *growing* families, have rapidly changing housing needs, jobs, and incomes and are thus inclined to be relatively mobile and to bulk large in the market for moderate-priced new suburban housing.[30] As a result, the counties with the largest proportions of children under 5 are Nassau, Somerset, Middlesex, Bergen, and Morris—in all of which there has been highly active new residential construction in low-density suburban developments and in which the rate of population growth has recently been well above the Region's average.

The influence of family structure on residence choice can be seen in Table 41, where the urban places in the Land-Use Survey Area are shown by groups, with each place classified by both its income level and the proportion

TABLE 41 Characteristics of Urban Places in Land-Use Survey Area, According to Income and Proportion of Children

Median Income ranking[a]	Number of places	Dwelling units per acre of residentially developed land, 1954-55	Per cent of dwelling units in multifamily structures, 1950	Average access-zone rating	Per cent increase in dwelling units, 1950-54	Per cent of residential land developed, 1954
Places with low proportion of population under 15 (less than 22.5%)						
Total	34	11.9	32%	2.12	6.2%	83%
Top fifth	4	6.8	40	2.25	11.5	97
2nd fifth	3	5.6	19	2.00	10.4	83
3rd fifth	4	10.6	33	2.25	4.9	91
4th fifth	9	8.8	30	2.22	6.6	85
Bottom fifth	14	16.0	39	2.00	5.7	78
Places with medium proportion of population under 15 (22.5 to 24.5%)						
Total	38	7.8	18%	3.03	11.8%	70%
Top fifth	6	3.4	11	3.33	17.3	68
2nd fifth	5	4.4	18	3.40	18.5	62
3rd fifth	10	8.0	18	2.70	14.7	73
4th fifth	11	7.8	23	3.09	11.2	70
Bottom fifth	6	16.2	26	2.83	6.8	76
Places with high proportion of population under 15 (over 24.5%)						
Total	54	4.6	12%	3.19	19.0%	55%
Top fifth	16	3.5	10	2.94	21.9	61
2nd fifth	17	5.1	12	3.24	18.4	57
3rd fifth	11	5.2	6	3.09	21.8	56
4th fifth	5	8.7	16	3.40	5.0	60
Bottom fifth	5	4.1	21	3.80	23.5	36

[a] The places are sorted into the same income groups here as in Table 38 above, except that the "bottom tenth" category of places is not separately tabulated here.

Source: Age data are from U.S. 1950 *Census of Population;* for other series, see source note to Table 38.

of its population under age 15. All the relations are necessarily obscured to a considerable extent by the fact that we have been obliged to classify whole communities rather than use households or families as units. Even so, it is possible to see in Table 41 the basic effect of household age-structure differences upon residence choice at each income level.

In each income class shown in the table, the communities with a low proportion of children tend to be those in which there is good access but high densities; and where the proportion of children is high, the access-density position is reversed.[31] In any given income bracket, a larger proportion of children is associated also with a greater preponderance of single-family dwellings, and with *newer* communities and housing, if one may judge from the rate of increase in dwelling units, the proportion of land developed, and the "access-to-Manhattan" ratings.

But there are differences between the upper-income and the lower-income communities which are worthwhile noting. The highest-income communities in the Land-Use Survey Area tend to be small, low-density, and relatively new, *regardless* of the proportion of children. What is more, for the upper-income communities, residential densities are sharply different as we move from a low to a medium proportion of children. But, in the lower income ranges, there is no very great change in community characteristics until the proportion of children shifts from medium to high.

What we see reflected here, no doubt, is the easier choice of high-income families, which shows itself in a greater readiness to find a low-density community as soon as children appear. The greater choice of this group is seen in still another way in the table. When the proportion of children is low or middling, higher-income communities tend to be slightly more remote than lower-income ones; but where the proportion of children is high, higher income seems to be used partly to buy better access, for the higher-income communities in the lowest third of the table are *closer in* than the lower-income ones. Here again we have a suggestion of the greater latitude of choice of the higher-income groups. If a low-income family with many children wants to find really spacious quarters, it has to seek them in relatively remote or inconvenient locations.

SYNTHESIS: THE REGION'S COMMUNITY TYPES

Having considered the effect upon residence choice of the three critical factors—job types, income level, and children—we can now trace their combined effects in determining "who lives where" in the Region.

The inner part of the Core—Manhattan and parts of adjacent counties—is peopled mainly by two contrasting types of household. First, there is a preponderant mass of bottom-income unskilled manual and service workers, including most of the Region's members of "disadvantaged" recent in-migrant groups. They are there because of the supply of obsolete, dilapidated, and highly compressed housing; because their jobs are mainly in Manhattan and nearby heavy-industry zones, and the subway affords cheap access; because they are excluded from most Inner Ring suburbs by social counter-pressures as well as by lack of rock-bottom housing; and because they find some community solidarity and better job opportunity within the focal cluster and its huge and variegated labor market. The other conspicuous element in the inner Core (far smaller, and mainly confined to certain sections of Manhattan) consists of wealthy and mainly childless people in the professional and executive categories, who value quick access to their Manhattan jobs and also the many avocational attractions of the Region's center, and who have been able to afford the high costs of luxury-apartment redevelopment.

A little farther out, in the outer parts of the Core and the most urbanized parts of the Inner Ring, the population is predominantly lower-middle in income, with both extremes under-represented. The housing here is somewhat less old and more spacious than in the inner Core and includes some relatively new apartments. Occupationally, these communities consist mainly of lower white-collar commuters to Manhattan and semiskilled industrial workers employed in the Inner Ring and Core.

Going farther out in the Inner Ring, there is a gradual

rise in income level and improvement in the newness and quality of housing, with the single-family house becoming predominant. The proportion of skilled industrial workers relative to semiskilled and unskilled rises, with a similar upward shift in the status of the white-collar groups, and a rising proportion of households with children. Interspersed in the pattern are the older, zoning-protected, upper-class suburbs populated largely by Manhattan-employed professional and executive workers.

Still farther out (in the outer parts of the Inner Ring and some of the inner edges of the Outer Ring) is a zone of active new construction, almost entirely in single-family houses on fairly ample lots. These suburbs house primarily upper-income people with children who want space and can afford new housing. A considerable proportion, by the time we reach this zone, work in the Inner Ring rather than the Core. Here are interspersed, too, some rather low-income communities (largely old industrial cities and towns), populated by unskilled manual and service workers with suburban jobs and, predominantly, with children.

Finally, in the more outlying parts of the Region we find a few exclusive exurbs where high-income families with children have accepted remoteness from Manhattan in order to get space, privacy, and neighborhood homogeneity. Most other people living that far out, however, work nearby in the outer suburbs; and economic and other links with the Region's center become more and more tenuous as we approach the largely arbitrary outer boundary.

SPREAD OF THE PEOPLE

If the last two chapters are solidly based, we now have a fairly adequate notion of who lives where in the Region and why. But our main objective has still to be reached. What are the forces that will be changing the population pattern in the decades just ahead? What changes are these forces likely to produce? To find answers to these questions, everything we have learned about the present distribution of people in the Region will prove useful. But it will also be useful to look at the way in which population patterns in the Region have been changing.

THE CHANGING POPULATION MAP

In most American metropolitan areas, a dramatic redistribution of population has been occurring during the last few decades.[1] The New York Metropolitan Region is no exception. Chart 9 offers one way of viewing some of the major shifts. Despite the great growth in the Region's total population since 1900—a growth of over 175 per cent—some important areas of the Region have declined in population. Manhattan's central business district* has lost about half its peak population in an almost uninterrupted decline since 1910.

As the Region's population has increased in numbers, therefore, the growth of the swarm has not been just a simple magnification in all dimensions. The picture of an enormous concentration near the center and a general tapering off toward the edges—a picture to which we were first introduced in Map 1 of Chapter 1—has persisted.

* See Map 3.

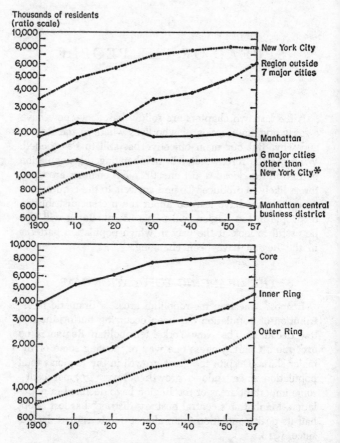

CHART 9

Distribution of Population in New York Metropolitan Region, 1900–1957

Thousands of residents (ratio scale)

New York City
Region outside 7 major cities
Manhattan
6 major cities other than New York City ✻
Manhattan central business district

Core
Inner Ring
Outer Ring

✻ Newark, Jersey City, Bridgeport, Yonkers, Paterson, and Elizabeth. The 1957 estimates for the four New Jersey cities are based on births and deaths only, and do not take account of migration; complete data would probably show that the six cities as a group, between 1950 and 1957, either gained very little population or actually declined.

Source: U.S. *Census of Population*, 1900 through 1950. The 1957 estimates are based on U.S. Special Census of April 1, 1957 (Series P–28, No. 1036), and on population estimates by state departments of health.

But with each decade, for at least three or four decades, this "density gradient" has been getting less steep. If we think of the population distribution as represented by a roughly conical mountain, with density as height, this peak developed gentler slopes as it grew in bulk. Maturity has brought "executive spread."

This trend can be seen in Chart 10, where the progression of densities in various zones is shown for 1920, 1940, and 1955.[2] In that chart, small areas (individual municipalities and groups of municipalities) were classified according to the amount of time required for a rail commuter trip to Manhattan in 1956, and densities of population per square mile of land area are shown for each time-class on each of three dates. There is a clear trend toward a flatter density gradient, particularly since 1940.*

If New York City had been included in Chart 10, the flattening of the density profile over time would of course have been even more pronounced, in view of the fact that the most central areas of the Region have long since ceased to grow and have actually been thinning out in population.

This shift in densities has not been produced by any simple pattern of population growth in the Region. For example, it would be wrong to suppose that the areas of fastest growth in the Region were uniformly those with the lowest population density. What seems to have happened is that at different stages in the Region's development, a

---

* The time-distance zones used in Chart 10 are the same ones used in Chapter 6 (see Table 23, note b, p. 124). They are fixed areas, since each place was classified according to its time-distance from Manhattan as of 1956. Commuting times by rail did not change very much during the period covered by the chart. Municipalities were grouped where necessary in order to avoid distortion of results through annexations and other boundary changes; but Nassau County was omitted altogether because the multitude of municipal boundary changes made it impossible to compare densities for identical parts of the county throughout the period. New York City was omitted for different reasons—because of difficulties in arriving at a comparable measure of commuting time, and because the densities run so much higher in New York City that the chart would have lost greatly in clarity.

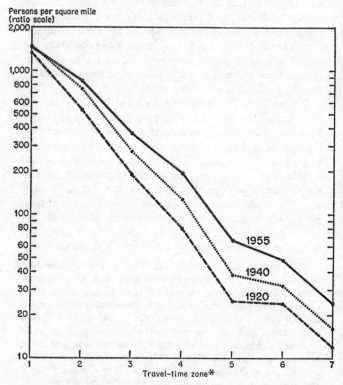

CHART 10
Relation Between Population Density and Approximate
Travel Time to Manhattan, New York Metropolitan
Region, 1920, 1940, 1955

(New York City and Nassau County excluded)

Persons per square mile
(ratio scale)

1955

1940

1920

Travel-time zone*

* Each additional time zone after the first represents about 15 minutes additional travel time.

ring of maximum population growth rate has existed; and as the decades have gone by this ring has moved farther out from the center of the Region.

Indications of that shift can be seen in Chart 11. Here we examine four periods of population growth: 1920 to 1930, 1930 to 1940, 1940 to 1950, and 1950 to 1955. In each period, the counties are arrayed across the chart in order of population density, in this case leaving unusable swampy and hilly terrain out of the calculation. The counties with sparsest populations are at the left and those with highest densities at the right. Certain counties with particularly conspicuous growth behavior have been identified by name. By following the four panels, the eye can discern where the greatest rate of population growth took place in the Region in each period, in relation to the density or sparseness of population in the areas.

In the 1920's, as Panel 1 shows, some counties in both the Core and the Inner Ring exhibited very high rates of growth. There was no pronounced relation between density and growth. The lowest-density counties (those in the Outer Ring) grew at rates varying relatively little from the Region average, with no spectacular performers among them. The "tidal wave" of metropolitan expansion[3] had evidently not yet reached the Outer Ring in the 1920's. In the Core, the rapid transit extensions that had begun to push into Queens in the preceding decade were an important factor in spurring Queens' belated growth.[4]

In the slow-growth decade of the 1930's, there appeared a definite tendency for growth to be most rapid where density was lowest. The Outer Ring counties on the whole showed faster growth rates than the counties in either of the higher density zones, though Nassau and Queens continued to expand at a rapid clip.

In the war decade of the 1940's, the tendency for growth to be greater in the sparser counties was a little more evident still. Suffolk, Monmouth, Somerset, and Morris Counties in the low-density Outer Ring moved into the highest-growth category, though Nassau was still the star performer.

The period 1950–1955 shows the relation of growth to

CHART 11 Relation Between County Population Densities

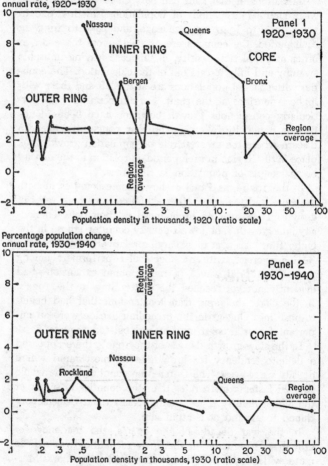

Note: Population density in this chart means population per square
ing 10 per cent).

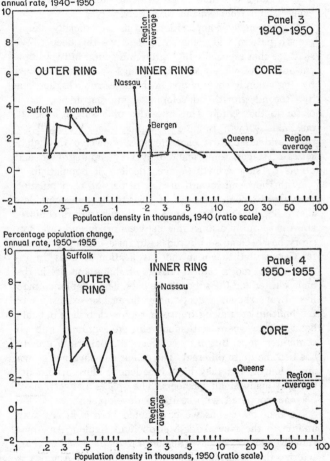

mile of usable land (that is, excluding swampy land and slopes exceed-

sparsity still more clearly defined. Among the Core counties, all but Queens grew more slowly than the Region (in fact, Manhattan, Brooklyn, and Hudson grew not at all). The Region's top rank in growth rate shifted outward in Long Island from Nassau to Suffolk.

A great many complexities in this superficially simple growth pattern will come to light as we dig deeper. We shall see that especially high growth is found in two different and rather widely separated "rings"—one characterized by single-family construction in the outer suburbs, and one by "second growth" development in apartments, much closer to the center. Thus the idea of a single "ring" of maximum growth is an oversimplification. We shall see that residential areas characteristically evolve through a series of stages, some marked by very rapid growth and others by slow growth or even decline of population.

With the trend toward greater dispersion of population over the Region, contrasts of density have become less sharp. Subdivisions have appeared in potato-farm country, and the formerly distinct line between urban and rural territory has become so blurred as to raise baffling problems for Census statisticians in the classification of areas. In another sense, too, a radical change of shape appears in the main cluster and the subordinate ones. The population map has always shown a good many finger-like extensions of the built-up area along transport routes, dribbling out into bead-strings where settlement clustered around railroad commuter stops. But in recent years the pattern of growth has become quite different. The extensions have not grown much longer, but they have broadened, blurred, and developed many small offshoots. The spaces between have become peppered with scattered development.

None of the trends we have noted here is in any way unique to the New York Metropolitan Region. As Amos Hawley and others have demonstrated, these shifts characterize the "Changing Shape of Metropolitan America."[5]

HOW NEIGHBORHOODS EVOLVE

So far, we have simply been describing some of the most conspicuous changes in the Region's over-all settlement pattern. Volumes more could be added by way of description, tracing historical trends in the particular residence patterns of different income, ethnic, or occupational groups and the changing complexion of the Region's myriad neighborhoods. But a closer examination of processes of change, if it is to be fruitful to our understanding, must be directed toward explanation and not mere description.

In the search for significant causal relations hypothesis must play a part. Our next task is to develop a concept of the whole process of the evolution of the metropolitan population pattern which can be tested by its ability to account for the observed facts and which can serve to suggest the directions that further development is likely to take.

The shifting pattern of metropolitan residence areas has often been schematically described in terms of gradually widening concentric zones pushing out in all directions from a growing central business core like ripples from a splash. Nonresidential "downtown" land uses, pre-empting the very center of the metropolitan area almost exclusively, expand into the immediately surrounding old residential areas, and also extend an aura of blight far beyond the range of their actual land-taking. Housing nearest the center is mainly slum—because it is the oldest, because it is cramped, because the street traffic and other aspects of downtown development make it undesirable for residence, and because it comes to house a concentration of disadvantaged people who are shunned as neighbors by those more fortunate or longer in residence. These slum characteristics are persistent, even cumulative, since the economics of slum property deters extensive replacement, modernization, or even maintenance of the antiquated housing.

The near-central slum area, eroded from the inside and along its main streets by competing land uses, and having to accommodate an influx of bottom-income people, expands outward into the next nearest and next oldest zone, mainly by the down-grading and conversion of old apartments and houses to higher densities. This pressure, as well as over-all population growth, forces the population of the next zone to push outward in turn, and so it goes till we reach the out-crawling fringe of urban development where new houses replace farms, woodland, or golf courses.

This highly simplified picture is not unrelated to reality in the New York Metropolitan Region, but it needs a good deal of modification to take account of observed facts. In the first place, there is not just one high-density commercial center but many, of different orders of magnitude; there is not only Manhattan but Newark, Jersey City, Paterson, Passaic, Elizabeth, New Brunswick, and many other old cities. The widening ripples come, then, not from a single pebble dropped into a puddle, but from a scattered handful of large, middling, and small pebbles, each a focus of expansion. Secondly, the pattern does not really shape up into neat concentric circular zones, because of manifold variation in transport facilities, topography, zoning, and so on which "distort" the picture. Thirdly, people do not just "shove over" from one block to the next, like a row of dominoes falling, but often move to a quite different part of the metropolitan area once they decide to move at all. New residential developments too, as we have already seen, do not simply extend the built-up area into the countryside in solid sequence, but "leap-frog" across intervening vacant land in order to use sites better matched to the current demand for new housing. Finally, the housing supply responds to changing demand in several alternative ways.

We can get a realistic view of what has been happening in the New York Metropolitan Region by identifying areas in sequential stages of development. Some of the oldest communities in the Region have evolved through the whole succession while other less "mature" parts of the Region are still in earlier stages. Our hypothesis is that the historical pattern of sequence, as exhibited in cross-section in the present structure of the Region, does have enough predictive value to be useful, if we can allow for certain evident changes in the impact of such basic determinants as means of transport.

What then are the stages of evolution we can identify, and where in the Region are they found?

Stage 1 is residential development in single-family houses. This stage, the earliest of all, is just beginning to appear in some outlying parts of the Region, is currently in full swing in the outer parts of the Inner Ring, and was passed long ago in most of the Core and in the central parts of the large Inner Ring cities, notably Newark. Table 42 shows that new residential construction in the outer counties of the Region is primarily single-family. In every Outer

TABLE 42   Percentage of New Dwelling Units in Single-Family Structures, New York Metropolitan Region, First Half of 1958

Entire Region	54.1	Union	70.9
		Richmond	75.5
Core	9.3	Nassau	81.3
Manhattan	None	Outer Ring	87.9
Brooklyn	1.7	Fairfield	72.0
Bronx	12.0	Middlesex	72.2
Queens	20.6	Dutchess	78.9
Hudson	59.1	Rockland	94.9
		Somerset	95.4
Inner Ring	65.9	Suffolk	96.2
Essex	35.2	Morris	98.1
Passaic	55.1	Orange	98.3
Westchester	56.0	Monmouth	98.4
Bergen	69.5	Putnam	100.0

Source: Regional Plan Association, *New Homes in the New Jersey–New York–Connecticut Metropolitan Region* (RPA Bulletin 90, Number 3), December 1958.

Ring county, more than 72 per cent of the new housing covered by permits issued in the first half of 1958 was in one-family structures, and all of the counties with more than half of their new housing in multifamily structures in that period were Core counties except Essex.

The progressive shift in the zone of most active new residential development is suggested by Chart 11, since very rapid population growth is associated with this first stage in development rather than with any subsequent increases in density that may occur through redevelopment or conversion. Thus, in the 1920's, Queens was the area in which this stage was most apparent. By the 1940's, the big boom in Queens was over, and Nassau and Bergen Counties had been joined by such Outer Ring counties as Suffolk and Monmouth in passing into the first stage. Since 1950 the zone of most active development of new residential land has moved still farther out, especially on Long Island. As recently as the early 1950's, two to three houses were being built in Nassau County for every one in Suffolk; but in each year after 1955, more have been built in Suffolk than in Nassau.[6]

Stage 2 is a transition stage in which there is substantial new construction and population growth in the area, but in which a high and increasing proportion of the new housing is in apartments, so that average density is increasing. Much of the apartment construction replaces older single-family houses.

The zone of transition to a predominantly apartment pattern of housing can be traced in some detail in terms of the data for individual municipalities in the Land-Use Survey Area that was discussed in Chapter 6. (See Map 5, page 125, and Appendix J.) We find, first, a rather compact and inlying group of these municipalities where the process was already so far advanced by 1950 that more than half the dwelling units enumerated in the 1950 federal Census of Housing were in multifamily structures, here defined as structures for three or more households. These municipalities are all very close to New York City or are large old subcenters and their immediate suburbs. Nearly all were developed prior to the period of mass automobile commuting. In southern Westchester we find Yonkers, Mount Vernon, and Bronxville; in Nassau County, the tiny apartment community of Great Neck Plaza near the Queens line; and on the New Jersey side, most of the cities in Hudson County, the old cities of Newark and Passaic, and the suburb of East Orange adjoining Newark.

That is an indication of the extent of the outward spread of multifamily development by 1950. There has been significant further extension since then, with more communities entering Stage 2. Thus we can identify a "mature" group of places in the Land-Use Survey Area in which the proportion of units in multifamily structures in 1950 was already at least 10 per cent and in which an increased proportion of multifamily units appears in the "housing starts" of the period 1951–1955. This group includes two old and sizable Inner Ring cities (Elizabeth and Paterson) and some commuter settlements with exceptionally good access to New York City or to major Inner Ring subcenters. In Westchester there is the string of commuter stops on the Hudson Division of the New York Central (Hastings, Dobbs Ferry, Irvington, Tarrytown); the Harlem Division stops of Tuckahoe and White Plains; and the New Rochelle-Mamaroneck-Port Chester sequence on the New Haven Railroad. On Long Island the well served communities of Long Beach, Cedarhurst, Rockville Centre, Freeport, and Great Neck appear in the list. In a continuous band near Newark and Paterson we have Montclair, Orange, Clifton, and Rutherford.

To complete the picture of the transitional zone, we have to take account also of what is going on in areas closer in or farther out than our Land-Use Survey Area. In the Riverdale area of the Bronx, in eastern and southern Queens, and in Staten Island there has been active redevelopment into apartments. The same applies in the major Outer Ring centers such as Bridgeport, Stamford, Poughkeepsie, and New Brunswick, where a considerable proportion of the occupants work outside the Region's Core. Finally, there has been some new apartment development in other Outer Ring spots with special site advantages, primarily shore communities in Fairfield and Monmouth Counties.

Most of the areas where the transition process that we call Stage 2 is markedly evident, however, lie in the inner part of the Inner Ring and the outer fringes of New York City. According to our statistics for the first half of 1958, the construction of new multifamily buildings—defined now as structures for two or more families—predominated over the construction of single-family homes in a compact zone extending no farther out than a line beginning at Long

Beach, on the south shore of Long Island, and extending through Hempstead, Flushing, Norwalk, Rye, Yonkers, Maywood, Paterson, Rutherford, Belleville, West Orange, Irvington (New Jersey), Elizabeth, and Perth Amboy (plus offshoots in New Brunswick and Ossining).

Stage 3 is a down-grading stage, in which old housing (both multifamily and single) is being adapted to greater-density use than it was originally designed for. In this stage there is usually little actual new construction, but there is some population and density growth through conversion and crowding of existing structures. This stage appears most clearly in areas of recent "slum invasion" located on Manhattan's upper West Side, in sections of the Bronx and Brooklyn, and in certain old urban areas in and around Newark, Paterson, Passaic, Elizabeth, and the Hudson County cities.

Of course, the sequence to this stage from the preceding one is not always clean-cut. Thus in the down-grading stage there may be a certain amount of new housing construction too, involving the replacement of single-family homes by apartment houses at the same time that other structures are being subdivided. Moreover, Stage 2 does not inevitably lead to Stage 3: an area converted to apartments may not undergo any down-grading then or later. The Riverdale area of the Bronx, for instance, promises to hold its present quality for some time to come. The stretch of Fifth Avenue facing Central Park was almost entirely transformed from one-family residences to towering apartment buildings after about 1910 and has maintained its character. On the other hand, Riverside Drive, similarly redeveloped at about the same time, has been subject to down-grading.

The down-grading stage is often associated with the spread of districts occupied by more or less segregated ethnic and minority groups. In the spread of such districts, conversion of structures to accommodate more families plays a significant part, but not always a decisive one. Thus, the number of dwelling units in the 17-county Standard Metropolitan Area[7] with nonwhite household heads showed a net increase of about 100,000 between

1950 and 1956. Of this increase, at least 85 per cent appears to have been accounted for by net shift from white to nonwhite occupancy in dwelling units that were occupied in both 1950 and 1956 and were not converted. The remainder of the increase was split fairly evenly between conversions and post-1950 construction.[8] In particular areas of the Region, of course, the relative importance of conversions in the shifting character of neighborhoods was much greater than these over-all figures might suggest.

As we look at the changes in the Region's housing stock in the perspective of the last few decades, it is not possible to sort out in hard quantitative terms the roles that new construction, demolitions, conversions, and other processes have played.[9] For the period since 1950, however, the data are more adequate. In the Standard Metropolitan Area, the number of dwelling units rose from 3,954,000 in 1950 to 4,631,000 in 1956, a 17 per cent increase. This increase, as shown in Table 43, was the net result of many things— of new construction, of demolition, of conversion, of "merger" (the reverse of conversion), and still other processes. New construction, of course, was far and away the dominant element in the change, but the net addition in dwelling units due to conversions accounted for nearly one-tenth of the aggregate increase.

A considerable amount of light is thrown on the conversion process by the figures in the table comparing the characteristics of dwelling units before and after conversion with the characteristics of other dwelling units. The table shows that the units involved in conversion were in comparatively old structures; that though only half the units were renter-occupied before the conversion process, more than three-fourths were renter-occupied when conversion was completed; and finally, that the rentals charged for the converted units were far from low when compared with the units whose status was unchanged between 1950 and 1956.*

* The rent control laws in force in some parts of the Region could have produced some of these differences. Converted units and newly constructed units are not subject to such control.

TABLE 43 Characteristics of Dwelling Units Added, Lost, Changed in Form, or Reported in Same Form, New York Standard Metropolitan Area, 1950–1956

	Number of dwelling units (thousands)	Percentage in structures built before 1930	Percentage tenant-occupied	Percentage dilapidated structures[a]	Percentage in multi-family structures[b]	Percentage with nonwhite household head	Median value of owner-occupied property[c]	Median monthly rent[d]
Units reported in same form in both 1950 and 1956								
1950 characteristics	3,706	n.a.	67[e]	4	n.a.	6[e]	$12,800	$42
1956 characteristics	3,706	n.a.	66[e]	5	n.a.	9[e]	16,300	53
Units added by new construction								
1956 characteristics	737	0	42	1	43	5	17,200	97
Units involved in conversion								
Characteristics before conversion (1950)	51	90	50	2	53	6	13,100	47
Characteristics after conversion (1956)	109	90	77	3	100	9	...	64
Units added by other means[f]								
1956 characteristics	44	59	88	19	95	15	12,500	79
Units demolished								
1950 characteristics	72	40	96	42	88	46	n.a.	31
Units involved in mergers								
Characteristics before merger (1950)	71	84	62	6	100	10	...	38
Characteristics after merger (1956)	35	91	29	6	40	18	13,600	59
Units lost by other means[g]								
1950 characteristics	54	87	87	22	80	12	n.a.	38

Note: For notes and source, see bottom of page 191.

Table 43 also shows that dwelling units built since 1950 were higher in value or rent, in 1956, than units that had survived unchanged in status since 1950 or earlier. Only 5 per cent of the new units were occupied by nonwhite households in 1956, less than 1 per cent were rated dilapidated by that time, and more than half were in single-dwelling structures and owner-occupied.

The units lost by demolition, accidental destruction, abandonment, or loss of dwelling-unit status showed the opposite characteristics. They were relatively ancient, dilapidated, tenant-occupied, multifamily, and high in nonwhite occupancy. Nearly half the units demolished between 1950 and 1956, in fact, were occupied by nonwhites in 1950, and more than 40 per cent had been rated dilapidated at that time. The median rent of such units was also relatively low.

All of which brings us to *Stage 4*, the thinning-out stage. This is the phase in which density and dwelling occupancy are gradually reduced. Most of the shrinkage comes about through a decline in household size in these neighborhoods. But the shrinkage may also reflect merging of dwelling units, vacancy, abandonment, and demolition. This stage is characterized by little or no residential construction and by a decline in population.

To find the reasons for this thinning-out process, we

NOTES FOR TABLE 43

n.a. = not available.

a Percentage of dilapidated units among units for which condition was reported.

b Structures with two or more dwelling units.

c Owner-occupied nonfarm dwelling units in single-dwelling-unit structures, without business use and with only one dwelling unit included in the property. Some units, for which no data were available, were omitted from calculations.

d Median contract monthly rent in renter-occupied nonfarm units. Some units, for which no data were available, were omitted from calculations.

e Based on units reporting characteristics for both 1950 and 1956.

f Change to dwelling-unit status, or units moved to site.

g Change to non-dwelling-unit status, removal from site, abandonment, accidental destruction.

Source: Calculated from data in Bureau of the Census, *1956 National Housing Inventory, Components of Change, 1950 to 1956: New York–Northeastern New Jersey Standard Metropolitan Area* (Washington, 1958).

shall have to retrace our steps and have another look at the families which characteristically participate in the preceding stage of slum invasion. Those families are, on the whole, recently-arrived in-migrants to the Region, with low incomes and a limited housing choice. The limitations are imposed not only by their income levels but also by restrictions and prejudices against many of them in various parts of the Region, by an inadequate knowledge of the housing market, and by uncertain employment alternatives. At the same time, these in-migrants tend to be predominantly young married couples or marriageable individuals in their twenties, that being the time of life when mobility is much the greatest for all classes of people.[10]

Households with these characteristics expand rapidly in size through the arrival of children and also, commonly, by taking in relatives or other lodgers even more recently arrived in the City and seeking a foothold. As a result, at the stage when a down-grading neighborhood is having an increase in the number of dwelling units (that is, households) per structure, it is likely also to have—either at the same time or very shortly after—an increase in the number of persons per dwelling unit.

But once settled, the main couple of the household does not characteristically move soon again. The tendency to stay put strengthens fast after people pass their early twenties.[11] Also, as may be noted from Table 44, dwellers in central-city areas are distinctly less mobile than residents of other types of areas in the Region.[12]

Once the in-migrant couples have settled down and raised families, the continued aging of them and their neighborhoods leads to the "thinning-out" stage characteristic of slum areas after they reach peak density—a thinning-out provided in considerable part by the shrinkage of household size.

The thinning-out stage began several decades ago in some of the Region's oldest slums, and those areas are now far less crowded than they were, both in absolute terms and in comparison with more recently created slums. In Manhattan's lower East Side the population, after having risen from 339,000 to 532,000 between 1890 and 1910, declined in the next twenty years by more than half, reaching 250,000 in 1930.[13]

The thinning-out stage is in progress, but less advanced, in a good many other areas of New York City, as Map 6 shows. If we take the City Planning Department's Statistical Districts as the unit of area, it appears that population has declined since 1950 in every district of Manhattan; in all but the northern and eastern fringes of the Bronx; in all but a very few of the districts of Brooklyn; and in a number of Queens districts closest to Manhattan and

TABLE 44 Moving Rates in New York Metropolitan Region, 1949–1950[a]

	Percentage of population in 1950 which had moved during last 12 months	
	From anywhere	From elsewhere in same county
Region	14.7	5.2
Manhattan	13.3	5.0
Core outside Manhattan ...	8.8	4.1
Bronx	7.6	3.5
Brooklyn	7.8	4.1
Queens	11.0	4.5
Hudson	8.2	4.9
Inner Ring	14.3	6.7
Bergen	13.9	5.8
Nassau	19.8	6.2
Westchester	13.4	6.4
Union	13.2	6.6
Essex	11.9	7.3
Newark	11.4	6.9
Remainder	12.4	7.6
Richmond	15.9	7.5
Passaic	12.9	7.9
Outer Ring	16.2	7.3
Morris	12.9	5.4
Putnam	19.7	5.5
Somerset	13.3	5.8
Suffolk	23.1	6.5
Rockland	26.8	6.5
Middlesex	12.9	6.9
Dutchess	14.3	7.4
Fairfield	13.1	7.8
Orange	17.4	8.9
Monmouth	18.0	9.2

[a] "Moving" is defined here as having resided in different houses on the 1950 Census enumeration day and one year earlier. Persons less than one year old in 1950 were excluded from the population in calculating the ratios.

Source: Calculated from data in U.S. *1950 Census of Population, Characteristics of Population*, Tables 34 and 43.

Brooklyn. It also declined in the two Staten Island districts nearest to Manhattan, though this is not shown on the map.*

Further striking illustrations of the thinning-out stage are found when we examine Health Areas, which are smaller units than Statistical Districts. Manhattan has 89 Health Areas. Unpublished data from the City Planning Department, based on federal Censuses, show that, in 1950, thirteen of them had population densities exceeding 300 persons per gross acre (192,000 per square mile). In all but one of these, population declined substantially by 1957. The same was true of all five Brooklyn Health Areas with densities exceeding 150 per gross acre in 1950.

The importance of reduced household size in the thinning-out process in the highest density areas is reflected in a comparison of population and housing trends. Although population declined between 1950 and 1957 in Manhattan, Brooklyn, and the Bronx, according to federal Census reports, the number of dwelling units apparently went on increasing in each borough.[14]

We come at last to *Stage 5.* This is the renewal stage, in which obsolete areas of housing, after arriving at Stage 4, are being replaced by new multifamily housing. Quality and the effective use of space are improved, but the overall population density of the area affected may not change much. By and large, such redevelopment in recent years has tended to increase over-all densities somewhat in Manhattan projects and to reduce them a little in projects elsewhere in the City.

This stage has assumed importance only quite recently, but it is safe to assume that the renewal effort will grow in magnitude. It is most conspicuous in Manhattan, particularly in the oldest slum areas, though appearing also in parts of Brooklyn, the Bronx, and Newark. It takes

* Map 6 is based on 1950 and 1957 population figures which the Department of City Planning, New York City, developed from Census data. In Richmond (Staten Island), the only borough not shown on the map, the two northernmost districts decreased by about 4 per cent and the other four districts experienced gains ranging from 12 to 46 per cent.

MAP 6

Population Change in Four Boroughs of New York City,
by Statistical Districts, 1950–1957

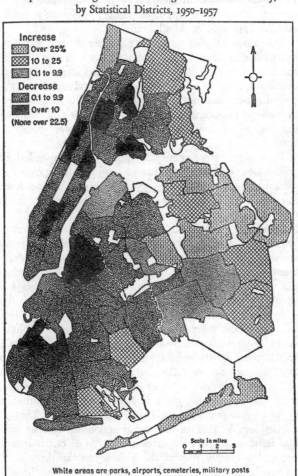

Increase
▦ Over 25%
▧ 10 to 25
▨ 0.1 to 9.9
Decrease
▩ 0.1 to 9.9
■ Over 10
(None over 22.5)

Scale in miles
0   1   2   3

White areas are parks, airports, cemeteries, military posts

mainly two contrasting forms: first, subsidized medium-income and low-income housing, and second, luxury apartments. So far, the unsubsidized luxury structures which have been built in the Region on the razed sites of decayed slums have appeared almost exclusively in the middle East Side of Manhattan.

Still another slum-renewal process, less important to date but with significant further potentialities in a few parts of the Region, is exemplified in Greenwich Village. Old areas of felicitous design and conveniently central location, originally high-income but deteriorated, are restored piecemeal to high-grade occupancy by extensive repair and remodeling, merger of dwelling units, and a little new construction.

To a large extent, however, Stage 5 has depended on public intervention: on the use of condemnation powers to assemble the site, on the use of public grants to bring down the site costs to levels at which medium-income rentals could be charged, and in some cases on the use of continuing operating subsidies to bring the rentals within reach of low-income families. About 500,000 people in the Region are now housed in structures falling in one or another of these categories, most of them in New York City. Though the effect of such programs on some neighborhoods has been of major importance, their impact on land use in the Region as a whole has been small. In Manhattan, Brooklyn, and the Bronx, where renewal programs of all sorts have made the greatest relative progress in the Region, the land area affected by the subsidized renewal programs adds up to about two square miles, or 1.4 per cent of the total.

Table 45 provides a broad picture of the new housing construction that took place in New York City's boroughs in the 12-year postwar period 1946–1957 inclusive. Though a considerable part of the construction in Queens and Richmond was of the types characterized in our Stages 1 and 2, the greater part of the building in the three most mature boroughs (Manhattan, Brooklyn, and the Bronx) comes under our Stage 5. It was nearly all apartment buildings, and a large fraction of it was publicly financed or subsidized housing for lower-income tenants, in old slum

TABLE 45   New Dwelling Units Constructed in New York City, by Boroughs, 1946–1957

(in thousands)

	All dwelling units	Publicly financed[a]	Privately Financed		Single-unit
			Multi-unit[b]		
			Land cost partly absorbed publicly[c]	Other	
New York City, total	364.6	80.1	5.4	217.7	61.3
Manhattan	67.1	25.5	4.3	37.3	d
Brooklyn	78.1	26.0	1.1	46.2	4.8
Bronx	48.7	17.2	0	24.1	7.4
Queens	158.5	9.3	0	107.7	41.5
Richmond	12.1	2.0	0	2.5	7.6

Note: Because of rounding, detail may not add exactly to totals.

[a] Financed by U.S., State, or City government.

[b] Structures with 2 or more dwelling units.

[c] Part of land cost was absorbed by U.S. and City governments under Title I of the Housing Act of 1954 and antecedent legislation.

[d] Actual number of units reported was 7.

Source: Based on data obtained from Dept. of City Planning, New York City.

areas. Finally, we can see that the rate of replacement of the housing stock is quite slow. The 194,000 new units of all types built in Manhattan, Brooklyn, and the Bronx during the 12-year period amounted to somewhat less than one-tenth of the total housing stock in those three boroughs, and of course some of the building represented net expansion rather than replacement. Only a fraction of 1 per cent of the dwellings were replaced per year, on the average.

By taking a closer look at Manhattan we can see how the various stages of change are affecting different neighborhoods. We saw in the map, just presented, that between 1950 and 1957 every Statistical District in Manhattan showed a decline in population. But if we again take smaller units of area—the 89 Health Areas of the borough —we find 14 of them registering population increases of 300 persons or more in that period. The bases for growth were different. In one Health Area in the East 60's and 70's, replacement of old buildings by new high-rise luxury apartments was the dominant factor in increasing over-all density. In six others (located in Inwood at the northern tip of Manhattan, in Harlem, and at the end of the Williamsburg Bridge), new high-rise low-income housing redevelopment was the main factor, offsetting the thinning-out that was going on in those areas during the interval. In six other areas, west of Central Park, there was little residential construction of any kind, and the increased density reflects our Stage 3 rather than Stage 5: with general down-grading, increase in Puerto Rican and Negro population, increasing size of household, and some conversions.[15]

These, then, are our five stages in the neighborhood cycle: (1) new single-family subdivisions, (2) apartment development, (3) down-grading generally associated with conversion, (4) thinning-out, and (5) renewal. Needless to say, the sequence describes what has happened only in general terms, and there are plenty of variations when we look at specific areas. For example, some fortunate areas (as already noted) have been able to stabilize their character short of the "down-grading" stage, or even short of the apartment-transition stage, in many instances by strongly supported zoning. Still other areas, like Harlem, have experienced not just a single slum-invasion-and-thin-out cycle, but several repetitions involving distinct new waves of in-migrants. (This picture is examined in considerable detail by Oscar Handlin, in his book in this series, *The Newcomers.*) Moreover, we ignore the process of invasion of residential areas by nonresidential uses—developments like the transformation of Park Avenue above Grand Central from a luxury apartment area to an area of sleek office buildings. These are special cases, many of them dealt with in other portions of this volume. In terms of the amount of land area involved, they represent only minor qualifications on the general patterns developed in this chapter.

THE FORCES IN MOTION

Though our five-stage conception is useful in understanding the development of the New York Metropolitan Region up to the present, we have no reason to assume that it will always work in the future in just the same fashion as in the past. The speed with which successive phases of development follow upon one another in particular areas, and to some extent even the sequence of the phases themselves, depend on the basic determinants of residence choice. These we have met before, in earlier chapters. Let us review them briefly and then try to see how changes in each of them alter the operation of the evolutionary sequence.

First there is *housing supply.* Shifts in the residence pattern depend partly on how the housing stock responds to demand—through construction, obsolescence, conversion, and in other ways. As we know, choice of residence is limited for most of the population because the stock of housing is very durable and only a small and highly unrepresentative part of the demand for housing is met by new construction. The stock of housing changes sluggishly in size and character, but it has responded differently in different periods in the past; and these responses on the supply side of the housing market have helped to shape the trends of population distribution in the Region.

Another basic determinant of housing choice is the need for *access.* Part of the explanation of the shifting of populations in the Region lies in the changing distribution of jobs, discussed in Part II of this book. But the impact of access considerations on residence choice depends not merely on where jobs are, but also on what means of travel are available and how people use them. Passenger-transport innovations are enough in themselves to alter the population map almost beyond recognition within a generation.

Finally, the changing *characteristics of the people themselves* have a great deal to do with shifts in the residence pattern. How people react to the bases of change already noted above—to the availability of housing, to the location of jobs and other access-objectives, and to travel facilities —depends on their effective demands for various types of living places and the degree of choice that they can exercise. These in turn reflect trends in levels of income and leisure, the age composition of households, conventional and individual tastes, and various restrictions on residence choice such as race prejudice.

Each of these three basic determinants of housing choice has undergone profound changes in the past. Their future changes—some of which we can venture to foresee—will inevitably make the processes of regional and neighborhood evolution work out in some new ways. We now take them up in detail, beginning with the supply-response of the housing market.

NEW HOUSING FOR WHOM?

Most of the Region's housing is the product of earlier eras, located and built to conform with the tastes and needs of its time. Data from the federal Census of Housing of 1950, as shown in Table 46, suggest that by now over half

TABLE 46 Age of Housing in New York Metropolitan Region in 1950

Percentage distribution of dwelling units according to year built

	1940–50 (0–10 years old in 1950)	1930–39 (11–20 years old in 1950)	1920–29 (21–30 years old in 1950)	Before 1920 (over 30 years old in 1950)
Region	12.5	12.0	28.4	47.1
Core	7.9	10.6	30.4	51.1
Manhattan	6.0	6.1	17.3	70.6
Bronx	7.7	12.8	41.9	37.6
Queens	16.4	19.0	41.3	23.3
Brooklyn	5.6	9.4	30.1	54.8
Hudson	3.0	3.2	20.2	73.6
Inner Ring	19.0	13.2	28.7	39.1
Richmond	10.3	9.4	35.3	45.0
Union	20.1	12.7	30.0	37.2
Essex	8.6	8.5	28.6	54.3
Passaic	14.1	8.9	23.6	53.4
Bergen	27.0	14.7	29.6	28.7
Westchester ...	10.3	15.4	29.9	44.4
Nassau	38.0	19.5	27.3	15.1
Outer Ring	19.7	15.6	19.5	45.2
Monmouth	17.4	14.2	25.8	42.5
Middlesex	22.0	10.4	24.5	43.1
Somerset	24.5	14.3	18.4	42.9
Morris	20.2	19.0	20.7	40.1
Rockland	17.6	14.3	17.6	50.5
Orange	10.8	11.5	11.9	65.7
Dutchess	13.1	11.4	13.2	62.3
Putnam	15.6	38.0	16.9	29.5
Fairfield	19.1	12.9	17.5	50.5
Suffolk	27.1	25.7	20.5	26.7

Source: U.S. 1950 *Census of Housing.*

of the Region's dwelling units are over 30 years old and date back to times when only a small fraction of the families in the Region owned automobiles. The proportion of these older dwellings is of course higher still in the Core counties taken as a group. Each successive residential development can be thought of as responding to the conditions of its period and depositing a record of the past a little like the growth rings in the cross-section of a tree trunk. Starting near the core of each old urban center and traveling outward to the zone where the surveyors tread gingerly through the cow pastures, we can view the whole historical sequence and we can even guess at the date at which any given neighborhood was "on the fringe."

The bulk of new residential construction in the Region, we have observed, takes one of four forms: single houses in new suburban developments, on vacant or near-vacant land; apartments replacing old single houses in a zone that can be loosely described as straddling the Core-Inner Ring boundary; privately-financed luxury apartments in highly central locations such as mid-Manhattan and the city of Newark; or subsidized low-income and middle-income apartments in renewal projects in fairly central areas, replacing old slums.

Who are the candidates for newly built housing? According to Table 43, presented several pages back, the owner-occupied dwelling units built in the Standard Metropolitan Area between 1950 and 1956 had a median value of $17,200 in 1956. That this is still a fairly realistic figure is suggested by Table 47, which gives some idea of the range of "asking prices" in the still more recent past for new single-family houses in various parts of the Region. These figures suggest that a large majority of the Region's families are currently priced out of the new single-family housing market.[16]

Unsubsidized new apartments are probably even less accessible to the bulk of the Region's population. Turning again to Table 43, we find that the rental units built in the Standard Metropolitan Area between 1950 and 1956 commanded a median rental of $97 a month in 1956. Since these units include a substantial amount of subsidized low-

TABLE 47   Advertised Prices of Sample of New Detached
Single-Family Houses for Sale in New York
Metropolitan Region, October 1957

County	Highest	Median	Lowest
Westchester and Fairfield	$46,000	$28,000	$15,500
Bergen	42,900	28,000	14,900
Nassau	46,000	22,500	16,000
Queens and Brooklyn	32,000	22,500	16,900
Suffolk	36,500	21,000	14,200
Rockland	45,000	20,000	16,500
Monmouth and Union	23,900	17,000	14,500
All above counties	46,000	23,000	14,200

Source: Sample survey of newspaper display advertisements
made in October 1957 by New York Metropolitan Region Study.
The total number of houses covered in the sample was 162; in
the individual counties and pairs of counties listed above, the
number varied between 11 and 48. The figures shown give only
a rough indication of price ranges, since "asking prices" are often
higher than actual sale prices, and since the sample was very
small.

income rental housing, it seems certain that rents in new
unsubsidized units were predominantly well over $100.[17]

A fraction of the lowest-income dwellers in old slums
have access to new subsidized apartments. But this still
leaves most people, in all income groups up to the top
sixth or so, getting their housing at second hand.

The basic outlines of this picture are not new. They may
in time be greatly altered by revolutionary advances in construction techniques or by a broadening of publicly supported urban renewal programs. But in the near future,
say in the next decade or more, it is likely that only relatively minor effects on population distribution in the Region will come directly from changes in the conditions gov-
erning the supply of new housing.

What are some of the changes that will produce these
"relatively minor" effects?

More and more new lower-income housing and some
middle-income housing can be expected in slum-renewal
areas in the largest urban centers of the Region on a sub-

sidized basis, with a progressive improvement of living conditions in such areas.

There seems no reason to expect more serious cost hurdles than at present to the building of more luxury apartments without subsidy in selected central areas; and, as we shall see, the demand for these is likely to increase and broaden, though that demand will be small in relation to the total housing picture for the Region.

The potential supply of new single-family houses is limited only in terms of nearness to urban centers. Even if new subdivisions are still more spaciously laid out than now, any foreseeable population growth over the next generation could find room well within the Region as presently defined.[18]

It is also to be expected that the gradual spread of apartments in replacement of old single-family homes will continue in the transition zone near the Core-Inner Ring boundary and that this zone of transition will move slowly outward.

Finally, of course, all existing housing will age and will become thereby riper for either down-grading or replacement, except in those all-too-rare cases where good design forestalls obsolescence.[19] In the next twenty years the part of the housing supply which will begin entering the obsolescence stage will be drawn largely from the units which were built between 1910 and 1930, when the Region increased in population by 4,000,000. The sheer size of this pool of housing, which probably is larger than any created during a period of comparable length in the Region's history, suggests that the impending increase in the supply of obsolescent housing may be very rapid. That probability is increased by the fact that most of the units erected in the 1910–1930 period were built without much regard for the existence of the automobile. A considerable change in the housing supply situation in the Region may therefore be in store.

But where and how people live will depend, as in the past, not only on the age and condition of the housing supply but also on shifts in demand.

ACCESS: THE REDISTRIBUTION OF JOBS

The recent trend has clearly been in the direction of a less centralized pattern of employment. We have concluded, in Chapters 2 through 5, that a still further suburban movement is in prospect in manufacturing and in wholesale and retail trade. Though office and business-service types of jobs may also disperse, they will probably remain much more highly centralized than other jobs. What do these trends imply in regard to residential shifts?

First, it is likely that more and more of the lower-income residents of Manhattan and other Core areas will find employment farther out. There is already, for example, such heavy "reverse commuting" from upper Manhattan as to approximately balance the rush-hour flow of traffic across the George Washington Bridge. This situation creates an increasing demand for Inner Ring housing in order to improve access to work, and the foreseeable effect is in the direction of some further equalization—both in densities and in neighborhood income levels—between the older slum areas in Manhattan and communities of the Inner Ring such as Mount Vernon, in New York, and Bloomfield and Irvington, in New Jersey, where access to industrial employment is good, racial-group restrictions are relatively weak, and plenty of obsolete housing is in process of down-grading.

We have already noted that a considerable amount of this shift represents "leapfrogging" rather than continuous flow. For some, it is a more logical jump from, say, Harlem to Mount Vernon or Montclair or Paterson than into middle-income apartment areas in the Bronx. There are several reasons for this. As we saw in Chapter 1, the outer boroughs of New York City are the most "bedroomy" counties of the Region, in the sense that the ratio of jobs to residents is lowest there. Their one great advantage as a place to live is that of cheap and rapid transportation to Manhattan. But a worker in an industrial plant located in the Inner Ring can get better access to his work by moving farther out. Outside the City, he can bid for space without competing with those who do need to be near the subway;

oftentimes this means he can find cheaper housing. To meet his needs, the old middle-income housing of many of the Inner Ring communities is easily convertible into cheap dwelling space.

Professor Handlin, in his volume in this series, concludes that the peculiarly disadvantaged Negro and Puerto Rican groups are likely to play an increasingly important part in the outward spread of populations formerly bottled up in the Region's highest-density areas. On several fronts, the restrictions upon residence choice for these people are being eased—through more enlightened housing and redevelopment policies, through improved access to home financing, through wider choice and wider geographical dispersion of jobs, through rising levels of income, education, and aspiration, and through some improvement in community acceptance. On the basis of these trends, Professor Handlin foresees that the great bulk of the future growth of the Region's Negro and Puerto Rican populations will occur outside Manhattan, with a considerable share of it even outside New York City and the other major cities of the Core and Inner Ring. The importance of this prospective change can be appreciated by contrasting it with the migration trends of the 1940's, which are shown in Table 54, page 224.

A second effect of the further suburbanization of employment in industry and trade involves middle-income people now living in the outer parts of the Core and the inner parts of the Inner Ring. To the extent that their jobs move farther out, their own choice of reasonably convenient residence locations also extends farther out—even into the Outer Ring. We can think of this category of people, in the context of our simplified sequence of stages, as keeping a step behind the outer fringe of new suburban development and getting their housing at second or third hand from somewhat wealthier people who are shifting to more remote, spacious, and modern developments in outer Suburbia or in Exurbia. We can also think of them as occupying some of the cheaper and higher-density new developments. The outward movement of their jobs and the increasing convenience and attractiveness of suburban shopping facilities further encourage these shifts.

So far, we get a picture of each population group, beginning with the central slum dwellers, helping to push the next group farther out from the urban centers of the Region as numbers expand, mobility increases, jobs suburbanize, and space standards rise. But when we come to the relatively well-off people who are the backbone of the market for new housing, we must conclude that *their* outward movement has little to do with the suburban drift of jobs. New single houses are built, in general, only where there is vacant land. The rapid outward migration of this group is impelled partly by the filling-up of vacant land in the inner suburbs, partly by the expanding standards of space requirements, and last but not least by the desire to escape from the encroachment of higher-density and lower-quality settlement. And here a dilemma arises. For commuters to Manhattan from the new-subdivision zone, which is already more than an hour's journey in some directions from Manhattan and still inexorably forging outward, the work-access factor comes back into the picture as a constraint and possible limit to spread.[20]

The dilemma affects high-income people in particular. The jobs of a great many of these, who are in executive, professional, and upper financial posts, seem rather firmly rooted in Manhattan (and to a smaller extent Newark, which presents a similar picture in some respects). These are also people who by virtue of their income, position, and background are more interested than the average inhabitant of the Region in access to Manhattan for reasons apart from the strictly vocational. Finally, these are the people most able and most disposed to want to live in an exclusive suburb if they live in the suburbs at all, and the only place to build new exclusive developments is in remote Exurbia. If the exurb of today, already an hour and a half or two hours out from town, threatens to be the suburb of tomorrow, and if the office cannot be suburbanized or commuting by helicopter arranged, the alternative of living in the city (at least during the work week) may commend itself more and more.

It is for this reason that we foresee further growth in demand for high-grade Manhattan apartments. A prospective strengthening of the basis for this trend implies also the likelihood of some broadening in its impact. In other words, it may gradually involve a high-income group extending somewhat farther down the ladder from the top. There are strong reasons, however, for expecting unsubsidized apartment development in Manhattan to remain distinctly luxury in character. One reason is the extremely high cost of acquiring and clearing sites, which results in the pricing of even small privately financed new apartments at levels few can afford.[21] Another reason is that people of more modest incomes and tastes are not faced with such an inordinate commuter journey or such a narrow choice of suburbs as the very wealthy, when they choose the suburban alternative.

ACCESS: CHANGING WAYS OF TRAVEL

So far we have discussed the prospective shifts in population distribution that will be geared to the supply of new housing and the changing distribution of jobs. In both connections, we have pushed aside a much more important factor of change than either; namely, the means of transport between home and job. It is useful to remember that the business and residential areas of the Region were laid out, and acquired lasting physical characteristics, in response to different historical stages in the evolution of the transport system. A familiar example from the early history of the Region persists in the peculiar shape of blocks in most of Manhattan; the multitude of crosstown streets and the wide distance between avenues reflect the assumption by early planners that movement up and down the island would be principally by water.[22] Again, the density and layout of most of the cities and older suburbs in the Region were based on the transport facilities available before the automobile came into general use.

Like previous improvements in passenger transport, the private automobile opened up much new territory to residential settlement and furthered the trend toward a more uniform pattern of densities in the Region. But in contrast to earlier improvements, the automobile increased the amount of space required per person in the process of transportation and gave rise to traffic congestion problems of unprecedented extent. Here for the first time appears a new means of travel too space-consuming to be used efficiently in existing downtown areas. Accordingly, the automobile has far exceeded earlier passenger-carriers in its spectacular effects on residential densities.

Table 48, covering the period in which mass use of the automobile was attained, highlights the automobile's increase and points up the adverse effects of the automobile on travel into the congested central area and upon other means of transport. Almost three times as many persons entered the southern half of Manhattan by automobile on a typical work day in 1956 as had been the case in 1924. But the total number of persons entering the area daily by all types of vehicles has apparently been declining for about a decade—partly a reflection of the diversion of trade to the suburbs.

The adverse effect on the financial position of public transit services is too well known to call for documentation here. In considerable part, it arises from the fact that the central-city travel diverted to automobiles has been mainly off-peak travel, leaving the public transit services with increasing proportions of their facilities used only a few hours a day, five days a week. This can be illustrated by the subway travel data, though the effect is even more marked on the commuter rail lines, whose off-peak business has become small indeed. Between 1948 and 1956, the number of subway passengers entering the Manhattan central business district during the interval from 7 to 10 A.M. dropped by 11.7 per cent, and the number entering during the remaining 21 hours of the day dropped by 20.8 per cent.[23]

The number of passenger automobiles registered in the Region is still growing rapidly. The total was 2,922,900 in 1950 and only five years later had risen by 30 per cent to an estimated 3,785,500.[24] What is of special significance is (1) that car ownership is rising faster than population, and (2) that it is rising not merely in the suburbs but

TABLE 48 Number of Persons Entering Manhattan Central Business District[a] in Vehicles on a Typical Business Day, by Mode of Travel, Selected Years, 1924–1956

	Thousands of persons					Percentage of total number				
	1924	1932	1940	1948	1956	1924	1932	1940	1948	1956
Total	2,343	2,697	3,271	3,691	3,316	100.0	100.0	100.0	100.0	100.0
Auto and taxi	249	430	503	577	736	10.6	15.9	15.4	15.7	22.2
Bus	...	40	150	290	246	...	1.5	4.6	7.8	7.4
Truck	82	86	116	80	92	3.5	3.2	3.5	2.2	2.8
Trolley	161	88	59	24	3	6.9	3.2	1.8	0.6	0.1
Rapid transit	1,531	1,752	2,169	2,389	1,970	65.3	65.0	66.3	64.8	59.4
Railroad (commuter) ...	217	216	206	283	233	9.3	8.0	6.3	7.6	7.0
Ferry (pedestrians)[b] ...	103	85	68	48	36	4.4	3.2	2.1	1.3	1.1

[a] Here defined for convenience as Manhattan south of 61st Street.
[b] Pedestrians are not counted unless they entered by ferry.

Source: Regional Plan Association, Bulletin 91, *Hub-Bound Travel in the Tri-State Metropolitan Region: Persons and Vehicles Entering Manhattan South of 61st St., 1924–1956* (New York, 1959).

also within New York City itself, though the City's population is no longer rising. Thus, in 1950, New York City had a car for every 6.9 people, and in 1955 a car for every 5.9 people. The rest of the Region had a car for every 3.4 people in 1950 and one for every 3.0 people in 1955.

It seems clear that people outside the Region's largest cities are, as a group, so well provided already with cars that they are free to consider the access advantages of various living places without being bound by the need to be near public transportation. The proportion of trips (both to work and for other purposes) that go from one suburban point to another suburban point is rapidly growing, and this traffic by its nature is predominantly automobile traffic, since both destinations and points of origin are so highly scattered that adequate public transport service cannot economically be provided. Only for commuting into the Manhattan central business district and a very few of the largest other "downtowns" of the Region are dwellers outside the Region's largest cities now dependent on public transport for part of their work journey. The group affected is not a significantly growing one, though its dependence on public transport may actually increase somewhat in future, since these people tend to settle at greater and greater distances from the Region's focal points. No very drastic further change in the travel habits of these suburban long-distance commuters seems likely in the foreseeable future, and access considerations will continue to influence their choice of residence in much the same way as now.[25]

It is the people now living in the major central cities of the Region who may have yet to face a substantial readjustment of commuting habits and residence choice. As we have seen, car ownership per capita is only half as high in New York City as in the rest of the Region. To some extent, this reflects inability to afford a car on the part of low-income workers; perhaps even more basically it reflects the fact that City people working in the City are better and more cheaply served by subsidized rapid transit and have less reason to own a car.

But, as noted elsewhere in this chapter, a growing proportion of the lower-income workers in Manhattan and other parts of New York City are getting jobs outside the City or on its fringes, and are getting to work by "reverse commuting." This is effected mainly by automobile (including car pools), largely because of the inadequacy of public transport to the diverse points of employment; and the growth of this type of commuting perhaps contributes to the recent growth in car registrations in the City.[26] For this growing group, the incentive to look for a home in the suburbs has markedly increased. In fact, the only remaining strong reason for staying in the City at all is the difficulty of gaining admittance to residence areas outside and of finding enough cheap housing—and we have already noted at various points in this chapter some ways in which those barriers to dispersal are weakening.

It may also be confidently expected that car ownership in the Region will for some time continue to expand faster than population, even if the estimated 1955 suburban ratio of one car to every 3.0 people can be regarded as near saturation. The reason is that the growth of population in the Region will occur almost wholly outside the limits of the larger cities; hence an increasing fraction of the Region's people will be dependent on family car ownership. This swelling horde of cars will continue to press for entry even into the jammed precincts of the Manhattan central business district. Some further increase in the number that can be accommodated there will doubtless occur, but this will depend on public policy decisions on transit and parking facilities which are not yet clearly shaped.

It can hardly be questioned that the pattern of new residential development everywhere in the Region (outside of the luxury apartments in and near the very center) will be based on the assumption of much more automobile ownership than in the past. The effect on new suburban development densities is not radically different whether the commuter drives all the way to work or only as far as a mass-transit station; the important thing is that he can leave and return to his home by car.

Table 49 suggests the general levels of density that have prevailed in the last few years in subdivision activity in some of the suburban counties of the Region where popu-

TABLE 49   Average Lot Sizes[a] in New Subdivisions in
Selected Suburban Counties, 1950–1957
(*in thousands of square feet*)

	1950	1951	1952	1953	1954	1955	1956	1957
Bergen	...	...	18.2	14.9	14.1	17.0	18.4	20.5
Middlesex	...	8.1	7.8	7.4	7.6	8.1	9.6	8.3
Morris	...	...	...	...	...	19.9	23.0	24.5
Passaic	11.2	11.8	11.5	12.4	17.8	13.9	12.9	20.7
Westchester	13.1	14.8	14.8	16.6	20.0	20.5	28.3	31.8
Cities	12.6	11.8	9.6	9.6	9.6	9.6	14.8	13.9
Villages	13.9	10.0	15.7	13.9	13.1	17.9	23.5	15.7
Towns (unincorporated areas)	13.1	18.7	17.9	21.8	26.1	25.7	35.3	43.1
Southern part of county	13.1	13.5	12.2	10.5	13.1	14.8	17.0	17.4
Northern part of county	12.6	17.0	25.3	26.1	25.7	24.0	40.9	57.5

[a] For all counties shown except Westchester, average lot sizes are net (that is, deducting streets and open spaces in subdivisions). The Westchester averages are on a gross basis and would have to be reduced by perhaps 15 to 20 per cent to make them comparable with those shown for the other counties.

Source: County planning board reports.

lation is increasing rapidly. It is clear that there is a wide range of densities between counties (and of course still more between individual developments); and also that, in most newly developed areas, lots are much more spacious than in older suburban developments. In terms of the number of dwelling units per residentially developed acre (the density measure used in various tables in Chapters 6 and 7), the 1957 county averages shown in Table 49 would correspond to densities ranging from about 1.2 to 4, with only Middlesex rising above a density of 2.

The rapid rise in lot sizes in the counties shown in the table is spectacular, but possibly misleading. The underlying trend is certainly in that direction, but in any short period of years various temporary factors in the housing market are likely to be reflected, and there would be no warrant for projecting into the future anything like the rate of increase in lot size suggested by the table.[27] Nevertheless it is highly probable that lot sizes will continue to expand somewhat over the long run.

Associated with the lower density of new development,

and likewise ascribable primarily to the use of the automobile, is the rapid trend toward a more widely diffused pattern of expansion of the Region's built-up area. Earlier in this chapter we noted that the long projections of urban settlement created by earlier rail commuter services, continuous in the inner suburbs and disintegrated into bead-strings farther out, have during the automobile age become a less dominant feature of the suburban population map, as newer automobile-oriented settlement has loosely filled in the spaces between the older strings of communities. Even before 1940, in fact, this trend was in evidence. In 1925, only 2 per cent of the Region's "closely developed" residential land was more than a mile from a rail station. But no less than 10 per cent of the area brought into close residential development between 1925 and 1940 was more than a mile from a station.[28]

INCREASED INCOME AND LEISURE

One of the most important past and prospective trends affecting the residential patterns of the Region is the rising level of living of its population—a rise apparent both in real income and in leisure time. These changes in living standards have given the Region's populations an increased command over personal transportation and more spacious living quarters.

Growth of per capita income in the Region has lagged behind the growth for the United States as a whole since 1929. Nevertheless the Region's per capita income rose at an average rate of 1.1 per cent per annum between 1929 and 1956 in "real" terms; and, for the period 1939 to 1956, it rose at an average annual rate of 2.3 per cent.[29] Over the long run, also, the relative standing of the lower income groups has tended to improve in respect not only to money income but also to public services, economic security, and leisure.

Both higher incomes and more leisure have affected housing demand in terms of quality. To be sure, housing construction costs have risen faster than the general price level and perhaps even faster than money incomes in the last few decades, so that the average householder cannot afford "more house" than he could a generation ago. But he can assert his preference for modern style and layout and for a bigger lot in more spacious surroundings. Thus, rising incomes and leisure are the basis for a demand for newer houses as such, and in general for more spaciously sited homes.

Perhaps the most significant aspect of this improvement is that the homes of the lower income groups no longer need be so closely bound to their jobs as was once the case. A study of journey-to-work patterns in New York City in 1907[30] indicated clearly that the poorer wage earners were under a strong compulsion to huddle close to their work places. Working long hours for low pay, they could ill afford either the time or the money to travel very far. In those days, commuting from suburbs to city was largely confined to the wealthy. This situation has radically changed with the shortening of working hours, rising incomes, and mass access to the automobile. Few workers now are so closely bound by work-access considerations as was the typical low-paid New York worker of half a century ago.

One major effect of this new-found freedom of the low-income worker is to widen the range of his housing choice and to quicken the abandonment or thinning-out of the worst and oldest slums as other properties in the Region become ripe for down-grading. In terms of the sequence we developed earlier, the crowding and down-grading stage (3) may become more diffused geographically and less acute where it occurs; and the thinning-out stage (4) may be accelerated.

A major effect of the low-income worker's rising living standards and greater mobility has been to reduce the peak density of the populations living in the crowded slums. With each decade, a different set of areas in the old cities has built up to the peak densities characteristic of our Stage 3. But it is highly significant that, over several decades now, these successive peaks in different areas tend to be less and less acute. Some indication of this phenomenon appears in Table 50. Though the data are rather fragmentary and may contain some minor technical distortions,

TABLE 50 Areas of Highest Density of Population in Manhattan, Brooklyn, and Hudson County, Selected Years, 1850–1957

	Manhattan		Brooklyn		Hudson County	
	Highest density area	Population per square mile	Highest density area	Population per square mile	Highest density area	Population per square mile
1850	6th ward	165,000	....	....	5th ward, Jersey City	59,250
1900	8th Assembly Dist.	400,000	16th ward	148,800	5th ward, Jersey City	75,500
1920	8th Assembly Dist.	261,000	14th Assembly Dist.	111,700	3rd ward, Jersey City	64,800
1930ᵃ ..	17th Assembly Dist.	217,000	6th Assembly Dist.	96,700	....	....
....	Health Area 67	295,000	Health Area 56	147,000	....	....
1940	Health Area 67	260,000	Health Area 56	141,000	3rd ward, Jersey City	56,400
1950	Health Area 67	232,000	Health Area 56	121,000	3rd ward, Jersey City	51,200
1957	Health Area 67	221,000	Health Area 56	107,000	....	....

ᵃ At any given time peak densities in terms of Health Areas run considerably higher than in terms of Assembly Districts (as illustrated for 1930 in the table), because Health Areas are much smaller. In Manhattan there were 23 Assembly Districts in 1920 and 1930; there are now 89 Health Areas. Figures in terms of both types of area are included for 1930 in the table, to establish that the trend of reduction in peak densities is uninterrupted since 1900 at least, in both Manhattan and Brooklyn.

Sources: Committee on Regional Plan of New York and Its Environs, *Regional Survey of New York and Its Environs*, Vol. II (New York, 1929); Regional Plan Association, Bulletin No. 7 (March 28, 1932), pp. 8–9; unpublished data from Dept. of City Planning, N.Y. City; also our estimates for Hudson County, 1940 and 1950.

the main point seems clear: the more recent local peaks
in the Region's density pattern are consistently lower than
earlier peaks were.

The central reason for this decline in peak densities is
the persistent long-run improvement in freedom of movement and latitude of housing choice for the population as
a whole. It is worth emphasizing that this basic explanation applies even in the case of population groups which
have not themselves acquired increased freedom of movement. Thus, even the family which is too poor to afford a
car and which belongs to a severely restricted ethnic group
is under less compelling pressure to concentrate at high
slum density than were families in similar circumstances
in the past—the reason being that the widened residence
choice and improved mobility of more fortunate groups
give them the means of moving rapidly out of the way of
expanding slum areas. In short, the mobility of middle-
income as well as lower-income people has helped in al-
leviating the bottling up of low-income people in congested slums.

One of the surest predictions that can be made is that
this long-run trend will persist, since the underlying causes
are still moving in the same direction. Various areas will
evolve into a slum condition of peak density, according to
the sequence outlined earlier in this chapter, and may then
undergo thinning-out or redevelopment or other relief; but
the peaks will continue to be less extreme. We are most
unlikely to see again in the Region, regardless of the relative smallness of slum-clearance and renewal programs,
any crowding of slum areas like that of 1900 or 1920, or
even 1950, and the most crowded slums of 1970 will be
roomier than those of the present.[31]

By the very same token, however, areas of "blight" will
continue to become much more extensive—at least if our
standards of what is considered blighted are adjusted in
keeping with a rising standard of aspiration. Slums, blight,
and low-income concentration have not been eliminated,
nor are they going to be in the near future, but they have
been diluted and dispersed to some extent, and will become considerably more so.

We have been stressing here the impact of rising incomes and increased leisure on the residence patterns of the lower and middle income groups, partly because the improvement in the *relative* position of those groups—in both income and leisure—has had particularly marked effects so far. But important gains have been and will be realized generally, from top to bottom of the income scale. For any class of people, more income and a shorter work week spell more freedom to live, if desired, farther from the place of work. This is the way in which people have in fact been responding; and, except perhaps for some of the very wealthy, it seems doubtful that the limits of journey-to-work tolerance have yet been reached.[32]

The movements of higher and lower income groups are strikingly reflected in the pattern of relative income levels in the various parts of the Region, as set forth in Table 51. The most prominent development shown there is the rapid decline in Manhattan's relative position. In 1939 (and, one may surmise, during most if not all of the Region's previous history), personal incomes in Manhattan averaged far higher than those of any other county of the Region. But, between 1939 and 1956, Manhattan's advantage over the average for the Region as a whole fell from 63 per cent to only 14 per cent. By 1956, two suburban counties (Nassau and Westchester) had attained much higher average incomes than Manhattan.

As noted in the preceding chapter, Manhattan's income distribution is a peculiar one, heavily weighted with the extreme groups of the very rich and very poor. Manhattan's relative decline reflects a large increase in numbers in the latter group, including predominantly unskilled Negro and Puerto Rican in-migrants.

The Core counties surrounding Manhattan, taken as a group, have not shifted much in income status relative to the rest of the Region. But individual Core counties have differed from one another in their trends. Average income rose in Queens at a faster pace than for the Region as a whole, while at the same time it lagged in the more "mature" areas of Brooklyn, the Bronx, and Hudson County. This difference is significant in view of the fact that

Queens is much more recently developed, with its main surge of growth dating only from the 1920's. There is a strong hint here of the tendency for higher-than-average incomes to be associated with active new construction, reflecting the familiar fact that dwellings are priced predominantly for people in the upper ranges of the income scale.

Another conspicuous development shown in Table 51 is the emergence of certain distinctively high-income suburban counties: first Essex and Fairfield, more recently Westchester, and most recently Nassau, Bergen, and Union. There has also been a rapid postwar rise in average incomes in such Outer Ring counties as Morris, Somerset,

TABLE 51   Relative Levels of Per Capita Personal Income in New York Metropolitan Region, by Counties, 1939, 1947, 1956

	Per capita income as percentage of average for entire Region		
	1939	1947	1956
New York City	109	106	99
Core	108	105	98
Manhattan	163	149	114
Rest of Core	91	91	93
Queens	79	93	106
Bronx	84	93	89
Brooklyn	101	91	89
Hudson	88	88	84
Inner Ring	88	97	111
Nassau	74	78	125
Westchester	93	103	124
Bergen	85	79	109
Union	85	85	109
Essex	102	121	104
Richmond	80	83	87
Passaic	72	102	86
Outer Ring	81	84	86
Fairfield	90	119	114
Morris	81	68	92
Somerset	73	58	89
Middlesex	69	68	83
Monmouth	86	74	82
Suffolk	76	73	72
Rockland	75	65	70
Orange	88	88	69
Dutchess and			
Putnam	75	83	62

Source: Estimates by New York Metropolitan Region Study.

and Middlesex, suggesting that well-to-do families were finding refuge in these areas as well.

Further evidence of considerable dissatisfaction with living conditions in the Core, and of a potential further demand for more suburban locations, emerges from certain findings of the recent sample journey-to-work survey described in Appendix K. In that survey, workers who had changed their county of residence in the last ten years were asked to indicate reasons for the move; and one of the possible reasons which respondents were invited to consider was "desire for more pleasant surroundings."

The responses were tabulated to show the relative frequency of the various reasons given for moving into and out of each county in the Region. Now if we find "desire for more pleasant surroundings" cited very often as a reason for moving *into* some county and very rarely as a reason for moving *out* of it, we may conclude that the county in question is highly regarded on that score. On the other hand, if the "pleasant surroundings" response appears predominantly among the reasons given for leaving a county, we may conclude that a generally dim view of that county's amenity prevails.

The striking conclusion of our analysis of these responses is that the *only* counties with definitely unfavorable ratings as to quality of surroundings are the five Core counties —Manhattan, Brooklyn, the Bronx, Queens, and Hudson. This is, of course, not necessarily a new preference on the part of the Region's population. But the results do tend to support the impression that the most central and most densely developed parts of the Region are presently regarded as providing the least satisfactory living places, access considerations aside; and this implies that the flight from these areas is likely to continue, and to extend perhaps to a wider range of income groups as housing in newer areas moves toward the conversion stage.

CHANGING AGE COMPOSITION OF HOUSEHOLDS

Another major factor can influence the distribution of population in the Region in the future, and has in the past; namely, the age composition of the Region's households.

Other chapters have demonstrated that the presence or absence of children in a household is a major factor in residence choice. The way in which a changing age distribution has figured in the redistribution of the Region's populations is seen in Table 52.

TABLE 52 Age Distributions in Areas of the New York Metropolitan Region Compared with Age Distribution of the Region, 1930, 1940, 1950

A. Percentage distribution of population by age groups
(Total population of each area = 100)

		0–4	5–14	15–24	25–44	45–64	65 and over
Region	1930	7.90	17.42	18.16	34.58	17.68	4.25
	1940	5.93	14.27	17.14	34.74	21.93	5.98
	1950	8.96	13.00	13.21	32.90	24.11	7.83
Manhattan ...	1930	6.10	13.85	17.76	38.76	19.34	4.19
	1940	4.70	11.21	15.20	38.14	24.45	6.29
	1950	7.09	9.61	12.80	34.76	26.99	8.74
Rest of Core ..	1930	8.32	17.79	18.89	34.74	16.59	3.66
	1940	6.15	14.71	17.55	35.19	21.08	5.31
	1950	8.86	13.27	13.73	32.63	24.17	7.32
Inner Ring ...	1930	8.23	18.43	17.54	33.51	17.80	4.49
	1940	6.14	15.10	17.32	33.59	21.65	6.19
	1950	9.83	13.87	12.62	39.96	23.12	7.60
Outer Ring ...	1930	7.97	18.71	17.01	30.45	19.61	6.24
	1940	6.15	14.67	17.53	31.10	22.51	7.84
	1950	9.51	13.86	12.99	31.77	22.85	9.01

B. Ratio of area percentage to Region percentage
(Region percentage = 1)

		0–4	5–14	15–24	25–44	45–64	65 and over
Manhattan ...	1930	.76	.80	.98	1.12	1.09	.98
	1940	.79	.78	.89	1.10	1.12	1.05
	1950	.79	.74	.97	1.06	1.19	1.12
Rest of Core ..	1930	1.04	1.02	1.04	1.00	.94	.86
	1940	1.04	1.03	1.02	1.01	.96	.89
	1950	.99	1.02	1.04	.99	1.00	.94
Inner Ring ...	1930	1.03	1.06	.97	.97	1.01	1.06
	1940	1.04	1.06	1.01	.97	.99	1.03
	1950	1.09	1.07	.96	1.00	.96	.97
Outer Ring ...	1930	1.00	1.07	.94	.88	1.10	1.47
	1940	1.04	1.03	1.02	.90	1.03	1.31
	1950	1.06	1.07	.98	.97	.95	1.15

Note: In upper half of table, because of rounding, rows may not add to 100.

Source: Calculated from U.S. *Census of Population* for years shown.

In the first half of Table 52, the population of each part of the Region is shown in percentage distribution by age groups. In the second half of the table, each of those distributions is compared with that for the whole Region to bring out the relative "excesses" and "deficiencies" of various age groups in different parts of the Region at each date.*

We have already noted the relative deficiency of children in Manhattan. This deficiency is conspicuous in Table 52; witness the low Manhattan figures for the two youngest age groups in the second part of the table. Thus in 1950, when 13 per cent of the Region's population consisted of children from 5 to 14 years old, the corresponding percentage in Manhattan was only 9.61—that is, only 0.74 times the Region percentage.

It is worth noting that this difference between Manhattan and the rest of the Region changes a little between 1930 and 1950: the relative deficiency in the school-age group (5 to 14) grows even larger. In the Core counties surrounding Manhattan, the tendency toward "underrepresentation" of children appears only since 1940 and with respect to the youngest age group. That part of the Region, with its access to especially varied job opportunities for those just entering the labor force, persistently shows some "excess" of persons aged 15–24. In both Manhattan and the rest of the Core, the proportion of older people (45 and over) was rising much faster than in the Region as a whole.

Age structure in both the Inner and Outer Rings showed trends basically opposite to those in the Core. The relative "excess" of children was heightened (especially in the case of those under 5 years), and the "excess" of old people (characteristic of semirural areas not yet embroiled in metropolitan development) was rapidly reduced.

Table 53 examines changes in age structure for a more

* A similar technique was used in the first two tables of Chapter 7 above (Tables 32 and 33), to measure the relative over-representation or under-representation of specific occupational groups in the jobs and resident populations of various parts of the Region.

recent period, 1950 to 1957, in those few counties where 1957 age data are at hand. In this case we do not have the Region's age distribution to use as a standard of reference as was done in Table 52; so we have compared the age distributions of the individual counties with that of New York City.

Table 53 shows no sensational new changes in relative age structure as among the City's boroughs, but does show signs of a still further flight of families with children to the suburbs, as here sketchily represented by Westchester, Suffolk, and Rockland Counties. This is spectacularly evident in the case of the most rapidly growing of the three suburban counties, Suffolk, where likewise the former relative excess of people 65 and over has vanished. It would appear that the greatest relative excess of old people is now in Manhattan (and perhaps some of the other large

TABLE 53 Age Distributions in Selected New York Counties of New York Metropolitan Region, Compared with New York City's Age Distribution, 1950 and 1957

A. Percentage distribution of population by age groups
(Total population in each area = 100)

		0–4	5–14	15–24	25–44	45–64	65 and over
New York City	1950	8.44	12.40	13.51	33.21	24.86	7.68
	1957	8.34	15.09	11.95	30.08	25.44	9.09
Manhattan ..	1950	7.09	9.61	12.80	34.76	26.99	8.74
	1957	7.07	12.28	11.31	31.86	27.38	10.09
Bronx	1950	8.27	13.43	14.02	31.79	25.20	7.29
	1957	8.40	15.42	12.67	28.46	25.77	9.28
Brooklyn	1950	9.03	13.42	14.13	32.77	23.25	7.41
	1957	8.85	16.00	12.50	29.58	24.14	8.92
Queens	1950	9.06	12.96	12.75	33.12	25.04	7.08
	1957	8.64	15.86	11.20	30.45	25.63	8.22
Richmond ...	1950	9.96	14.13	14.06	31.68	22.98	8.08
	1957	9.90	18.91	11.96	29.07	21.35	8.81
Westchester .	1950	8.92	14.04	12.84	31.22	24.72	8.26
	1957	9.44	17.41	10.63	29.25	24.76	8.50
Suffolk	1950	9.15	13.55	11.46	30.30	22.18	8.88
	1957	12.10	19.01	9.25	31.05	19.85	8.74
Rockland	1950	9.56	14.62	13.16	31.60	22.18	8.88
	1957	10.36	18.96	10.76	30.10	21.09	8.72

Because of rounding, rows may not add to 100.

B. Ratio of county percentage to New York City percentage
(New York City percentage = 1)

		0–4	5–14	15–24	25–44	45–64	65 and over
Manhattan ..	1950	.84	.78	.95	1.05	1.09	1.14
	1957	.85	.81	.95	1.06	1.08	1.11
Bronx	1950	.98	1.08	1.04	.96	1.01	.95
	1957	1.01	1.02	1.06	.95	1.01	1.02
Brooklyn	1950	1.07	1.08	1.05	.99	.94	.96
	1957	1.06	1.06	1.05	.98	.95	.98
Queens	1950	1.07	1.05	.94	1.00	1.01	.92
	1957	1.04	1.05	.94	1.01	1.01	.90
Richmond ...	1950	1.18	1.14	1.04	.96	.89	1.05
	1957	1.19	1.25	1.00	.97	.84	.97
Westchester .	1950	1.06	1.13	.95	.94	.99	1.08
	1957	1.13	1.15	.89	.97	.97	.94
Suffolk	1950	1.08	1.09	.85	.92	1.03	1.30
	1957	1.45	1.26	.77	1.03	.78	.96
Rockland	1950	1.13	1.18	.97	.95	.89	1.16
	1957	1.24	1.26	.90	1.00	.83	.96

Source: Computed from data in U.S. *1950 Census of Population* and reports of Special Censuses of April 1, 1957, conducted by U.S. Census Bureau.

old central urban areas) rather than in the Region's semi-rural outer counties as was the case even as recently as 1950.

In the preceding table a trend toward increased concentration of people 45 and over in Manhattan showed up prominently. Table 53 shows a similar trend in the Bronx between 1950 and 1957, at least for the group 65 and over. These figures have to be interpreted with great caution, however. They could conceivably suggest a return flow of older, well-to-do people to the convenient central neighborhoods. Alternatively the figures could reflect aging of the populations previously established in these two boroughs, with parents left behind as their children grew up and departed to the suburbs.

We surmise that the latter factor was probably much the more important in quantitative effect. This surmise cannot be firmly verified in the absence of specific data on the characteristics of migrants into and out of individual boroughs, but it derives some support from the figures in Table 54, representing net migration during the 1940's

TABLE 54   Estimated Net Migration to and from the New York Standard Metropolitan Area[a] and Its Central Cities, by Age and Color, 1940–1950

(all figures in thousands of persons)

Age group	Standard Metropolitan Area, total		Central cities (New York, Newark, Jersey City)		Rest of Standard Metropolitan Area	
	White	Non-white	White	Non-white	White	Non-white
All ages, total	−140	+279	−731	+239	+591	+40
0–14	+24	+42	−247	+25	+270	+17
15–24	+3	+64	−11	+56	+15	+8
Males ...	−33	+24	−26	+21	−7	+3
Females .	+36	+40	+15	+35	+22	+5
25–44	+33	+158	−219	+143	+251	+14
45–64	−123	+16	−171	+14	+48	+2
65 and over	−77	b	−84	b	+7	b

[a] Includes all of New York Metropolitan Region except Fairfield, Dutchess, Putnam, Orange, and Monmouth Counties.
[b] Fewer than 500 persons.

Source: Donald J. Bogue, *Components of Population Change, 1940–50: Estimates of Net Migration and Natural Increase for Each Standard Metropolitan Area and State Economic Area*, Studies in Population Distribution, No. 12 (published jointly by Scripps Foundation for Research in Population Problems and the Population Research and Training Center, University of Chicago, 1957), Table V, p. 133.

into and out of the Region's three largest cities combined. From these three "central cities," New York, Newark, and Jersey City, the general loss of population included a heavy outflow of people 45 and over, with only a very small net inflow in one category of such people—non-whites aged 45–64.

What one does *not* find in any of the figures here presented is any suggestion of a reversal in the long-standing flight of the growing family from the older areas of the Region to the more sparsely settled suburbs. Some recent spot surveys have seemed to indicate that, for all the outward flight of families, a return to the cities was in the making;[33] that ex-city dwellers were beginning to find that the charms of Suburbia were a will-o'-the-wisp, that the care and feeding of the lawn was a chore beyond en-

durance, and that the city had not so repellent an at-
mosphere for children after all. That such individual cases
exist there can be no doubt. But their total effect on the
major trends has been so insignificant as to be lost in the
tidal wave of outward movement.

What now can we foresee about prospective changes in
the age structure of the Region's households and the effect
of these changes on the residence pattern?

Changes in the age structure of individual households
are reflected, roughly at least, in the changing age structure of the population in the aggregate. The age distribution of the Region's population, like that of the nation's
metropolitan areas generally, differs significantly from that
of the United States population as a whole. Metropolitan
populations have lower proportions of both children and
old people, and they have higher proportions in the age
groups which make up the bulk of the labor force. These
differences are rather consistent and stable, though, as the
years go by, metropolitan age distributions will somewhat
more closely resemble those for the whole United States
as the population on the nation's farms and in small towns
continues to dwindle in relative importance.[34]

No great problems are involved in projecting the number of adults in the United States as a whole over the next
two decades, since that number is not influenced at all
by the highly uncertain factor of changing birth rates and
is influenced very little by international migration. We can
use such projections, as set forth in Table 55, as rough indicators of the kinds of changes to be expected in the Region's age structure over that period.

Table 55 shows that since 1950 the 45-to-64 and 65-
and-older groups have been growing much the fastest;
these groups, on the whole, make for small household size.
But the growth rate of these groups will be slackening in
the foreseeable future, while the number of people in the
family-forming ages of 20 to 29 will grow at a spectacularly
accelerating rate.

Looking ahead to the period 1965–1975, then, it seems
reasonable to envisage another upsurge in marriage rates,
household formation, and demand for housing suitable for

TABLE 55 Projected Average Annual Percentage Rates of
Increase of Population in Selected Age Groups,
United States, 1950–1970

Age group	1950–1957	1957–1965	1965–1970
20–29	−0.1	1.5	4.0
30–44	0.1	−0.1	0.3
45–64	1.7	1.6	1.1
65 and older	2.6	2.3	2.2

Source: Calculated from data in Bureau of the Census, Current Population Reports, Series P–25, No. 187: *Illustrative Projections of the Population of the United States, by Age and Sex, 1960 to 1980*, Nov. 10, 1958.

families with young children. This prospect is based simply on trends in age distribution, rather than on such factors as "catching up" on deferred marriages and births or changes in desired family size, which were involved in the recent postwar increases in marriages, babies, and housing.

The trends just described, if reflected in the Region, would tend to contribute to the increased suburban spread in single-family developments, but with perhaps some shift in emphasis to less expensive types of houses, since people in the 20–29 age group will not have attained anything like their peak incomes. At the same time, the prospective slackening in growth of the 45–64 age group will tend to limit in some degree the possible importance of "back to the city" migration by working households whose children have grown up and left home. The trend in numbers of people attaining age 45 will closely parallel the birth trend of 45 years earlier, and the birth trend in the United States fell steadily until the late 1930's. Finally, the continued rapid growth of the "retired" (65 and older) group suggests a rise in demand for small-household housing located with reference to agreeable living conditions rather than access to employment centers.

SYNTHESIS: *THE PATTERNS OF CHANGE*

The most general and apparent trend of recent years is the one identified at the beginning of this chapter—wider diffusion of residence over the New York Metropolitan Region, with a thinning-out of density where it was highest, a slower drop-off of density with increasing distance from the Region's main centers, and a more spacious and more scattered pattern of new development on the fringe.

We have found several explanations for this shift. One is the recently accelerated trend toward wider suburban dispersal of many important types of the Region's jobs. More important, however, is the increased freedom that virtually all classes of the Region's population have attained in their choice of living places, which has led many to desert older and more crowded areas in favor of newer and more spacious ones. The increased freedom of residence choice that has been attained, and the still further freedom that certainly lies ahead, can in turn be traced to rising standards of income and leisure, the mass ownership of automobiles, and relaxation of some of the special barriers affecting the residence choice of racial and other minority groups.

The effect of all these factors has expressed itself essentially in a quickening of the characteristic progression of stages in neighborhood evolution, at all major points in the sequence.

Thus, new suburban developments have been taking advantage of a vastly widened choice of areas, and have adopted lower-density layouts, because of the latitude provided by automobile transport. This has almost explosively accelerated the expansion of the Region's developed land.

The burgeoning of the newer residential developments and their distinctive features have helped to speed the passing-on of housing in the older suburbs to a successor group of occupants less bent on modernity, space, or isolation.

In much of the Core, outward movement from middle-class areas in the cities has been accelerated partly by diminished dependence on urban mass transit to get to work, so that the desire for more space can be gratified without sacrifice of access. Here, and in fact at every stage in the procession, outward movement of specific kinds of people is impelled not only by the beckoning pull of newer areas as housing becomes available farther out, and by enhanced mobility, but also by the push of the next wave, particularly in areas facing increase in density through apartment development or down-grading.

Historically, even the dwellers in the oldest slums have felt this push from still more recent and poorer arrivals in the City. It seems likely, though, that this particular push may be diminishing greatly in significance. The major part of the further increase in Negro and Puerto Rican population in the Region is expected to occur outside the established areas of concentration. That trend, plus the accelerated relinquishment of housing by middle income groups in fairly old urban areas of the Region, and the growing urban renewal effort, produces a continuing dispersion of the Region's slums.

These changes are rapidly shifting more and more of the Region's population into a new suburban pattern, of a type hardly conceivable before the age of universal automobile ownership. The suburbanites will probably include a somewhat growing proportion of the people who work in the Region's major central business districts, and for that group the problem of reconciling access requirements and other residence preferences will become more rather than less acute. The upper-income members of this group are, by and large, those who already spend more time commuting than anyone else. Those who elect to solve the problem by return to a city apartment are so far a relatively tiny minority, affluent and past child-rearing. These two criteria of eligibility will continue to apply generally, and no massive "return flow" from suburbs to city can be foreseen; but on a modest scale this category of city-dwellers can be expected to grow. That trend, plus continued redevelopment of slum areas, will help set the tone for a rapid adjustment of living patterns in some of the Region's oldest residence areas more in keeping with present and future aspirations.

What is least clear in the prospect is the trend of development in the "gray" areas that comprise most of the less central parts of the Core, and their counterparts in the older large cities elsewhere in the Region. The aging multi-family housing of those areas suffers most of the drawbacks of congestion and high redevelopment cost that prevail in still more central areas, but lacks their unique access advantage. In terms of access, its appeal is to the subway commuters, a group now beginning to shrink in numbers. Employment opportunities within the gray areas themselves are unlikely to grow. On the other hand, the supply of obsolescent housing is likely to grow at record rates. The increasing fraction of the Region's population who work outside the Core will generally look farther out for their homes, while the shift of inner-Core dwellers into the gray areas may well fall far short of maintaining demand for all of the low-grade housing that will exist there. Renewal projects will accommodate more and more people in the inner Core itself, perhaps even at slightly higher densities per square mile if past Manhattan experience is a guide; and those who leave the inner Core will have a great deal more freedom to move into the single-family residential neighborhoods beyond the gray areas than they had in the past.

Our final chapter will throw some further light on how the various areas of the Region are likely to look in the future, in the light of all the evidence on both jobs and people that has been produced so far.

PART IV

9

THE JOBS, THE PEOPLE
AND THE FUTURE

The bits and pieces of projection that have appeared in this book, when added all together, do not offer a tidy prognosis of future developments inside the New York Metropolitan Region. Large pieces of the picture are lacking. For one thing, we have had almost nothing to say about future economic growth in the nation as a whole. Yet what happens to the cities, towns, and suburbs of the New York Metropolitan Region turns in good part on what happens in the rest of the country. If the people of America step up their interest in opera, or their reading of magazines, or their participation in the stock market, the central business district of Manhattan may well gain jobs as a result. If their future consumption patterns emphasize beer and cosmetics instead of magazines and opera, this will imply growth in suburban employment. And if the recreational interests of the nation turn increasingly to forest and seashore, or the nation's savings are diverted to more home ownership, these changing habits of national consumption will have their counterparts inside the Region as well.

Besides, any view of an economy as complex and varied as that of the Region has to be tested thoroughly for its internal consistency. A projection of future transportation patterns in the Region is inseparable from a projection of the location of future jobs and homes in the Region. And the projections of homes cannot be done independently of the projections of jobs.

The tasks of projection which we have just outlined call for extensive information and analysis, well beyond the

scope of this book. We do not propose to discharge those
tasks in any final way, therefore, until the capstone volume
in this series is written; there, all that we shall have
learned about the Region's future will be drawn together
systematically in order to support a set of projections for
the Region and its various parts. Yet a certain amount of
synthesis can be done at this stage, too. To be sure, such
synthesis must be framed in general terms rather than in
the quantitative form which our projections ultimately will
take. But, even without the basis for developing such
quantities at this stage, some of the tendencies which we
have isolated in this volume seem so powerful and so in-
variant as to suggest that they will survive on almost any
reasonable assumption about the other pieces of the puzzle.

THE CORE

As we now know, the five counties of the Core cover
an extraordinarily varied set of neighborhoods, some fairly
stagnant, some vibrating with change. Among the latter is
Manhattan's central business district, the scene of complex
cross-currents of growth and decline.*

MANHATTAN'S CENTRAL BUSINESS DISTRICT

Here, one can see a major shift taking place in the kinds
of economic activity which the district contains. Manufacturing and wholesale jobs are decreasing in number and
promise to continue their decline for reasons suggested in
Chapters 2 and 3. Retail jobs are also likely to decline
slightly, given the population trends sketched in Chapter 8. Office jobs in the central business district will probably expand in absolute numbers, though the district's
huge *share* of the Region's office jobs is likely to decline
further. In this volume we cannot say with confidence
whether aggregate employment in all activities can be ex-

---

* By this time the reader is familiar with our geographical
terms, but those who like to glance occasionally at maps will
find the Core, Inner Ring, and Outer Ring mapped on page 8,
and the Manhattan central business district on page 10.

pected to increase or to decrease in the central business district during the next few decades; the elements of growth do not differ so dramatically from those of decline as to point clearly to a net tendency. Besides, new drastic forms of government intervention could tip the scales—intervention to move goods-handling activities more rapidly out of the area, for instance.

But any considerable amount of growth in the activities of the central business district would soon run up against a major restraint—the inadequacy of passenger transportation facilities. To appreciate why transportation facilities could place a ceiling on economic activity in the central business district, we must review the forces affecting the composition of population in New York City. Inside the central business district and on its fringes, various currents can be discerned. Nonresidential uses continue to nibble away at the edges of residential neighborhoods. Inside those neighborhoods, the overriding tendency is the seemingly irreversible thinning out of inhabitants in run-down residential structures; as children come of age they leave the old neighborhoods for other surroundings. This tendency is modified somewhat by a modest increase in the number of people in expensive apartments and in brownstones converted for luxury living. It is modified also by the continuation of public programs of housing and urban renewal, which substitute new structures for some of the old housing stock.

Neither of these countervailing forces, however, promises to reverse a population decline in the central business district. In neighborhoods where they occur, the thinning-out process will probably be arrested. But neighborhoods which are redeveloped for high-income occupancy will not be so extensive as a ride along the East River may suggest. The number of candidates for high-cost living space in Manhattan is sharply limited by price, the number of subsidized dwellers by the size of public subsidies. Subsidized redevelopment will surely expand somewhat. But, if such redevelopment in the central business district during the next twenty years were to proceed at double the rate of the past decade, the added construction would be equivalent to about 11 or 12 per cent of that district's present housing.

Accordingly, the net trend of resident population in the central business district will probably be a further decrease in numbers; and, short of a very large change in the scope of publicly aided housing programs, the population also can be expected to age further. To see what these developments imply for passenger transportation to the central business district, we must anticipate our story a bit and look briefly at population changes in areas just beyond the central business district—areas like middle or upper Manhattan, middle and lower Bronx, and western Brooklyn and Queens. Here, too, as we suggest below, the predominant population tendency will be one of decline.

All these prospects point in one direction in their implications for passenger transport. They imply that the average daily trip to the central business district will lengthen. It will lengthen for two main reasons. One is the change in the mix of jobs in the central business district. As manufacturing, wholesale, and retail jobs fall off and office activities increase, the near-in, low-income areas will decline in importance as traffic-generating points, since office workers pay more for living quarters, on the average, and live farther out. The other reason is that these people—and middle-income families in general—will move even farther outward. The steady retreat of middle-income jobholders in the central business district from their homes in Manhattan, the Bronx, Brooklyn, and Queens to remoter localities would alter commuting patterns even without the change in the job mix.

The outward movement of some City dwellers will leave them still within the City limits. The prospective Narrows Bridge, for instance, offers the possibility that some of those leaving Brooklyn's older areas may cross the bridge to Staten Island instead of making the eastward trek to Queens and Nassau County as they have in the past. Whether within the City or outside it, however, many of those on the move will settle outside the range of the City subways.

Once beyond the subway's range, they will be faced

with the need to shift to some other form of transport. Their response at this point will be colored by the nature of the facilities which are available. Our assumption here —a large one, and not by any means the only plausible one—is that no dramatic innovations in suburban transport will have occurred: that the choice will still be that of using the private car or public bus on comparatively congested roads, or of going by suburban train to City terminals. If this is the case, some of the erstwhile subway users outside the subway's range will shift to the rail, others to the road.

They certainly cannot all choose the rail, especially since the suburban railroads have every incentive to drag their feet in increasing their peak-hour capacity and even to reduce that capacity where they can. Thus, short of some major change in technology or public policy, automobiles and buses can be expected to take up some of the growth. Some—but not much. The capacity of the main arteries into the central business district and the capacity of the streets and parking areas of the district constitute major limitations on automobile and bus commuting. If the growth of the facilities is slow enough, the expansion of office activity in the central business district may be held down, and an added incentive for locating repetitive standardized office work in other areas may be created.

Of course, as the city fathers recognize that the capacities of arteries and parking areas are constituting a block to the growth of the central business district, they may well respond with some vigor. For instance, they may allow Manhattan's parking garages to grow at a faster rate than they have permitted in the past, reckoning that it is futile to use the control of garage space as a way of encouraging the use of the City's mass transit facilities. On top of this, new lanes will be added to critical radial highways. But, all told, it would take unusual effort to prevent the inadequacies of motor transport facilities from acting as a significant restraint on the growth of employment in the central business district. Here we assume that such unusual effort will not be forthcoming, but it is an assumption which is readily subject to challenge.

THE REST OF THE CORE

The rest of the Core, surrounding the central business district, is as varied in character as any part of the Region. In certain parts of the Core, a process of downgrading and conversion is in full swing. Here, a generation or two of children will be raised, to be followed by the gradual thinning out and aging of populations so evident in the oldest slums. But the thinning-out phase is already the dominant one for large stretches of the Core. Some areas in Bayonne, N.J., the southwest Bronx, and western Brooklyn have already reached the advanced stage of residential obsolescence found in Manhattan's Lower East Side. Even areas like Harlem, which have seen more than one cycle of slum families, have joined in the thinning-out process, as Negro families have begun to break through the ring of restrictions which has confined them to such areas. True, there are still a few neighborhoods of the Core outside the central business district—neighborhoods set off from their surroundings by natural or artificial barriers, by relative newness, or by especially felicitous design—which have managed to cling to their middle-income character and may hang on for much longer. Here and there also, one may find a high-rise, high-rent development in these areas, perched close to a strategic highway not many minutes (though perhaps a number of miles) from the central business district. But from all appearances these neighborhoods will be islands in a generally deteriorating environment.

Once more, the extent and character of subsidized redevelopment programs are a big imponderable. Once more, it is well to have some magnitudes in mind. Though New York City's public housing projects to date represent a prodigious effort, still they shelter only a little more than 5 per cent of its population. Successive programs of the next twenty years will no doubt be even larger in scope, especially as the less intensive use of the dwellings in these areas lowers the public cost of site acquisition. But we do not foresee a program so large as to offset the factors creating the population decline in the Core.

What about *jobs* in the Core areas outside the central business district? Those in the retail trades will grow no more than sluggishly and may well decline. As for manufacturing jobs, if our analysis of the locational forces affecting their distribution has any validity, there is little reason to anticipate much rise in their number in any of these Core areas. Here and there, a few new plants may be built, especially at the outer edges of the Core. More common, however, will be shifts in the use of existing structures; large plants will abandon some of their facilities and small ones may take up some of the vacated space; plants in some industries will grow under the spur of growing national demand while others will decline. Redevelopment for industrial purposes may occur in a limited way, although we shall assume on the basis of our discussion in Chapter 2 that such efforts will be quite limited in scope. On balance, manufacturing jobs in these areas could rise a little but there is no basis for expecting much expansion. Trucking and warehousing facilities also may expand a little on the edges of Hudson County, Brooklyn, the Bronx, and Queens. But the orders of magnitude suggest that the total job expansion to be anticipated in these areas is not very large.

The foregoing picture differs significantly from that customarily painted for New York City. True, other projections have taken cognizance of the fact that the City's population is unlikely to grow much in the decades ahead. But so far as we are aware, they have rarely reflected the possibility of an actual decline, particularly one continuing over several decades. Our projection foresees the likelihood of such a decline, in both population and jobs. This could raise new political issues, but that is a subject to be treated elsewhere in this series.*

THE INNER RING

THE OLD CITIES

A conceptual bridge between the Core and the Inner Ring is provided by the older satellite cities in the Inner

* Robert C. Wood, *1400 Governments.*

Ring. For, in some ways, cities like Elizabeth, Passaic, Paterson, and old Yonkers have the flavor of portions of the Core outside the central business district. Formerly independent service centers for consumers and local business, they have since been engulfed by the suburban growth around them and by-passed by high-speed modern highways. Many of the middle-income families once making up their populations have aged and shrunk or have departed for the suburbs. Many of the plants within their jurisdiction have become outdated. Their central business districts now compete with suburban shopping areas to capture the retail customer. And this competition is on a footing which handicaps the old cities, where obsolescent street patterns impede easy automobile travel and obsolescent shops suffer by comparison with new layouts in the suburbs.

The elements of growth in the old cities, to the extent that they appear, promise to be much like those in portions of the Core outside Manhattan's central business district. Some warehousing and wholesaling operations previously conducted from more centrally located points in the Region may grow in the less congested portions of the Inner Ring cities; they are likely to experience no difficulty in finding good storage space there. Small manufacturing plants are likely to find quantities of useful factory space left behind by their original owners.

Again, the movement of jobs has implications for the movement of populations. Low-income jobs are heavily concentrated in goods-handling, in consumer trades and services, and in some highly competitive lines of manufacturing. These jobs have been shifting outward from the Core and promise to keep on shifting outward. Workers in these jobs, more than higher-paid workers, have a strong incentive to avoid a long and costly journey to work each day. Therefore, they will also have a strong incentive to settle in the space being vacated by middle income groups in the old cities of the Inner Ring. Low income groups formerly concentrated in New York City and Hudson County, notably Negroes and Puerto Ricans, will find an increasing reason to move into the Inner Ring cities. Indeed, there will probably be a growing tendency for new migrants from Puerto Rico and the South to make such cities their very first stopping point in the Region.

Because of the relatively low average level of their incomes, the growth of Negro and Puerto Rican populations in some of the old cities of the Inner Ring will require the down-grading of structures in some neighborhoods—doubling-up of families, conversion into rooming houses, and the like. Accordingly, population densities may increase here and there in such cities. But population densities will not always increase. As Chapter 8 suggests, there are strong grounds for the view that conversions, down-grading, and public construction will increase the total supply of low-income housing in the Region faster than the demand for it during the next decade or two. What is more, there are indications that some cities plan to enforce ordinances which could place a damper on excessive doubling-up. So the densities generated by low income groups in the suburban cities may not be very high. Any population growth among low income groups could easily be so modest, therefore, as to be offset by the aging of middle-income groups elsewhere in the City. In the long-established portions of such cities, where new residential construction is inhibited by lack of land and where population density is already high, net declines in population are likely to ensue.

The City of Newark, along with other cities in the Inner Ring, shows many of the tendencies just described; yet in some ways it is a special case. It is like downtown Brooklyn in that its claim as a service center for a large hinterland was very strong before the era of the automobile. Newark's central business district contained a major nucleus of shopping facilities, business offices, and cultural activities of the sort typical of an independent metropolis. When the automobile era arrived, Newark's position justified the development of an extensive bus network converging on its business district. And in still other ways Newark retained earmarks of its early role. Some elements of the analysis of the central business district of Manhattan, therefore, apply as well as to the central business district of Newark.

There are major differences, however. The growth of the communication-oriented activities which Manhattan attracts is largely a function of growth in the nation. The growth of those which Newark or Brooklyn attracts is largely a function of growth in a limited hinterland. What is even more important, perhaps, is that many of the activities in Manhattan's central business district are less subject to the effective competition of the suburbs than those in Newark. For example, Manhattan's money-market activities and its tourist attractions have no counterparts anywhere else in the Region. Newark's central business district, therefore, lacks some of the elements of vitality which are present in Manhattan. Sustained activity in Newark's central business district is likely to depend upon the success of civic efforts to attract nonprofit cultural, educational, and governmental functions, rather than upon its attractiveness as a center for other forms of office activity.

OUTSIDE THE OLD CITIES

The economic life of the suburban areas outside the Inner Ring cities can only be projected by an exceedingly careful analysis which begins at the national level. The growth in national demand for given products is likely to be a major influence in determining the different rates and patterns of industrial expansion in different areas. A full treatment of Suburbia's future must wait for the larger framework in which the final report in this series will be written.

A few things, however, are reasonably clear. There will be considerable growth in the number of jobs and the number of homes in the suburban areas. Some suburbs— including those which acquired the tone of high-income neighborhoods only a decade or two ago—will resist the invasion, using zoning and other ordinances to prevent rapid growth and higher densities. But there is bound to be a bending of such standards, especially in older areas where the obsolescence of the housing is creating a turnover in the residents. Suburbs once known as "exclusive" will gradually surrender their old estates to the subdivision developer and to higher densities. Some suburbs long dedicated to barring industry will reverse that policy and become suitors of industry, in order to meet the higher governmental costs that will go with serving the needs of their lower-income inhabitants.

The scramble for industry, of course, will not be confined to aging suburban municipalities. The newer communities in the Inner Ring (and Outer Ring, for that matter), burdened by the need to expand their schools, streets, and sewers, will participate in the hunt. But their capacity to attract industry through competitive local tax concessions is likely to be reduced with time—reduced in the sense that local taxes on real property will constitute a smaller part of the total state and local tax bill.

Suburban communities may change in still another way. Here and there, multifamily structures will likely appear in communities now lacking them. Apartment buildings are not altogether new in the suburbs of the Inner Ring. They have always been prominent in the towns and villages of southern Westchester County, for instance. But the new wave of multi-unit construction promises to be different.

Twenty or thirty years ago, apartment buildings in Westchester County were fairly high-density buildings, reflecting the fact that automobile ownership was not widespread and that two-car families were rarer still. For the most part, such structures were built shoulder to shoulder, within walking distance of the railway stations and the village shopping centers. To a considerable extent, they housed families that preferred an upper-income neighborhood without the tribulations of home ownership.

The new multifamily building, however, will probably be located largely upon the assumption that its inhabitants need not be within walking distance of the suburban railway station. The families which bid for such space will be heavily weighted by two groups: people in their fifties or older who have reared their families in the vicinity and who are anxious to remain there without the burdens of maintaining their outsized houses; and couples in the early years of marriage who do not need the space in a private dwelling or who lack the means of buying one. These two groups will increase substantially in number in the decade or two ahead. What they are likely to demand and what they are likely to get in good part will be low-rise, low-density structures of the garden apartment variety at prices which high-middle-income people can afford. The Inner Ring's old cities, too, may conceivably be able to capture some of this market. But the extent to which they do so will depend in part on their ability to provide cleared building sites at reasonable cost; this implies governmental subsidy in most cases. And it will also depend—unless social attitudes go through a revolutionary change—on the extent to which these sites are insulated from the low-income neighbors surrounding them.

The travel patterns suggested by this kind of development in the New York Metropolitan Region are fairly clear. We have already indicated that radial trips to Manhattan will lengthen, on the whole. The same will be true of radial trips to Newark, for the same reasons. Thus the number of radial trips to both places, originating in the suburbs, will increase. But, with jobs growing only slowly in the two great centers and growing rapidly in the suburbs, radial trips will increase in number much more slowly than trips within suburban areas or from one suburban area to another. Passenger transportation, therefore, will become more diffused. Belt highways linking one suburban area with another will be in considerable demand. The importance of the Narrows Bridge, for instance, may prove to be its role in linking Staten Island with the newer areas of Long Island, rather than its contribution to trips terminating in Manhattan. Accordingly, in the absence of major innovations in mass transit, the opportunities for the institution of added facilities of that sort will be limited, and the use of the motor vehicle will continue to expand.

THE OUTER RING

Though the Outer Ring is generally associated with open spaces, it has to be remembered that the open spaces are punctuated with some fairly old and substantial cities. Bridgeport in Connecticut and New Brunswick in New Jersey, for instance, are long established urban centers, with many of the attributes of those discussed earlier.

Most of the land of the Outer Ring, however, lacks the well-defined attributes of the old city centers. Very little of the open area is committed, as yet, to any particular pattern of growth, and only a fraction is likely to become so committed in the next decade or two. In such a situation, where available land in a broad zone far exceeds the demands likely to be made upon it, projection for any specific portion of the zone is especially difficult; isolated initial decisions of one sort or another can set the tone and timing of the portion's development.

Nonetheless, the shape of future events in some parts of the Outer Ring is already beginning to emerge. The easterly portion of Suffolk County, jutting out into the Atlantic, will not be able to match the Region's southwest edges as a site for some types of manufacturers, especially those anxious to hold down freight costs in shipments to national markets. But the growth of air freight will slightly mitigate the disadvantages of Long Island. And, if a causeway were thrown between the Island and New England—a possibility not to be ruled out—another slightly mitigating force would be introduced. Development in Middlesex County at the southwesterly edge of the Region will merge with the industrial and research activities reaching up from Trenton and Princeton. Nevertheless, it is well to emphasize that even 25 years from now the densities of both jobs and people will still be much higher in the center than at the edges of the Region.

Twenty years ago, new highways brought places like Chappaqua and Mt. Kisco into tolerable commuting distance of Manhattan by automobile. More recently, the New York Thruway tapped hitherto remote portions of Rockland County, and the Connecticut Turnpike is being tied into the New York City network. Spurred by the giant federal highway program, new highways will penetrate into additional areas. Whether these areas will in fact become commuting points for jobholders in Manhattan will depend primarily on the extent to which the City expands its capacity for carrying commuter traffic and parking commuter automobiles. The growing use of the helicopter will add somewhat to this trend toward speedy access, though high operating costs may limit the extent of its adoption for some time to come. Each transportation development of this kind opens up new possibilities for the well-to-do exurbanite with ties to Manhattan; which of these possibilities he chooses depends on where he can expect to find the peers he seeks for neighbors.

Meanwhile, the high-speed highway will also affect the location of middle-income housing. For occupants of this kind of housing in the Outer Ring, ties to Manhattan or Newark are not nearly so important as ties to the plants and businesses of the Inner Ring. The highways are important, therefore, not so much because they improve access to the center as because they bring large new tracts of undeveloped land into the market for mass builders of moderately priced colonies. Accordingly, such highways encourage more leapfrogging in the choice of sites and more spacious sites as well. The fact that interchanges and exits on these high-speed roads are sometimes very widely spaced—witness the 13-mile stretch between the Harriman and Newburgh exits on the New York Thruway—encourages the leapfrog process.

One can envisage, therefore, a highly selective process of site locations, even more selective than what has been going on so far. Flat terrains with sandy soils will get first attention; areas encumbered by steep slopes or rocky outcroppings will be passed over much more readily than before. This suggests that the attractions of areas like Monmouth County and western Suffolk County will continue to grow. Though the *valleys* of Rockland County and Westchester County may be attractive for this sort of development, some of their steeper terrains may be long neglected. The incentive to fill in space that was by-passed in earlier waves of development, such as the undeveloped areas of Staten Island, will be somewhat blunted. To put it differently, some of the growth which might have occurred in the Inner Ring in an earlier era—an era when highspeed highways were rare—will now take place in the Outer Ring.

In the next decade or two, then, the demand for space will grow; but this demand will be readily supplied by improved transportation. Freed from the need to be close to the centers of the old cities—unbound from spatial restraints by the wider use of the automobile and the truck —the people of the Region and many of the enterprises on which they live will devour space at a faster rate than ever before.

FROM PROJECTION TO REALITY

It is easy to slip into the use of the future tense; the future is so much less clumsy and so much more authoritative than the conditional. Yet no one will be deceived by the copious use of the future tense in this chapter. What we have stated as expectations could be set aside in reality by the unpredictable or the improbable. There is no need to recite the whole list—wars, depressions, acts of God, and so on—but there is real point in stressing the fact that unpredictable changes in the role of governmental policy or wholly novel efforts on the part of private groups are among the forces which could alter the future structure of the Region.

The task of this book has been to analyze and project, not to evaluate and decry. But as some of the events foretold in these pages come to pass, they could engender governmental or private responses much stronger than we have so far been accustomed to witness. Implicit in our analysis has been the assumption that some programs of governments and private groups would change: that urban redevelopment programs would grow somewhat; that transportation facilities would improve somewhat; and so on. But no unprecedented programs of change have been taken for granted.

The developments which these projections foretoken— the unbinding of some of the activities of the metropolis from the compulsions of centrality, the deterioration which outward movement leaves behind—could well spark greater changes in public and private policy than could have been reasonably assumed. These pages, therefore, carry the seeds of the forces which may make reality very different from the projections. In that event, in describing what might have been, this book will have served one of its major purposes.

APPENDICES

APPENDIX A

Employment Estimates

I. EMPLOYMENT BY CATEGORIES

Table A-1, accompanying this appendix, shows employment in the New York Metropolitan Region as of March 15, 1956, by counties and by chief categories of employment such as manufacturing and wholesale trade. The figures include full-time and part-time employees, and also the self-employed. These are the employment statistics that were used in preparing Tables 1 and 2, which appear in Chapter 1.

The principal source of the data in Table A-1 is *County Business Patterns, First Quarter 1956*, compiled by the U.S. Bureau of the Census and the U.S. Bureau of Old-Age and Survivors Insurance. But we have had to supplement this source because *County Business Patterns* excludes certain kinds of employment. *County Business Patterns* gives the numbers of wage-and-salary employees; it includes most employees who are under Social Security; thus, on a national basis, *County Business Patterns* covers about 62.4 per cent of total paid civilian employment, according to the Census Bureau. It does not include employment in most agricultural pursuits, forestry and fisheries, interstate railroads, and government. Also excluded are domestic workers, the self-employed, employees of organizations which were not required to enter the Social Security program but elected to do so, and seamen on ocean-borne and coastwise vessels whose home port is in the New York Metropolitan Region. (*County Business Patterns* does report a national total for seamen, but not one for the Region.)

All these groups, however, are embraced in Table A-1,

TABLE A-1 Employment in Counties of New York Metropolitan Region by Categories of Industries, March 1956 (in thousands)

	Total employment	Manufacturing(a)	Wholesale trade(a)	Financial community(b)	Other office workers in office buildings(c)	Consumer trades and services(d)	Contract construction(e)	Other employees(f)
Region, total	6,699.8	1,889.9	453.5	320.2	895.6	1,244.0	241.8	1,654.8
New York City	4,051.2	947.5	344.3	251.4	683.5	729.6	115.3	979.6
Core, total	4,301.5	1,072.5	357.9	255.1	701.8	763.2	122.2	1,028.8
Manhattan	2,717.5	531.5	268.6	220.0	609.7	412.4	59.7	615.6
Central business district	2,475.9	518.3	264.4	213.6	531.1	394.2	54.5	499.8
Brooklyn	664.9	230.3	34.1	13.7	31.4	147.6	21.7	186.1
Queens	398.4	124.1	27.2	9.1	27.3	97.7	20.4	92.6
Hudson	289.1	134.5	14.6	4.8	19.7	42.2	7.6	65.7
Bronx	231.6	52.1	13.4	7.5	13.7	63.3	12.8	68.8
Inner Ring, total	1,572.3	518.4	70.5	51.3	133.1	319.8	78.5	400.7
Essex	424.7	136.4	25.2	28.0	37.8	80.3	14.6	102.3
Nassau	284.9	69.2	9.7	6.4	22.2	69.6	20.7	87.2
Westchester	229.8	51.3	8.8	5.8	26.3	54.2	15.0	68.3
Bergen	222.5	89.1	8.7	3.2	15.4	42.7	12.9	50.5
Union	201.5	85.6	9.9	3.3	16.7	33.3	8.4	44.4
Passaic	170.1	77.3	7.2	3.5	13.3	31.1	6.2	31.5
Richmond	38.8	9.5	1.0	1.1	1.4	8.6	0.7	16.5
Outer Ring, total	826.0	299.0	25.1	13.8	60.7	161.0	41.1	225.3
Fairfield	249.4	111.3	9.3	4.5	16.7	44.7	12.2	50.8
Middlesex	137.2	65.0	4.0	1.5	8.9	20.6	6.3	30.9
Suffolk	112.7	23.9	2.7	2.1	9.5	26.2	8.3	40.1
Monmouth	68.8	14.3	2.5	1.5	4.8	20.9	4.2	20.6
Dutchess	61.7	21.7	1.8	1.0	5.1	10.3	1.9	19.8
Morris	61.4	19.7	1.3	1.2	6.2	12.9	2.7	17.4
Orange	58.1	15.9	2.0	1.1	4.3	12.1	1.7	21.0
Somerset	38.7	15.6	0.9	0.4	2.0	6.3	1.9	11.5
Rockland	30.9	10.8	0.6	0.4	2.7	5.4	1.5	9.5
Putnam	7.1	0.8	...	0.1	0.5	1.6	0.4	3.7

except seamen. Employment in the groups that are not included in *County Business Patterns* has been estimated from other sources. Where possible, we relied on separate estimates by the Bureau of Old-Age and Survivors Insurance; estimates by the state labor departments of New York, New Jersey, and Connecticut; or data collected by the New York Regional Office of the U.S. Bureau of Labor Statistics. Where estimates could not be derived from those agencies, we made our own.

Sometimes *County Business Patterns* included employees in its county totals but could not classify them by industry. We have distributed these by categories of employment according to the proportion of the number of *firms* in each category in the counties involved. In addition, employees shown only by economic activity on a statewide basis had to be allocated to the various counties, and still other employees in the state totals who were classified as to neither county nor industry had to be distributed by counties and industries.

The following further explanations are keyed to the column headings in Table A-1.

(a) *Manufacturing and wholesale trade.* The figures in Table A-1 for these two categories are not strictly comparable with those in the tables in Chapters 2, 3, and 4 because those tables represent, not total employment, but employees covered under state unemployment insurance programs. The limitations of the state data are discussed in Part II of this appendix.

Manufacturing employment in Table A-1 includes ordnance. It does not include employees in central administrative offices—a group which we have placed in "other office workers in office buildings." The figures for both manufacturing and wholesale trade exclude the self-employed, who are placed instead in the category of "other employees."

(b) *Financial community.* This category in Table A-1

Notes are in text of this appendix. For example, those for manufacturing and wholesale trade are in paragraph (a), those for the financial community in paragraph (b), and so on.

includes the same groups of employees as in our Table 18, which appears in Chapter 4. The two tables differ a little in the total number of employees, however, because they are from somewhat different sources. In Table 18 the figures relating to the Manhattan central business district are based on data obtained from the Department of City Planning, New York City, referred to in this appendix under the heading "Breakdown of Employment for Areas Within New York City." Further methodological detail for the financial category of employment will appear in a forthcoming book on the financial community in this series.

(c) *Other office workers in office buildings.* A breakdown of the 895,600 workers in this category of Table A-1 is shown in Table 19, found in Chapter 4. Our figures are based on numerous incomplete sources and therefore the data are at best very rough estimates. The 895,600 includes several types of employment:

1. Central offices. Included here are central administrative office employees of several industry groups, except the financial community. Manufacturing central office employment data are from *County Business Patterns, First Quarter 1956,* while retail and mining estimates are based on the *1954 Census of Business, Manufacturers, and Mineral Industries,* "Central Administrative Offices and Auxiliaries," Preliminary Report, Series P-CAO 1. The number of office workers in water transportation was partly derived from the occupation characteristics for water transportation employees shown for the New York Standard Metropolitan Area in the *1950 Census of Population.* About 15 per cent of these employees, excluding seamen on vessels in foreign trade, were estimated to be in central offices. In air transportation about 15 per cent of all employees were also assumed to be in central offices. For interstate railways, 10 per cent of the employees who were on payrolls in New York City were assumed to work in central offices.

2. Services closely identified with central offices (advertising, accounting, auditing, and bookkeeping services, employment agencies, legal services, architects, and engineering firms). For these groups, *County Business*

Patterns employment data were supplemented by employment data obtained from state unemployment insurance programs. The number of self-employed lawyers by counties was based on *Martindale-Hubbell Law Directory, 1956,* since the scope of *County Business Patterns* excludes the self-employed. Estimates of other self-employed in services associated with central offices were based on unpublished estimates of the total number of self-employed classified by industry in the nation as a whole, obtained from the Bureau of Old-Age and Survivors Insurance. The proportions of this employment in selected services were applied to estimates of self-employment in the New York Metropolitan Region, also based on data obtained from that bureau. The Region total was distributed to the counties by the pattern found largely in the other employment in services closely identified with central offices.

3. Public utilities. The Bell System provided figures on its telecommunications office workers in the New York Metropolitan Region. Switchboard operators are considered to occupy office space. Bell System office workers in the employ of manufacturing and laboratory subsidiaries are not included in the office worker totals. As for gas, electric, and other utilities, we assumed that a fifth of their employees are working in offices.

4. Real estate offices and combinations of real estate, insurance, loan and law offices were assumed to be primarily in office buildings. Our estimate of the number of self-employed operators was based on the data obtained from the Bureau of Old-Age and Survivors Insurance (referred to in paragraph 2, above).

5. Government. The Department of City Planning, New York City, furnished estimates of the number of federal, state, and local government employees working in private office buildings and in tax-exempt government structures in each borough of New York City. On the basis of those figures, we estimated that 27 per cent of the governmental employees in Manhattan work in office buildings, and in the other four boroughs of the City, about 13.5 per cent. Elsewhere in the Region the rela-

tion between office workers and total is also assumed to be 13.5 per cent. The "Government" category also includes employees in New York City of foreign governments and foreign and international organizations: these estimates were obtained from the New York City Department of Commerce and Public Events, and practically all were estimated to occupy office building space.

6. Nonprofit organizations. These are principally educational, scientific, and religious organizations; fraternal, political, and professional groups; trade associations; labor, civic, and social organizations. Employment in those organizations in this broad category that are required by law to participate in the Social Security program was obtained from *County Business Patterns*. Employment in those nonprofit organizations that elected to become part of the Social Security System was obtained from unpublished estimates by the Bureau of Old-Age and Survivors Insurance. Three-quarters of the employees in both classes of organizations—those required to participate in the Social Security program and those with elective coverage—were assumed to be in office buildings.

7. Employment data for radio and television offices, news syndicates, and motion picture production and distribution, obtained from *County Business Patterns*, were supplemented by figures on employment reported under state unemployment insurance programs, where data were not available in sufficient detail in the federal source.

8. Other office workers. This group consists of adjustment, credit and collection agencies; duplicating processes; mailing and stenographic services; and one-half of business and miscellaneous services not classified elsewhere.

(d) *Consumer trades and services.* "Consumer trades" is synonymous with retail trades and excludes central administrative office employees, who appear in the category entitled "other office workers in office buildings." Consumer services include services of a personal kind (such as hotels, laundries, barber and beauty shops, automotive and other repair services, and amusement and recreation facilities).

The total of consumer trades and services in Table A-1 includes estimates for self-employed proprietors; these estimates are based on U.S. *1954 Census of Business*, "Retail Trade" and "Selected Services." Self-employed proprietors are also included in Table 20 (found in Chapter 5), which is based on the same *Census of Business*, supplemented by our own employment estimates for several consumer services in Outer Ring counties.

Table A-1 and Table 20 differ in their estimates of employment in consumer trades and services, for these reasons: Paid part-time workers are included in Table A-1 but not in Table 20; Table A-1 is for mid-March 1956 and Table 20 for mid-November 1954; and, because employment was measured at different times of the year, the figures are affected by seasonal considerations.

Table 2 (in Chapter 1) includes the consumer trades and services employment data of Table A-1 and therefore has a somewhat broader coverage than Chart 4 (in Chapter 5) which conforms with the consumer trade estimates in Table 20 and excludes part-time employees.

(*e*) *Contract construction.* Employment in this group is based on *County Business Patterns* and excludes self-employed contractors, who are placed in "other employees," described in the next paragraph.

(*f*) *Other employees.* This category is represented by the final column of Table A-1, and includes (1) the portions of the following not located in office buildings: public utilities and transportation (including interstate railways), government, nonprofit membership organizations, and real estate; (2) those self-employed who are not in office buildings or engaged in consumer trades and services; (3) domestic workers; (4) agricultural workers and services; (5) medical and other health services, private education, museums and art galleries; (6) miscellaneous services not included in other categories.

BREAKDOWN OF EMPLOYMENT FOR AREAS WITHIN NEW YORK CITY

County Business Patterns lists employment by industries for the counties of New York City as a group. The distribution of employment for areas within New York City was derived in the following crude manner:

1. The Department of City Planning, New York City, estimated employment in broad industry groups in each borough of New York City for 1955 based on federal employment censuses for 1954; on a tabulation of the records of the New York State Department of Labor for workers in industries covered by unemployment insurance for 1955; and on a special borough tabulation of covered employment by that department for September 1950. The special borough tabulation covered establishments of 12 or more employees. We supplemented the resulting estimates with information from the U.S. *1954 Census of Business* ("Selected Services").

2. The proportions of New York City's employment in each borough by industrial category were applied to our employment estimates for New York City for 1956, derived from *County Business Patterns* and other sources.

3. Similarly, the September 1950 proportions of Manhattan's employment categories that were located in its central business district, as we have defined it in Map 3, were applied to our crude estimates of industrial employment in Manhattan in 1956. (In the September 1950 tabulation by the New York State Department of Labor, employment in various types of activity was given by Census Tracts.) Of the total of 2,475,000 employed persons who are noted in our estimates as working in the central business district, roughly 5 per cent are estimated to work elsewhere in New York City, but are carried on payrolls in the central business district. No attempt has been made to distribute these jobs by borough and industry.

II. LIMITATIONS OF "COVERED" EMPLOYMENT DATA

Part I of this appendix discussed the sources of our estimates of employment in the Region on March 15, 1956. We also prepared employment estimates for several industries over a period of years. To do this for these earlier dates, we were obliged to rely in some cases on unpublished employment data obtained from state sources.

The departments of labor of New York and New Jersey provided us with industry employment data for each month of the third quarter of 1947 and 1956. Similar employment data for the third quarter of 1956 were provided by the Connecticut labor department, from which we also obtained first quarter 1956 manufacturing employment figures. All these figures, however, include only "covered" employment, by which is meant employees in activities covered under the state unemployment insurance programs. As a result, they include only establishments with four or more employees. (The data obtained from the New York State Department of Labor for 1956 included establishments with three or more employees, but in order to achieve comparability we adjusted the figures for the New York counties to a "four-or-more" basis.)

In our manufacturing tables from the above sources (Tables 3, 6, 9, 10, 13, and 14), certain classes of employees are excluded even though they are participants in unemployment insurance programs. These are: employees in central administrative offices of manufacturing firms; employees of United States government shipyards; and employees of the ordnance industry.

Even with all the limitations mentioned in the foregoing paragraphs, the "covered" manufacturing employees in our tables exceed 90 per cent of all manufacturing employees outside of central administrative offices, though for wholesale trade the coverage is lower.

Our manufacturing estimates in Tables 3, 6, 9, 10, 13, and 14 are based on state covered employment data for the third quarters of 1947 and 1956 (or for 1956 alone), with the following exceptions:

1. We estimated 1947 employment for individual industries in Dutchess, Putnam, and Orange Counties.

2. Fairfield County, Connecticut, employment is for the first quarter of 1956, while for 1947 we estimated comparable first quarter data from *County Business Patterns, First Quarter 1947*.

Estimates of wholesale trade employment in Tables 16 and 17 are also based on covered employment data, with the following exceptions:

1. The distribution of New York City's employment between Manhattan and the rest of New York City is based on borough data for 1948 and 1954 obtained from the U.S. *Census of Business* for 1948 and 1954, "Wholesale Trade."

2. Employees in Social Security Board Code 52, mixed wholesaling and retailing operations, were not included.

Wholesale employment as reported by the New York State Department of Labor includes all employees of central offices of manufacturing establishments wherever a substantial part of the activity of those offices was selling. The number of such central-office employees was roughly 35,000 in 1956. In our use of covered employment data we left these employees in the wholesale category, but in Table A-1 we placed them in "other office workers in office buildings" along with other central-office employees. In New Jersey and Connecticut, where the number of such employees is believed to be relatively small, the state governments included them in manufacturing and thus they are counted as manufacturing employees in our tables based on covered employment data. Again, in Table A-1 they are included in "other office workers in office buildings."

APPENDIX B

Population Estimates

For 1900 to 1950, county population estimates at ten-year intervals in the decennial censuses. For other years prior to 1950, our county population estimates were made by interpolating between Census years. For the period after 1950, interpolations were made between the 1950 Census totals and those obtained from the Special Census taken in many of the New York counties of the Region in April 1957, in connection with applications for federal aid to local schools. We also used unpublished 1955 estimates of population of the counties of the Region made by the Bureau of the Census in connection with civil defense problems and a Census estimate of the population of the New York Standard Metropolitan Area as of April 1957 ("Population of the New York-Northeastern New Jersey Standard Metropolitan Area: April 1957," *Current Population Reports*, Series P-25, No. 161, August 1957).

Our interpolated estimates for the population of the New Jersey counties after 1950 were checked against estimates made by the Public Service Corporation and those made by several county planning boards. In some instances we modified our estimates in the light of the information obtained from those sources.

The 1956 estimates we made appear in Table 1. Our estimates for this and other years were also used in the preparation of Tables 24 and 51 and of Charts 1, 2, 4, and 9.

APPENDIX C

Factory Construction Costs at Alternative Sites

Following are estimates of the cost of constructing a hypothetical modern factory for 720 employees in Manhattan and in other locations in the New York Metropolitan Region.

The Manhattan plot we have selected for this theoretical purpose is a block bounded by 29th and 30th Streets and Ninth and Tenth Avenues. This block has an assessed value of $13 per square foot, which is fairly low for the central business district. The assessed value of $13 per square foot must be increased by 25 per cent to cover present market price, acquisition cost, and clearing cost, bringing the actual cost to $16.25 per square foot. The block is 200 by

800 feet, a total of 160,000 square feet. The land cost of the site then would be 160,000 × $16.25 = $2,600,000.

The structure hypothetically erected on the site is a metal-working plant with dimensions and specifications developed in accordance with modern industrial plant requirements, taking into account the restraints imposed by the dimensions of the block.

For comparative purposes, there is also presented an alternative plan for a plant of equal floor space located outside Manhattan, assuming a site consisting of 15 acres of undeveloped land. The site is assumed to be located on a main highway and to be accessible to a railroad siding. The cost of the raw land is $10,000 per acre, but another $10,000 per acre is required to develop the site and bring in the necessary utilities, raising the total cost of the land to $20,000 per acre.

The alternative plan outside Manhattan involves somewhat different specifications. Though the total floor space is approximately the same as the hypothetical Manhattan plant, the shape of the building is changed in order to obtain the most economic proportions. The land provides a

TABLE C-1 Comparative Costs of Manufacturing Plant at Two Locations

	City plant	Suburban plant
Square feet of floor space	238,000	237,000
Land cost	$2,600,000	$300,000
Building cost[a]	$3,403,000	$2,861,000
Total cost	$6,003,000	$3,161,000
Total cost per square foot	$25.25	$13.34
Rent equivalent per square foot (@ 12%)[b]	$ 3.03	$ 1.60
Rent equivalent per employee (@ 323 sq. ft.)	$979.00	$517.00

[a] Building cost in the city plant is calculated at $14.30 per square foot and at $12 per square foot in the suburban plant. The difference is due to the fact that the latter building has 20 per cent less wall space per foot of floor space, and the fact that the open space would permit more expeditious delivery and handling of construction materials. The second building also includes a railroad spur, 500 feet in length, at $35.00 per linear foot.

[b] The 12 per cent figure includes operating and maintenance expenses, as well as depreciation, taxes, and return on capital. However, it does not include a provision for vacancies which is included in the return required for a loft building whose space is leased out, as noted in Appendix E.

density of 40 employees per acre and is a little higher than the medians shown in a survey by the Urban Land Institute (Dorothy A. Muncy, *Space for Industry*, Washington, D.C., 1954, Table 7, p. 12) but it is equal to the land space per employee shown by migrating industries in a Regional Plan Association study of 1956 (*Regional Plan News*, March 1957). The comparative costs for both structures are shown in Table C-1.

Typical industrial site costs in various locations of the Region are shown in Table C-2.

TABLE C-2 Typical Costs of a Ten-Acre Industrial Site in New York Metropolitan Region, 1957 (thousands of dollars)

	Median	High	Low
Bronx	1,100	1,300	950
Queens	870	1,750	550
Brooklyn	850	1,300	450
Bergen	650	900	100[a]
Nassau	450	900	80
Essex-Hudson	450	900	100[a]
Westchester	250	650	25[b]
Suffolk	225	550	80
Rockland	50	80	25[b]
Morris	40	60	20
Monmouth	30	50	15

[a] Undeveloped marsh lands.
[b] Rough terrain requiring improvement, which is typical of the areas.

Sources: Opinions of industrial real estate brokers and advertisements.

APPENDIX D

Factors Influencing Variability in Construction Costs

The statistical measurement and isolation of the factors entering into building costs are extremely difficult. This is illustrated by the fact that, although labor is a considerable part of total construction costs, comparisons of wage rates do little to explain construction-cost differences between

TABLE D-1   Cost of Constructing a One-Story "Standard" Factory Building in Selected Areas of New York Metropolitan Region, 1956

Area	Dollars per square foot
Essex	13.62
New York City	14.30
Hudson	14.30
Union	14.30
Passaic	14.45
Nassau	14.75
Westchester	14.95
Bergen	15.65

Source: Base figures for New York City from Turner Construction Company, *50 Years of Buildings by Turner* (New York, 1952), adjusted to New York City for 1956 by the Boeckh index for brick-on-steel-frame factory buildings. See E. H. Boeckh, *Boeckh Index Calculator Tables* (Washington, D.C., 1951) and monthly supplements. Figures for other counties derived by the relations shown in F. W. Dodge Corporation, *Dow Index Calculator* (New York 1941) and monthly supplements.

TABLE D-2   Hourly Wage Rates (Including Fringe Benefits) in Building Trades, Selected Counties of New York Metropolitan Region, 1955[a]

Area	Brick- layer	Car- penter	Plas- terer	Iron worker	Laborer	Plumber, elec- trician, etc.	Total unit[b]
New York City	$4.05	$3.94	$4.05	$3.98	$2.73	$4.05	$47.59
Nassau	4.24	3.83	4.24	3.98	2.73	3.95	48.22
Westchester	3.65	3.55	3.65	3.98	2.60	3.74	44.88
Bergen	3.95	3.50	3.95	3.98	2.70	3.62	46.62
Essex	3.85	3.61	3.86	3.98	2.80	3.71	47.24
Passaic	3.97	3.60	3.97	3.98	2.80	3.62	47.38
Hudson	4.15	3.76	3.86	3.98	2.80	3.64	47.61
Union	3.95	3.50	3.95	3.98	2.60	3.62	45.80

[a] Going rates as reported by building trades employers' associations in the respective areas. These conform closely to union rates as published by the U.S. Bureau of Labor Statistics.

[b] Combined in the approximate proportions to their use in construction, in accordance with the following factors: bricklayers, 1.47; carpenters, 1.00; plasterers, 1.85; iron workers, 1.85; laborers, 8.00; plumbers, electricians, and so forth, 0.25. Factors from E. H. Boeckh, *Boeckh Index Calculator Tables* (Washington, D.C., 1951) and monthly supplements.

areas. Compare, for example, the construction-cost data in Table D-1 with the wage data in Table D-2.

Some of the factors that elude specific statistical measurement are: productivity of labor; skill in management; equipment used; jurisdictional claims (in some areas, a concrete mixer may be operated by a concrete laborer, and in others, by an operating engineer; or, a small hoist may be operated by a labor foreman rather than an operating engineer); safety measures required, such as sidewalk protection and site enclosures; access and storage for material deliveries; availability of specialized skills (installations of certain types, such as those required for skyscrapers, may require a team of experienced installers who may be sent from distant points for the purpose, with fare and travel-time allowance).

Generally speaking, basic material costs are the same throughout the Metropolitan Region. Such differences as exist are due largely to delivery charges. For instance, Douglas fir lumber comes from the West Coast to New York by intercoastal steamer at a net cost (in 1957) of about $32 per thousand board feet, as against a carload rail rate of about $35. Thus, the farther the construction site may be from the water terminals, the higher the delivered cost, until a point is reached that equalizes with the rail charges. (The rail rate is a single commodity rate that applies to all points east of Chicago and north of the Ohio and Potomac Rivers.)

Steel and cement usually incur a greater hauling cost in the city, but the amount of this differential is negligible compared to the total costs of the building. In fact, the net carload price on cement is lower for New York than for Boston, Dallas, Los Angeles, and Kansas City. Prices of reinforcing steel are higher in nine other large cities than they are in New York.

APPENDIX E

Cost of Constructing a Loft Building

TABLE E-1 Estimated Cost and Return in Construction of a Nine-story Loft Building, Located in Manhattan Between West 20th and West 30th Streets, 1957

Total land—half a block, 200 feet by 400 feet	80,000 square feet
Less: off-street loading area	5,000 square feet
Total square feet of building (9 × 75,000 gross feet)	675,000 square feet
Total rentable space (90% of total gross feet)	607,500 square feet
Costs	
Land, at $16.25 per square foot cleared	$ 1,300,000
Building, at $16.50 per square foot (gross)	$11,137,500
Total	$12,437,500
Annual return required: 18%[a]	$ 2,238,750
Rent per rentable square foot	$3.68

[a] The 18% figure includes operating and maintenance expenses, as well as depreciation, taxes, provision for vacancies, and return on capital.

Source: New York Metropolitan Region Study estimates.

APPENDIX F

Computation of Tax Levels

(Notes for this appendix follow notes on Chapter 8.)

The state and local tax levels presented in Chapter 2 are based on data drawn from a sample of 25 manufacturing establishments. Though we generally refer to them simply as "firms," they are in some cases less in scope than an entire firm. Each of these firms was hypothetically located at 64 locations in the New York Metropolitan Region and a tax level computed for each firm at each location, using 1955 tax rates. Then the dollars-and-cents figures were translated for purposes of comparison into index numbers. That is, the average burden of each firm at all locations was stated as equal to 100.0 and then each firm's level at every location was computed in terms of this average.

The 25 firms are actual companies located in the New York Metropolitan Region, though we withhold their names because some of their figures are confidential. The relevant financial data for each firm are given in Table F-1. Hypothetical firms could have been constructed,[1] but the method used here possesses the advantage of being based on real operating companies located in the area being studied. It is not claimed that the sample is an accurate reflection of the Region's industry. After interviewing 75 firms and circularizing about 75 others, we settled on 25 which were willing to supply complete or nearly complete data relevant for tax purposes. Were it not for the fact that our average tax levels seem to be so highly representative of most of the individual firms, as shown in the last four columns of Table F-2, the haphazard nature of the

TABLE F-1   Financial Structure of 25 Sample Firms
(arranged in the order of their gross receipts)
(in thousands of dollars)

Gross receipts	Annual payroll	Net worth	Net profit	Property value	
				Real	Personal
$200,287	$82,000	$99,000	$23,296	$29,000	$56,247
73,000	21,000	44,000	11,565	14,000	29,400
57,873	21,958	79,000	9,706	12,164	24,083
50,863	14,554	18,320	4,884	11,010	13,160
32,043	7,346	10,000	2,847	5,225	8,908
30,052	9,584	10,115	3,214	5,700	6,825
22,855	4,093	17,500	2,713	6,617	11,424
21,585	12,075	32,173	3,544	8,000	19,284
13,432	9,515	6,515	1,119	1,848	6,398
10,100	1,175	2,371	1,294	750	1,608
8,619	5,879	2,645	1,449	303	5,406
7,360	2,340	2,007	736	419	1,743
7,236	1,690	1,756	380	864	823
7,131	1,305	3,222	1,497	1,210	1,314
5,643	1,638	2,100	360	600	731
5,200	2,925	1,530	294	457	3,427
4,612	936	2,274	171	1,137	640
3,000	216	950	150	888	500
2,818	1,016	424	40	675	1,634
2,812	668	3,012	200	1,800	1,237
2,685	552	1,108	403	772	685
2,500	538	420	80	240	752
2,407	423	410	77	565	631
2,190	563	45	759	250	448
299	177	43	11	35	92

Note: A few firms did not provide the value of their personal property; in those cases informed estimates were made.

sampling method might have left us in great doubt as to
the meaningfulness of our results.

Actually there is a fairly wide distribution according to
type of industry and size of company. The industries represented are: fabricated metal products; food and kindred
products; instruments, photographic and optical goods,
and watches; electrical machinery, equipment, and sup-
plies; paper and allied products; machinery except electrical; printing and publishing; chemical and allied products; and miscellaneous manufacturing. In Table F-1 it will
be observed that the gross receipts range from $200,287,-
000 down to $299,000.

It happens that about half of the 25 firms are actually
located in New York State and half in New Jersey but their
real geographical distribution has little significance since
our computations are based on setting down each firm
hypothetically at 64 well distributed locations.

LOCATING THE FIRMS

The 64 locations were selected for illustrative purposes,
not with the idea of rating all the communities in the Region but simply to give a meaningful picture of relative
tax levels. The 64 are distributed by states as follows: 31
in New Jersey, 29 in New York, 4 in Connecticut. All of
the locations either already contained industrial activity or
had zoning regulations permitting such activity. The locations had to be pinpointed geographically because of the
maze of tax jurisdictions in the Region, especially in the
New York counties surrounding New York City, for in those
counties many municipal services are provided by special
districts. Such districts are not coterminous with one another nor with any general governmental jurisdiction. In
Nassau County, for example, there are approximately 400
taxing jurisdictions and, as a result, firms on opposite sides
of a street may have three or four tax rates in common—
such as the county rate, the town highway rate, and school
district rate—while they differ in rates for street lighting,
garbage collection, and fire protection.

The various taxes applicable at each location were applied to the appropriate data of each firm at each location.

The average of the 25 firms was then calculated for each location. Table F-2 lists the 64 locations, ranked according to index figures signifying these averages.

TABLE F-2   64 Locations in New York Metropolitan
Region Ranked According to Tax Levels of
25-Firm Sample

	Average tax level		Number of firms with ranking between:			
	Index	Rank	1–16	17–32	33–48	49–64
Jersey City, N.J.	160.1	1	22	2	1	0
Union City, N.J.	141.3	2	21	1	3	0
Newark, N.J.	140.6	3	22	0	3	0
Bridgeport, Conn.	133.8	4	20	4	1	0
Stratford, Conn.	129.7	5	17	7	1	0
Manhattan (in New York City) .	129.6	6	22	2	3	0
Bronx (in New York City)	129.1	7	22	2	1	0
Norwalk, Conn.	125.9	8	16	6	3	0
Brooklyn (in New York City) ..	122.3	9	18	6	1	0
Irvington, N.J.	119.9	10	20	2	3	0
Orange, N.J.	116.9	11	18	3	4	0
Queens (in New York City)	115.4	12	13	7	5	0
Hicksville, N.Y.	114.6	13	18	2	5	0
Richmond (in New York City) ..	111.0	14	10	9	5	1
New Rochelle, N.Y.	110.8	15	17	3	5	0
Buchanan, N.Y.	110.0	16	17	2	6	0
Carle Place, N.Y.	109.2	17	12	7	6	0
Glen Cove, N.Y.	107.8	18	7	12	6	0
Farmingdale, N.Y. (Suffolk County portion)	107.7	19	7	11	7	0
Mineola, N.Y.	106.6	20	4	14	7	0
Ramapo, N.Y. (bet. Thruway & Piermont Branch of Erie R.R.)	106.2	21	4	13	8	0
Elizabeth, N.J.	104.8	22	9	11	5	0
Pelham Manor, N.Y.	104.7	23	2	14	9	0
Asbury Park, N.J.	104.2	24	11	8	6	0
Mount Vernon, N.Y.	103.4	25	2	13	8	2
Lyndhurst, N.J.	102.7	26	7	6	12	0
New Cassel, N.Y.	102.1	27	2	12	7	4
Rahway, N.J.	101.6	28	7	5	13	0
Ramapo, N.Y. (east of Suffern) .	101.3	29	0	13	8	4
Roosevelt Field, N.Y.	101.2	30	0	13	8	4
Bloomfield, N.J.	100.1	31	10	2	13	0
East Orange, N.J.	99.4	32	3	9	12	1
White Plains, N.Y.	98.8	33	0	13	7	5
Beacon, N.Y.	98.6	34	0	13	7	5
Port Chester, N.Y.	98.4	35	0	12	5	8
Bay Shore, N.Y.	98.4	36	0	11	6	8
Morristown, N.J.	97.6	37	7	4	14	0
Belleville, N.J.	97.2	38	5	7	13	0
Plainfield, N.J.	95.7	39	3	9	13	0
Montclair, N.J.	95.4	40	1	11	13	0
Woodbridge, N.J.	92.3	41	0	9	11	5
Passaic, N.J.	92.1	42	0	9	11	5
Perth Amboy, N.J.	91.6	43	0	11	7	7
Lindenhurst, N.Y.	91.2	44	0	5	8	12
Paterson, N.J.	90.9	45	0	7	10	8

	Average tax level		Number of firms with ranking between:			
	Index	Rank	1–16	17–32	33–48	49–64
Farmingdale, N.Y. (Nassau County portion)	90.7	46	0	5	8	12
Kenilworth, N.J.	88.8	47	1	6	5	13
Danbury, Conn.	88.6	48	1	4	9	11
Harrison, N.J.	88.6	49	0	6	9	10
Hackensack, N.J.	88.0	50	0	6	6	13
Clarkstown, N.Y. (south of Thruway)	87.8	51	0	3	10	12
Union, N.J. (Union County) ...	87.5	52	2	5	3	15
Orangetown, N.Y.	85.9	53	0	3	5	17
Clarkstown, N.Y. (east of Spring Valley)	85.5	54	3	3	5	17
New Brunswick, N.J.	84.9	55	0	5	3	17
Yonkers, N.Y.	82.6	56	0	3	3	19
Poughkeepsie, N.Y.	82.6	57	0	1	5	19
Kearney, N.J.	81.1	58	0	2	6	17
Garfield, N.J.	79.5	59	0	4	2	19
Hillside, N.J.	77.6	60	0	1	3	21
Linden, N.J.	74.8	61	0	0	4	21
Ridgefield, N.J.	72.1	62	0	1	3	21
Clifton, N.J.	69.3	63	0	0	3	22
Teterboro, N.J.	47.0	64	0	0	0	25

COMPUTING PROPERTY TAXES

Property taxes are applicable to all locations. In New Jersey and Connecticut, the localities tax both real and personal property, and New York local governments tax only real property. The primary difficulty in computing property taxes for the 25 firms at the 64 locations is in discovering the relation of assessed to true value.[2] We knew the "true value" or at least a good approximation of it, but we did not know what the assessed value would be in a given locality. Since tax rates apply to assessed value, it was necessary to use equalization ratios in order to obtain tax rates which we could apply to true value. In the case of real property, official equalization ratios were used when available, and the true-value tax rates thus obtained were applied to the actual land and improvement values of the sample firms. Since these values are in dollar terms the tax levels computed are inaccurate to the degree that land and building values differ from one part of the Region to another. Further, equalization ratios are averages and there is without question a wide variation in the ratio of true to assessed value within the same jurisdiction. These variations are held in bounds only by the alertness of taxpayers to discriminatory practices.

Part of the variation in the ratios of true to assessed value is between rather than within classes of property; this is eliminated when ratios are available for different classes of property. In the case of New York locations, an equalization ratio for industrial property was employed, and a combined ratio for industrial-commercial property was used for New Jersey. Informed sources in New Jersey believe that commercial property is assessed at a higher ratio than industrial, and, if this is correct, the tax levels for New Jersey are slightly overstated. In Connecticut it was possible to obtain only a general equalization ratio and Connecticut levels are incorrect to the degree that industrial property is assessed at ratios different from other kinds of property.

In New York State, including New York City, the equalization ratios used are determined by a state agency which independently assesses a sample of properties in each jurisdiction in the state and on the basis of this sample determines an equalization ratio for each jurisdiction.[3] In New Jersey the equalization ratio is derived from actual sales figures; these are compared to the *assessed* value of the property sold and a ratio is computed which is based on all property sold in each jurisdiction.

The problem of obtaining equalization ratios for real property is small compared to that of obtaining them for personal property. Since New York does not levy a tax against personal property, the problem exists only for locations in New Jersey and Connecticut.

One tax study contains the following comment on personal property taxation: "Local custom and practice have developed for valuing tangible personalty by various standards which do not always lend themselves to definition." Definition is indeed difficult because "The common practice among the States where this class of property is subject to the local property tax is to assess it largely by negotiation between the assessing officials and the taxpayers."[4] As if in confirmation of this view a branch man-

ager of a large industrial firm being interviewed for the
present study said, "We negotiate this one."

A few of the firms refused to provide the true value of
their personal property despite assurances that the information would be kept confidential. Competing firms cannot
easily compare assessed values of personal property, and
even the smallest risk was considered too great. In these
few cases, informed estimates were made.

As pointed out in the notes to Chapter 2, a recent study
based on a sample of 3,560 firms in New Jersey compared
the assessments of corporate personal property with the
book values of the property they represented. Of these
firms, 107 were assessed at less than 1 per cent of book
value, and 207 were assessed at over 100 per cent. The
unweighted average of the ratios was 23.29 per cent.[5] The
author of that study made available the data from which
he derived these figures, and on the basis of this information it was possible to compute a median ratio of assessed
to true value for this class of property for each jurisdiction
in New Jersey.

For Connecticut it was impossible to use even this approximation, since all that is available is the general equalization ratio for all classes of property.

CORPORATE TAXATION

In 1955, the year for which the state and local taxes
were computed, all three states covered in this study employed a form of corporate taxation; New York and Connecticut had a corporate income tax and New Jersey a
corporation franchise tax. New Jersey had not yet adopted
a corporate income tax.

In both New York and Connecticut there are alternative
means of computing the income tax, and the alternative
which produces the larger return is the one which must
be used. In this study the alternative used for both states
is the "per cent of net income." The basic rate is 5.5 per
cent of net income in New York and 3.75 per cent in
Connecticut.

UNEMPLOYMENT COMPENSATION

Normally omitted from comparative studies of tax burden is the unemployment compensation tax. When all employers in all states paid the same rate such omission was justified. Rates today, however, are dependent on two sets of circumstances, one pertaining to the state as a whole and the other pertaining to the individual employer.

The tax rate is dependent in the first instance upon the level of funds in the state unemployment fund. For each of various levels there is a series of tax rates. And the rate in this series paid by the employer is determined by his individual merit rating, based on his past record of payments. In all three states, the factor determining which series of rates is applicable is the ratio of the fund to the state's total taxable payroll. For example, in New Jersey, employers pay maximum rates if this ratio is less than 2.5 per cent; their rates drop by successive steps as the ratio increases; and if the ratio is 12.5 per cent or over, minimum rates go into effect.

The amount in the unemployment compensation fund at any time is a result of benefits paid out, and those payments, in turn, are determined not only by the amount of unemployment but also by the liberality of benefits and the ease of qualifying for the benefits available.

For the sample firms in this study the actual unemployment compensation rate obtained from the firm was used for all locations in the state where the firm is physically located. In each of the other two states the rate used for all locations is the appropriate industry rate plus or minus the percentage by which the firm's actual rate varies from its industry average in its home state.

Table F-3 presents the industrial averages of unemployment compensation rates in the three states.

THE NEW YORK CITY GROSS RECEIPTS TAX

The only important local tax other than property is the New York City gross receipts tax which is levied at the rate of 0.25 per cent of the gross receipts.

This tax is imposed on trades, professions, and busi-

TABLE F-3   Unemployment Compensation Tax Rates for
Selected Industries in New York, New Jersey, and
Connecticut, 1955

Industry group	Average tax rates		
	New York	New Jersey	Connecticut
Ordnance and accessories	1.88	2.16	1.35
Primary metal industries	1.19	1.28	1.11
Fabricated metal products	1.65	1.58	1.24
Machinery (except electrical)	1.30	1.38	1.17
Electrical machinery, equipment, and supplies	1.61	1.76	1.36
Transportation equipment	1.86	2.02	1.16
Instruments, photographic and optical goods, watches	1.13	1.65	1.49
Food and kindred products	1.21	1.53	.99
Tobacco	1.50	2.17	1.18
Textile mill products	1.88	1.93	1.66
Lumber and wood products	1.66	1.65	1.05
Furniture and fixtures	1.67	1.85	1.44
Paper and allied products	1.28	1.31	1.02
Printing and publishing	1.01	1.22	.77
Chemicals and allied products	.88	1.00	.86
Petroleum and coal products	.66	.77	1.04
Rubber products	1.16	.98	1.21
Leather products	1.29	2.10	1.50
Stone, clay, and glass products	1.17	1.61	1.01
Miscellaneous manufacturing industries	1.84	2.10	1.39
Retail trade, not elsewhere classified	1.42	1.33	.87

ness, with certain exceptions. Certain commission-type
businesses, financial businesses, and certain investment
companies pay on the basis of their gross income at lower
rates. There is no tax if receipts are less than $10,000.

TAXES NOT INCLUDED IN THE STUDY

Omitted from consideration in this study have been the
New York State personal income tax, the New York City
and Connecticut sales taxes, workmen's compensation
taxes, the New York State truck mileage tax, and the
disability benefits tax applicable in New York and New
Jersey.

The personal income tax in New York may induce firms
considering alternative locations of equal merit to avoid
New York State in order to save its employees from having
to pay it. One study of comparative tax levels counts the

total personal income taxes of a firm's employees as a part of the firm's taxes.[6] In justification it is claimed that the existence of the personal income tax is taken into consideration by unions in negotiating for higher wages. Analysis of comparative wage rates in the New York Metropolitan Region, undertaken in another study in this series, does not justify such a claim.

Sales taxes levied by New York City and Connecticut are omitted from the study because goods used in production by manufacturing firms are not subject to this tax.

Workmen's compensation had to be left out because of differing classifications of employees in the three states. The fact that the insurance may be with a state fund or a private insurance company, or accomplished through self-insurance, adds a further complication.

Also omitted was the New York State truck mileage tax, which is based on a maximum gross weight of loaded units, or unladen weight of units operating without any load. It is difficult to tie this tax down to specific firms since many employ outside trucking companies.

In addition to unemployment compensation, New York and New Jersey collect a small tax for temporary disability benefits. The cost of providing disability benefits in excess of contributions collected from employees is borne by the employers. An employer may provide disability benefits by (a) insuring with the state insurance fund; (b) insuring with a stock or mutual company; (c) being a self-insurer; or (d) participating in an approved disability plan.

Because of the many different ways employers may meet the legal obligations of the disability benefit program, it has not been possible to include their cost in total tax levels. The tax on employees in New York and New Jersey is the same, with employer supplements being fixed amounts in New Jersey and flexible in New York. Probably the costs are approximately the same in the two states.

APPENDIX G

Lists of Special Industries for Three Periods

(1900–1922, 1929–1939, and 1947–1956)

Following are our lists of the communication-oriented, nuisance, water-transport, and raw-material-consuming industries mentioned in Chapter 3. We have classified some industries both as nuisance and as water-transport industries.

I. COMMUNICATION-ORIENTED INDUSTRIES

1900–1922

Jewelry and precious metals
Men's hats and caps
Textile knit goods
Textile small wares
Women's cloaks and suits
Women's neckwear
Women's dresses and waists

1929–1939

(The name of each industry is followed by its code in the U.S. 1929 *Census of Manufactures*. The numbers in parentheses are the corresponding codes in the 1939 *Census of Manufactures*.)

Women's clothing, not elsewhere classified, 210 (430–439, 441–443, 446, 449, 461–466, 485, 486)
Embroideries, 219 (488, 490, 491)
Knit goods; gloves and mittens, cloth or cloth and leather combined, made from purchased fabrics, 224, 234 (351–357, 480, 481)

Men's hats and caps, except felt and straw, 228 (425)

Millinery, 239 (451)

Trimmings, not made in textile mills, and stamped art goods for embroidering, 246 (492, 493)

Wool pulling and hairwork, 250, 1617 (2093, 2094)

Toys, not including children's wheel goods or sleds, games, and playground equipment; sporting and athletic goods, not including firearms or ammunition; billiard and pool tables, bowling alleys, and accessories, 302, 1642, 1648 (2041, 2042, 2049)

Labels and tags; engraving, steel and copperplate, and plate printing; engraving, wood; lithographing; photo-engraving, not done in printing establishments; printing and publishing, book and job; printing and publishing, music, 406, 504–509 (831–833, 851, 861, 862, 871, 891–893)

Printing and publishing, newspaper and periodical, 510 (811, 812, 821, 822)

Stereotyping, 512 (894)

Leather goods, not elsewhere classified; pocketbooks, purses and card cases, 906, 908 (446, 1271, 1272, 1299)

Jewelry, 1210 (1551, 1552, 2071)

Feathers, plumes, and artificial flowers, 1601, 1613 (2074)

Buttons, 1606 (2061)

Fancy and miscellaneous articles, not elsewhere classified; combs and hairpins, not made from metal or rubber; ivory, shell, and bone work, not including buttons, combs, or hairpins; theatrical scenery and stage equipment; 1609, 1612, 1621, 1646 (2071, 2073, 2083, 2099)

Fur goods, 1615 (470)

Lapidary work, 1623 (1553)

Models and patterns, not including paper patterns, 1625 (2092)

Signs and advertising novelties, 1640 (2085)

1947–1956

(The name of each industry is followed by its number in the Standard Industrial Classification, 1945, established by the Bureau of the Budget.)

Knit outerwear mills, 2253
Men's, youths', and boys' cloth hats and caps, 2325
Women's and misses' blouses and waists, 2331
Women's and misses' dresses, 2333
Women's and misses' suits, coats (except fur coats), and skirts, 2337
Women's neckwear and scarfs, 2338
Millinery, 235
Fur goods, 237
Belts, 2387
Pleating, stitching, and tucking for the trade, 2395
Trimmings, stamped art goods, and art needlework, 2396
Embroideries, except Schiffli-machine, 2398
Periodicals, 272
Books: publishing, publishing and printing, 2731
Commercial printing, 275
Lithographing, 276
Service industries for the printing trade, 279
Handbags and small leather goods, 317
Jewelry, silverware and plated ware, 391
Games and toys (except dolls and children's vehicles), 3941
Costume jewelry, costume novelties, buttons, and miscellaneous notions (except precious metal, and also excluding needles, pins, hooks and eyes, and similar notions), 396, excluding 3964
Signs and advertising displays, 3993
Hair work, 3994
Models and patterns (except paper patterns), 3998

II. NUISANCE INDUSTRIES

1929–1939

(The name of each industry is followed by its code in the *1929 Census of Manufactures*. The numbers in parentheses are the corresponding codes in the *1939 Census of Manufactures*.)

Meat packing, wholesale, 123 (111, 112)
Chemicals, not elsewhere classified, 608 (981, 982, 999)
Fertilizers, 614 (970)
Glue and gelatin, 616 (990)
Grease and tallow, 617 (991)
Paints and varnishes, 626 (911, 912)
Soap and glycerin, 631 (941)
Tanning materials, 632 (980)
Lubricating oils and greases, not made in petroleum refineries, 704 (992)
Rubber goods other than tires, 802 (1191, 1199)
Forgings, iron and steel, 1107 (1492)
Wire drawn from purchased rods, 1126 (1441)
Nonferrous metal alloys and products, not including aluminum products, 1212 (1520, 1591, 1599)
Secondary smelting, nonferrous metals, 1217 (1532)

1947–1956

(The name of each industry is followed by its number in the Standard Industrial Classification, 1945, established by the Bureau of the Budget.)

Meat products, 201
Industrial inorganic chemicals, 281
Industrial organic chemicals, 282
Soap and glycerin, 2841
Paints, varnishes, lacquers, japans, and enamels; inorganic color pigments, whiting, and wood fillers, 285
Gum and wood chemicals, 286
Fertilizers, 287
Grease and tallow, 2886
Glue and gelatin, 2894
Petroleum refining, 291
Reclaimed rubber, 303
Rubber industries other than tires and inner tubes, rubber footwear and reclaimed rubber, 309
Primary smelting and refining of copper, 3331
Secondary smelting and refining of nonferrous metals and alloys, 334

Rolling, drawing, and alloying of nonferrous metals, 335
Miscellaneous primary metal industries, 339

III. WATER-TRANSPORT INDUSTRIES

1929–1939

(The name of each industry is followed by its code in
the 1929 *Census of Manufactures*. The numbers in parentheses are the corresponding codes in the 1939 *Census of
Manufactures*.)

Lubricating oils and greases, 704 (992)
Ships and boat building, steel and wooden, including re-
    pair work, 1410 (1931, 1932)

1947–1956

(The name of each industry is followed by its number
in the Standard Industrial Classification, 1945, established
by the Bureau of the Budget.)

Sugar, 206
Industrial inorganic chemicals other than sulfuric acid and
    alkalies and chlorine, 2819
Miscellaneous industrial organic chemicals, 2829
Inorganic color pigments, 2852
Petroleum refining, 291
Gypsum products, 3272
Primary smelting and refining of copper, 3331
Ship and boat building and repairing, 373

IV. RAW-MATERIAL-CONSUMING INDUSTRIES

1947–1956

(The name of each industry is followed by its number
in the Standard Industrial Classification, 1945, established
by the Bureau of the Budget.)

Hydraulic cement, 324
Structural clay products, 325
Cut-stone and stone products, 328
Minerals and earths: ground or otherwise treated, 3295
Sand-lime brick, block and tile, 3296

APPENDIX H

Comparative Cost of Office Space

This appendix compares the cost of air-conditioned office space in Manhattan and in Westchester County in 1956.

In Manhattan, the average office employee uses 188 square feet of space, according to an unpublished survey prepared for the New York City Planning Commission. The average rental per square foot per year in air-conditioned buildings built after World War II is $5.10; this is the average for four such buildings located in the central business district of Manhattan but not in special "prestige" locations, according to data obtained from the appraisal department of a leading insurance company. Annual office space rental per employee in such an office building would be $958.80 (188 square feet at $5.10).

If a company with 400 employees is assumed to build its own offices in the White Plains area of Westchester, it will require 20 acres of land at about $25,000 per acre. This represents the average experience of 8 firms; see Frederick P. Clark, "Office Buildings in the Suburbs," *Urban Land,* July–August 1954, p. 3. Some 249 square feet of building space will be required for each employee, according to this source.

The capital cost of the building is computed at $22.50 per gross square foot, based on Turner Construction Company data and adjusted by the E. H. Boeckh Index and the "Dow Index Calculator." Assuming that the funds to purchase land and construct the building are burdened with a 5 per cent financing charge, the annual cost associated with financing is $1.38 per year. Maintenance and operating costs, including depreciation, are estimated at an additional $3.60 per square foot per annum, based on the 1957 "Experience Exchange Report" of the Building Owners and Managers Association of the New York Area.

The comparative costs would then be as follows:

Westchester:

Land, 20 acres at $25,000 per acre	$ 500,000
Building, 400 employees at 249 square feet—99,600 square feet, at $22.50 .	$2,241,000
Total land and building cost	$2,741,000
Annual interest cost per square foot, at 5% .... $	1.38
Annual maintenance and operating cost, including depreciation, per square foot .... $	3.60
Total annual expense per square foot .. $	4.98
Cost per employee per year ($4.98 × 249) .... $	1,240.00

Manhattan:

Rent per employee per year ($5.10 × 188) .... $	958.80

APPENDIX I

Estimating Equations for Employment in Consumer Trade and Service Lines

The equations which follow are least-squares estimates fitted to the 1954 employment data in each indicated consumer trade and service line in 19 counties of the 22-county Region; the omitted counties are Manhattan, Brooklyn, and Essex. In each instance, the 1954 county population and employment estimates used were those found in the Regional Plan Association's Bulletin No. 87, *People, Jobs and Land 1955–75* (June 1957). In each case, "employment" in any line was taken from the *1954 Census of Business*, Retail Trade series, and consisted of the sum of full-time, paid employees in the work-week nearest November 15 and proprietors of unincorporated businesses.

In the county employment estimating equations in Table I-1, P represents population in the county in thousands, E represents total employment in the county in thousands, and H represents the number of one-family dwelling units in the county. The coefficients of correlation measure the degree of relation between county employment in each retail line and the independent variables presented in the corresponding estimating equation.

TABLE I-1 Retail Equations and Coefficients

	Equation	Coefficient of correlation
Food stores	$-404 + 9.57\,P$	$+.997$
Eating and drinking places	$621 + 6.74\,P$	$+.96$
Apparel stores	$60 + 3.71\,P$	$+.96$
Cleaning, laundry, clothing repair establishments	$-225 + 5.24\,P$	$+.96$
Miscellaneous repair services	$-191 + 1.99\,P$	$+.96$
Parking	$-95 + .53\,P$	$+.94$
Motion picture theaters	$-23 + .68\,P$	$+.97$
Jewelry stores	$14 + .96\,E$	$+.92$
Furniture and furnishings stores	$-22 + 8.56\,E$	$+.98$
Drug stores	$-21 + 4.23\,E$	$+.97$
Liquor stores	$-14 + 2.12\,E$	$+.96$
Variety stores	$41 + 4.04\,E$	$+.95$
Department and dry goods stores	$-25 + 8.27\,E$	$+.88$
Auto and accessory sales stores	$248 + 10.10\,E$	$+.94$
Gasoline service stations	$49 + 7.31\,E$	$+.93$
Auto repair facilities	$4 + 3.46\,E$	$+.97$
Barber and beauty shops	$-245 + 9.68\,E$	$+.84$
Lumber, hardware, and building materials	$61 + .004\,H + 4.94\,E$	$+.91$
Other retail stores	$151 + 13.37\,E$	$+.96$

APPENDIX J

Land-Use Measurements

Land-use measurements employed in Chapters 1 and 6 were prepared for the New York Metropolitan Region Study by the Regional Plan Association from a large number of sources, including aerial photography, existing land-use maps, and other sources. Land in the Core and in Inner Ring counties, except in upper Passaic and upper Westchester, excludes bodies of water such as lakes and reservoirs but includes marshes. For the Outer Ring counties and upper Passaic and Westchester, however, land measurements include such water.

Land-use measurements for the individual counties in the Region were made as of various dates between 1953 and 1956. The differences in time result in inconsequential differences in the proportion of a county's land used for a given purpose. The land-use data for counties in New Jersey are for 1954, for New York City 1955–56, for Suffolk 1954, for Rockland 1953, and for the remaining counties 1955. Where population data are used in conjunction with land use, as in Table 24 (Chapter 6), such data are as of approximately the same dates as the land-use data.

For the Land-Use Survey Area shown in Map 5, land-use information was tabulated by individual municipalities; for most other parts of the Region outside New York City, comparable detail is not available.

APPENDIX K

Journey-to-Work Survey

This survey was conducted for the Regional Plan Association in early 1956 by an organization retained for the purpose. The survey had a number of objectives, one of which was to determine the journey-to-work patterns of persons working in the New York Metropolitan Region. Accordingly, responses were sought to such questions as the county of residence and county of employment of each person covered in the survey, the amount of time involved in daily commuting trips, and the occupation of the respondent.

To obtain these responses, a sample of firms was selected from those in the Region reporting employees covered under the unemployment insurance programs of the several states. The sample was designed to obtain responses, by counties, of roughly one per cent of covered employment. Some counties, however, were more heavily sampled than others, the coverage running from 0.67 per cent to 2 per cent. Each county sample was stratified by size-of-firm groups, to ensure that the smaller firms were given adequate representation and weight.

Firm response rates varied from 0 to 100 per cent among the different size groups in the various counties. Employee response rates for firms in the various counties varied from 5 to 70 per cent of the employment of such firms. In general, firm response rates were higher from the groups of larger firms and higher from groups of firms in the central counties of the Region.

The results were blown up by the indicated ratios: First, each firm's reports were blown up by the reciprocal of the response rate of employees in the firm; second, the expanded figure was blown up again by the reciprocal of the response rate of firms in each size group in each county. Finally, the resulting figures were enlarged again to bridge the difference between covered employment and total employment in each county, the latter figure being an estimate for 1955 developed by the Regional Plan Association, Inc. These estimates of total employment, it should be noted, differ somewhat from those which would have been obtained if the methodology used in the compilation of Table A-1 for 1956 had been applied to 1955.

Some rather obvious biases exist in the resulting data. First of all, the results as presented in Table 29, in Chapter 6, contain a forced correspondence with total employment by counties but no forcing was done to obtain a correspondence with the working population resident in each county. Disparities between working resident figures by counties as obtained from the blown-up sample, and the working resident figures by counties as estimated independently were very large. Manhattan's residents were under-represented in the sample by about 34 per cent, the largest such aberration in the list of counties. The average

TABLE K-1   Distribution of Workers Employed in Counties

County of residence \ County of work	Manhattan	Bronx	Queens	Brooklyn	Hudson	Richmond	Union	Essex	Passaic	Bergen	Westchester	Nassau
Manhattan ...	440.2	16.1	33.0	31.9	5.4	1.9	1.4	7.4	0.2	8.7	12.8	3
Bronx	364.6	163.5	29.5	31.8	4.2	2.1	...	1.5	0.8	6.0	15.5	4
Queens	487.3	12.6	212.6	211.5	5.1	...	1.3	5.0	...	6.9	2.7	29
Brooklyn	504.4	11.7	43.9	336.1	6.5	0.5	0.3	8.6	...	6.4	0.4	9.
Hudson	75.5	...	2.9	0.7	102.8	...	7.5	18.1	1.8	12.4	...	..
Richmond	48.7	...	0.4	2.2	3.9	30.5	0.2	0.7	...	0.4	...	..
Union	28.2	...	...	0.7	13.4	...	108.8	34.4	1.4	2.1	...	..
Essex	43.4	...	2.0	...	28.1	...	16.5	243.8	16.4	6.2	...	..
Passaic	9.7	...	...	2.2	1.7	...	0.2	6.3	92.0	16.1	...	..
Bergen	119.7	9.5	5.2	5.7	50.9	...	1.5	16.2	20.0	115.4	0.9	..
Westchester ...	117.0	9.5	2.8	2.5	1.8	...	0.5	...	...	0.9	183.7	..
Nassau	160.7	2.0	48.4	30.1	1.0	...	...	...	0.8	0.8	3.9	222.
Monmouth	6.9	...	...	2.8	4.9	...	2.0	4.4	...	0.2	...	..
Middlesex	4.4	...	...	0.4	7.4	...	18.2	10.0	0.8	...	...	..
Somerset	2.5	...	...	...	0.2	...	4.1	3.0	2.8	...	...	..
Morris	11.9	...	...	...	6.4	...	6.4	12.5	4.7	1.1	0.4	..
Rockland	5.1	...	1.0	...	...	...	...	...	0.8	2.5	...	..
Orange	...	...	...	...	0.2	...	...	...	...	...	...	..
Dutchess	0.6	...	...	...	...	...	...	...	...	...	...	..
Putnam	2.4	...	...	...	...	...	...	...	...	...	1.2	..
Fairfield	23.7	0.1	...	...	...	...	...	...	...	...	...	..
Suffolk	21.9	...	4.5	1.5	...	...	...	...	...	...	...	14.
Total living and working in Region	2,488.8	225.0	386.2	660.1	243.9	35.0	168.9	371.9	142.5	186.1	223.4	283.

^a This tabulation includes only those who

difference for the 22 counties of the Region was 17 per cent.

There are indications also that clerical and sales employees are over-represented in the sample while shop and factory employees are under-represented. These biases arose from two practices on the part of firms participating in the survey. Despite instructions to the contrary, some firms circularized their office staffs but not their plant staffs. Others circularized suburban commuters but not other employees. These practices affected the results as indicated above.

The journey-to-work patterns derived from the survey, by counties, are presented in Table K-1.

f New York Metropolitan Region[a] (in thousands)

Monmouth	Middlesex	Somerset	Morris	Rockland	Orange	Dutchess	Putnam	Fairfield	Suffolk	Total Region
...	...	...	...	...	1.3	...	...	2.1	3.9	569.4
...	...	...	0.2	0.2	...	...	...	3.6	0.8	628.7
...	...	...	...	0.4	...	...	...	...	0.9	986.1
...	...	0.8	0.1	0.1	...	...	...	...	...	929.4
...	...	...	0.2	...	...	...	...	...	...	221.9
...	4.6	0.3	...	...	...	...	...	...	...	91.9
...	12.7	2.8	0.4	...	...	0.1	...	...	...	205.0
...	0.6	1.5	3.2	...	...	...	...	...	...	361.7
...	0.1	0.4	6.4	...	1.6	...	...	...	...	136.7
...	0.9	...	0.4	3.9	...	...	...	...	...	350.2
...	...	...	...	0.1	6.1	1.7	0.3	12.7	...	339.6
...	...	...	...	...	...	...	...	...	13.9	484.2
60.7	4.7	...	0.1	...	...	...	...	...	...	86.7
1.1	86.4	4.7	...	...	...	...	...	...	...	133.4
...	3.6	20.7	0.6	...	...	...	...	...	...	37.5
...	...	0.4	37.1	...	...	...	...	...	...	80.9
...	...	...	...	19.8	1.3	...	...	...	1.6	32.1
...	...	...	...	0.2	35.1	...	...	...	...	38.9
...	...	...	0.2	...	...	42.5	0.2	...	...	43.5
...	...	...	...	...	...	2.1	3.4	...	...	9.1
...	...	...	...	...	...	...	0.1	196.3	...	222.1
...	...	...	...	...	...	...	...	...	79.5	121.4
61.8	113.6	31.6	48.9	24.7	45.4	49.8	4.0	214.7	100.6	6,110.4

both live and work within the NYMR.

APPENDIX L

Calculation of Indices of Occupational Specialization and Work-Residence Separation

The various indices cited in the text and presented in Tables 32, 33, and 37 are all designed to show the degree to which a specified job type is "over-represented" or "under-represented" in the jobs or the resident workers of a specified county or urban municipality. "Over-represen-

tation" of a job type in the employment of a county means
that the job type constitutes a larger fraction of the total
employment of that county than it does of the total employment of the whole New York Metropolitan Region.
Similarly, "over-representation" of a job type among the
resident workers of a given county means that the job type
constitutes a larger fraction of total resident workers in
that county than it does in the whole Region. Each coefficient is a *percentage ratio* of the share of a job type in
a specified county or municipality to the share of that job
type in the Region as a whole; thus, coefficients greater
than 100 show "over-representation," or positive "specialization" in the job type in question, while coefficients below
100 show "under-representation" or relative deficiency.

All data are for the year 1950. The basic data on employed resident workers by job type and location were
taken directly from the U.S. *1950 Census of Population,
General Characteristics of Population,* Tables 35, 39, and
43.

The Census designations of the occupational categories
used are as follows:

Professional, technical and kindred workers
Managers, officials, and proprietors, excluding farm
Clerical and kindred workers
Sales workers
Craftsmen, foremen, and kindred workers
Operatives and kindred workers
Private household workers, combined with service work-
    ers, except private household
Laborers, except farm and mine

The following groups were omitted (all being of small
importance in the Region):

Farmers and farm managers
Farm laborers, unpaid family workers
Farm laborers, exclusive of unpaid family workers, and
    farm foremen
Occupation not reported

For each occupational category, the number of resident workers in each county was expressed as a percentage of the total in the Region. A similar county breakdown of the Region's total was prepared for the resident workers in all nonfarm occupations combined.

The coefficients of occupational specialization of residents were then calculated from these percentage distributions. For example, 4.43 per cent of the Region's total of operatives lived in Fairfield County while 3.62 per cent of the Region's total of all types of employed nonfarm workers lived in Fairfield County. The residents' specialization index for operatives in Fairfield County is accordingly 4.43 divided by 3.62, or 122.4 per cent.

The same basic procedure was used for the urban places of 2,500 or more population in the Land-Use Survey Area, but with an additional adjustment. It was found that the index figures showed a much wider range of variation for some occupations than for others—being, for example, quite wide for the managerial and professional groups and quite narrow for the clerical and sales groups. Consequently, if the urban communities in the Land-Use Survey Area had been sorted out into job-type specialization categories on the basis of assigning each community to the category for which its index was highest, almost no communities would have been assigned to the sales or clerical specialization categories. In order to get a more balanced distribution, reflecting relative specialization, the coefficients were adjusted to eliminate the effect of this difference in dispersions. For all the coefficients for a given job type, the standard deviation was computed. The coefficient for that job type for a given community was then expressed as a deviation from 100 per cent and divided by the standard deviation—that is, was expressed as a deviation from average, in "standard units." This had the effect of giving the *adjusted* coefficients about the same dispersion for one job type as for another, and communities were then assigned to occupational specialty categories on the basis of their highest adjusted coefficient.

The coefficients of specialization of the *jobs* in the various counties (as distinguished from those described above, which relate to the employed *residents*) had to be obtained via a procedure involving some very rough estimation, since employment figures by location of jobs are incomplete and inaccurate and are classified by industry rather than by occupation. In view of these data deficiencies, only the crudest indication of the distribution of jobs by job type can be achieved.

The procedure began with estimates of 1950 employment in the Region, for New York City and individual counties outside the City, as prepared by the Regional Plan Association and shown in its Bulletin 87 (June 1957), pp. 48 ff. The industry categories used were the following: Construction; Finance, insurance, and real estate; Manufacturing; Retail trade; Personal and business services; Transport, communication, and public utilities; Wholesale trade.

Agriculture, forestry and fishing and the residual "all other" category of employment were omitted.

In the Regional Plan Association tabulation on which these job estimates are based, New York City appears only as a whole, not broken down by boroughs. Accordingly, the City totals were roughly distributed among the five boroughs, for each industry group, by using the borough shares of total City employment in similar industry groups in Table 1 of the *Bulletin* of the New York Department of City Planning, December 1955: *Employment Distribution and Concentration in New York City*. Substantial errors may have been introduced at this stage in view of the fact that the industry groups and their coverage were not quite the same for the Regional Plan Association and Department of City Planning estimates.

These procedures yielded a tabulation of 1950 employment by county and industry category. The next step was to distribute the jobs in each industry into occupational categories. For this purpose, the *1950 Census of Population* cross-tabulation by industry and occupation (*Detailed Characteristics of Population,* Table 84) was used. Two tables were extracted from these Census data: one for the New York State portion of the New York-Northeastern

New Jersey Standard Metropolitan Area, and one for the New Jersey portion.

For each of those two major parts of the Region, the workers in each of our industry groups were broken down percentagewise by occupational category, and these breakdowns were applied to the previously obtained estimates of county employment by industry to produce a table of county employment by occupational type.

Several further elements of possible error entered at this stage. In particular, our procedure involved the assumption that the occupational structure of any given industry group in the *jobs* of *every* New Jersey county of the Region corresponded with the occupational structure of that industry group among the employed *residents* of the whole New Jersey part of the Standard Metropolitan Area—and a similar correspondence of industry structure by occupation in each New York and Connecticut county with that of the New York State part of the Standard Metropolitan Area.

The resulting set of estimates of county employment by job type was then treated in the same way as the data for employed residents of the counties by job type, to derive coefficients of specialization for each county and each type of job represented in its employment pattern.

APPENDIX M

Relative Income Levels of Communities by Occupational Type

The relation between occupation and income level, as shown in Table 36, can also be measured for the 126 urban communities of the Land-Use Survey Area that are classified according to occupational specialization in Table 35. If we array the communities in each specialization category in order of median 1949 income of families and unrelated individuals, and then take the median of those medians, results are as follows:

Managerial	$5,141
Professional	4,382
Sales	4,167
Clerical	4,202
Craftsmen-foremen	3,806
Operatives	3,401
Laborers	3,204
Service	3,616

The relative income ranking of the groups as thus measured diverges somewhat from that shown in Table 36, particularly in assigning a higher income standing to the service group and in reversing the ranking among the clerical, sales, and craftsmen-foremen categories. Several explanations suggest themselves for this divergence.

In the first place, the figures cited above are for whole communities while those of Table 36 refer to individual workers. Secondly, the Land-Use Survey Area covers only part of the Region. It omits four New York City boroughs (Queens, Richmond, the Bronx, Brooklyn), where (as Table 33 showed) a high proportion of the lower-white-collar clerical subgroup are congregated. It likewise omits Manhattan, the focus of the biggest concentration of low-income service workers.

Thirdly, the figures cited in the first paragraph above refer to families and unrelated individuals rather than to employed individual workers as such. Differences in family labor-force participation therefore play some part in the divergence of ranking between those figures and those of Table 36.

Fourthly, clerical and sales people, being "white-collar," are perhaps more likely than even the skilled industrial workers to prefer communities that also have a high proportion of the higher-income white-collar groups (managerial and professional). This would tend to raise the income ranking of communities that are categorized as specialized in clerical and sales workers.

Finally, for somewhat different reasons (job access rather than cultural affinity or emulation), many of the service subcategories are drawn to high-income communities even though the service workers themselves are low-paid. We find, for example, among the "service-specialized" communities of the Land-Use Survey Area such places as Mamaroneck and Rye (city) in Westchester, Cedarhurst and Great Neck in Nassau, and South Orange in Essex County—all well up in the income scale as communities.

NOTES

CHAPTER 1: CITIES AND SUBURBS

1. The concept of these 22 counties as an entity already has currency because of its prior use by the Regional Plan Association. See, for example, *People, Jobs and Land 1955-1975*, RPA Bulletin No. 87, June 1957. The total population is estimated at 15,375,000 as of April 1, 1956 (see Table 1), and has been growing by roughly 200,000 a year since 1950.

2. Other large metropolitan areas exhibit similar patterns. A study based on the 1940 census shows that in Standard Metropolitan Areas of one million or more population, the central cities had a population density 26 times as high as that of a surrounding zone of about 35 miles' radius. Population per square mile declined steadily as distance from the central city increased. See Amos Hawley, *The Changing Shape of Metropolitan America* (Glencoe, Ill., 1956), p. 39.

3. Based on a survey by Regional Plan Association. "Land suitable for development" means all land except swampy and steeply sloping terrain. For further details see Chapter 6 and Appendix J.

4. Based on a survey by Regional Plan Association. See Appendix J.

CHAPTER 2: LOCATIONAL PRESSURES ON MANUFACTURING

1. Committee on Regional Plan of New York and Its Environs, *Regional Survey of New York and Its Environs*, Vol. 1A, "The Chemical Industry," "The Metal Industry" (New York, 1928). Also E. E. Pratt, *Industrial Causes of Congestion of Population in New York City* (New York, 1911), Chapters 3 and 4, *passim*.

2. Regional Plan Association, *Regional Plan News* (New York), March 1957. Brooklyn Chamber of Commerce, Annual Report, June 1, 1954, to May 31, 1955, p. 5. Division of Business Research, School of Business Administration, Seton Hall University, *Reasons for Relocation, New Jersey Manufacturing Firms, 1955* (South Orange, New Jersey, 1955). Horace J. DePodwin, "New Jersey's New Manufacturing Establishments

Review of New Jersey Business (Rutgers University), 14:4, 5 (April 1958).

3. The rate of outmovement was also related in part to the size of plants of the industries concerned. See later discussion. But the tendency described here existed quite independently of the size factor.

4. A similar analysis was done for plants located within the large cities of the Inner and Outer Rings. For such plants, the amount of plot space per worker barely changed over time.

5. These figures have been derived by a "standardization" process that is designed to eliminate the effect that changes in the mix of industries have upon the averages. To apply this procedure, it was necessary to limit the figures to 11 major industry groups; for each of these groups, there are two or more plants in our sample which took possession of their premises in each of the following periods: prior to 1922, 1922–1945, and 1946–1956. Plants in other industry groups were excluded. As a consequence, although data were available for 296 plants outside the large cities, only 239 plants are included in this compilation.

6. See Appendix C for a presentation of the underlying calculations, and Appendix D for a discussion of factors influencing variability in construction costs. The competitive pressures which have raised the price of land in the congested areas of the older cities to astronomical levels for factory purposes are suggested by another calculation. If the same plot in Manhattan were used for a modern ten-story elevator apartment building, the investor could achieve an acceptable return by charging a rental of $47.50 per room per month, a figure not inconsistent with the current rental rates.

7. In appraisal reports to the Mayor's Slum Clearance Committee (of New York City), the statement is repeatedly made that it is practically impossible to assemble a site of two acres or more anywhere in Manhattan without resorting to condemnation proceedings. (See acquisition appraisals by the Committee on Slum Clearance in reports to the Board of Estimate on the redevelopment plans for Corlears Hook, Morningside Gardens, and others.) In the built-up portions of the Bronx, Queens, Newark, and Jersey City the situation is about the same.

8. See Appendix E, which demonstrates why the construction of a new loft-type building in downtown Manhattan is practically foreclosed by current building costs. Using current land costs in the area between West 20th Street and West

30th Street as a basis for valuing the site, we calculated that space in the new structure would have to rent for about $3.75 annually per square foot. If the land could be obtained at no cost, the figure still would run at more than $3.35. If generous property tax provisions were made, the figure might come down as low as $3.00. But this is still much higher than prevailing rental rates.

9. Regional Plan Association, Bulletin 91, *Hub-Bound Travel in the Tri-State Metropolitan Region: Persons and Vehicles Entering Manhattan South of 61st St., 1924–1956* (New York, 1959).

10. One can compute the average plant size in each segment of the Region on a basis which assumes that the mix of industries in all segments of the Region is the same. Using this approach—employing the number of plants which an industry has in the Region as a whole as the industry's weight—we find that the average number of employees in New York City's plants, about 35, was much lower than that for any county in the Region outside New York City.

11. In making generalizations of this sort, of course, one has to be careful to define what he means by an "industry." Do "women's shoes" constitute an industry? Or must we look on expensive women's shoes as a different industry from the inexpensive lines, because the production processes and the planning horizons are so different? And if the latter, do the industry categories we have used above carry out these distinctions adequately? There is no ironclad means of dealing with the problem. The outputs of any two establishments commonly differ from one another in subtle ways, even when one thinks of them as coming from the same "industry." Yet, despite this fact, we are inclined to think that the size differences indicated in the text are not the product of this conceptual pitfall.

12. Data for six other metropolitan areas also show a smaller average size of plant in the central city than in the remainder of the area, suggesting that forces similar to those in the New York Metropolitan Region may be at work in other large metropolitan areas. But the ratio between the average size of plant in the suburbs and that in the central city is larger for the New York Metropolitan Region than for the Baltimore, Boston, New Orleans, Philadelphia, St. Louis, or San Francisco-Oakland-Stanford metropolitan areas.

13. Compare the discussion by George J. Stigler, "The Division of Labor Is Limited by the Extent of the Market," *Journal of Political Economy*, 59:187–191 (June 1951).

14. See D. B. Creamer and H. K. Brunck, "The Diffusion of Manufacturing Employment," in *Migration and Economic Opportunity* (University of Pennsylvania Press, 1936), pp. 329–332.

15. T. M. Whitin and W. H. Peston, "Random Variations, Risk, and Returns to Scale," *Quarterly Journal of Economics*, 68:605 *et seq.* (November 1954).

16. In all such measures of locational change, of course, there is always the risk that the observed shift may be due to a problem of industry mix, that is, to the possibility that the various constituent industries in any group grew at different rates. Where such different growth rates occur, New York City's share of the total group can drop, even though its share of each constituent industry be unchanged. Throughout the analysis, tests were made to ensure that any seeming change in a group share was genuine, in the sense that it was not generated by different and changing mixes.

17. U.S. *Census of Manufactures,* 1947 and 1954.

18. In a study of 3,560 New Jersey corporations, it appeared that personal property assessments ranged from less than one per cent to more than 100 per cent of book value, a variation which fairly reflects the results which would have been obtained if "true value" had been used in place of "book value." See James A. Arnold, Jr., "The Personal Property Tax," *New Jersey Municipalities* (October 1956), pp. 5–8.

19. See below, Chapter 8.

20. For a fuller discussion of this subject, see the volume in this series by Robert C. Wood, *1400 Governments.*

CHAPTER 3: THE SPECIAL MANUFACTURING INDUSTRIES

1. The over-all effect of this pattern of operation has been to limit capital use in these industries. Though national manufacturing as a whole employs 9.6 horsepower per worker, the analogous figure is only half a horsepower in the apparel industry and less than 2 horsepower in commercial printing, lithographing, games and toys. Estimates are based largely on U.S. *1954 Census of Manufactures*, Vol. 1, *Summary Statistics*, Chapter 7, "Horsepower of Power Equipment," Table 2.

2. Seasonality adds another dimension in variability to these industries. The seasonal swing in employment in New York City in the apparel industries as a whole—an exceedingly crude classification which combines a variety of seasonal patterns—

appeared to be about 13.5 per cent in 1956. The high-to-low seasonal swing in 19 other broad manufacturing categories in the New York Standard Metropolitan Area was 9.1 per cent on the average.

3. E. E. Pratt, *Industrial Causes of Congestion of Population in New York City* (New York, 1911), p. 125.

4. Based on industry studies in: Committee on Regional Plan of New York and Its Environs, *Regional Survey of New York and Its Environs*, Vols. 1, 1A, and 1B (all New York, 1928). For this early period, the industries we count as "communication-oriented" are not so numerous and not so sharply defined as those we list for the later periods. See Appendix G for the lists we used for 1900–1922 and the later periods.

5. The 1929 and 1939 percentages are based on U.S. *Census of Manufactures* for those years. They represent the ratio of New York City employment to that of the New York Industrial Area, which consisted of New York's five counties, plus Westchester, Bergen, Passaic, Essex, Hudson, Union, and Middlesex.

6. See *Made in New York*, ed. Max Hall (Cambridge: Harvard University Press, 1959).

7. Committee on Regional Plan of New York and Its Environs, *Regional Survey of New York and Its Environs*, Vol. 1A, "The Chemical Industry" (New York, 1928), p. 19.

CHAPTER 4: THE WHITE-COLLAR CORPS

1. Jacob Knickerbocker, *Then and Now* (Boston, 1939), p. 39.

2. Figures are available for New York City in 1939, showing a breakdown of operating costs for various wholesale lines. For a "beer and ale" category, the data show distribution costs running at 26 per cent of total operating costs, and for the general grocery line the comparable figure was 20 per cent. See U.S. *1939 Census of Business*, Vol. 2.

3. This figure does not include employees of manufacturers' sales branches and agencies. Comparable data for such organizations were not available in this period.

4. Newark, Jersey City, Elizabeth, Paterson, Yonkers, and Bridgeport.

5. The twelve major areas covered were the metropolitan areas of Baltimore, Boston-Lowell-Lawrence, Buffalo, Chicago, Cincinnati, Cleveland, Detroit, Los Angeles, Philadelphia, Pittsburgh, St. Louis, and San Francisco-Oakland.

6. In Manhattan, the average wholesale establishment occupies about 2,800 square feet of floor space—the equivalent of an area only 53 feet square. The average manufacturing plant in Manhattan demands over twice as much space, even though it is far smaller than plants in other parts of the Region.

7. These data exclude savings banks. But such banks have only 14 per cent as much employment as the commercial banks in the Region.

8. This outward shift from the central city could also be detected in the other large metropolitan areas. We found that in the same period, the central cities of seven selected Standard Metropolitan Areas—those of Baltimore, Denver, New Orleans, Philadelphia, St. Louis, San Francisco, and Washington, D.C. —increased their aggregate banking employment by 38 per cent, while their surrounding areas increased theirs by 78 per cent.

9. A sample study of commuting patterns in the Region in 1956 (described in Appendix K) shows that Manhattan still draws the bulk of its female office and clerical workers from within the five-county Core of the Region. The 1956 figure was close to 87 per cent, compared with less than 70 per cent for other categories of Manhattan workers.

10. The 895,000, however, do include some 35,000 central-office employees who were also included in the wholesale employment given in Table 15 because of the dominant selling function of those central offices.

11. See our note 9, above.

12. Regional Plan Association, Bulletin 91, *Hub-Bound Travel in the Tri-State Metropolitan Region: Persons and Vehicles Entering Manhattan South of 61st Street, 1924–1956* (New York, 1959).

13. The New York City Tax Commission reports that the number of structures in Manhattan classified by the Commission as loft buildings dropped from 7,380 to 6,272 in the eleven years following its 1947–1948 fiscal year.

14. Observations about the changing use of loft space are based on unpublished data especially compiled for the New York Metropolitan Region Study by the Research Department of the Real Estate Board of New York, Inc.

15. For all types of employees, the average space per employee in New York City office buildings increased about 20 per cent between 1947 and 1958, according to a survey conducted by Herman E. Krooss for the New York Metropolitan Region Study.

CHAPTER 5: THE PURSUIT OF CONSUMERS

1. For the period 1953–1956, data from the federal Bureau of Old-Age and Survivors Insurance, compiled on a basis somewhat different from that of the Census data, reflect the continued absolute and relative decline of the Core. Between the two dates, employment in the Core in consumer trades and services fell by 26,400 jobs, while the Core's share of the Region's employment fell from 67 to 64 per cent.

2. U.S. Dept. of Commerce, *Central Business Districts and Their Metropolitan Areas: A Summary of Geographic Shifts in Retail Sales Growth, 1948–54*, Area Trend Series—No. 1, 1957.

3. The figures on retail buying by visitors are fairly fragmentary, but estimates by the New York City Convention and Visitors Bureau and surveys by various groups such as *Playbill* magazine suggest that at least one-fifth (probably somewhat more) of consumer trade and service sales in Manhattan's central business district are now accounted for by out-of-town visitors.

4. In each case, the relationships for 1954 are associated with coefficients of correlation in excess of 0.85. Since the distribution of the data involved is not badly skewed as a rule, these relationships seem highly significant.

5. Minus a small correction term. The formulas for food stores and other lines are given in Appendix I.

CHAPTER 6: SPACIOUS LIVING VS. EASY ACCESS

1. This and other figures on land types cited in the text are from Regional Plan Association, Bulletin 87, *People, Jobs and Land 1955–1975* (New York, 1957). Most of the swampy land lies in (1) the Jersey Meadows in Bergen, Essex, and Hudson Counties, (2) the eastern part of Morris County in the Passaic River watershed, and (3) along the south shore of Long Island in Nassau County. Compare Map 7 on p. 14 of Bulletin 87.

2. Most of this category of hilly land lies (1) west of the Hudson in a broad belt bounded on the southeast by the Watchung Ridge, (2) scattered liberally through most of Dutchess, Putnam, Westchester, and Fairfield Counties, and (3) in the Palisades strip bordering the Hudson.

3. U.S. Bureau of the Census, Current Population Reports, Series P–28, No. 1156, *Special Census of New York City,*

April 1, 1957: Manhattan Borough by Census Tracts and Health Areas.

4. As pointed out in earlier chapters, Newark also exercises some features of the special access attraction that we attribute primarily to Manhattan, though the functional differences of the two centers are still profound.

5. In practice, considerable discretion exists in measuring "net density." Such a measure may be based on lot acreage alone or it may be based on lots plus streets and reserved open spaces. The measure may vary also in the extent to which it takes account of very scattered buildings.

6. Robert C. Wood, *1400 Governments.*

7. The distinction between multifamily and single-family dwellings is blurred by several intermediate types—row houses, semidetached, two-family, and low-rise garden apartments.

8. The amount of variation among individual neighborhoods is partly concealed in Table 28, since all the dwelling units of each municipality have been entered in a single access-density group.

9. In the New York Standard Metropolitan Area in 1950, 94 per cent of all *families* had one or more members in the labor force. The percentage of *households* represented in the labor force in the metropolitan area, however, is not reported. U.S. *1950 Census of Population,* Special Report P-E No. 2A, *General Characteristics of Families,* Table 40, p. 2A–162.

10. Compare, for example, Donald L. Foley, "Urban Daytime Population," *Social Forces,* May 1954; Leo F. Schnore, "The Use of Local Facilities in a Metropolis," *American Journal of Sociology,* 56:238–246; R. E. Schmidt and M. E. Campbell, *Highway Traffic Estimation* (Eno Foundation, Saugatuck, Conn., 1956), Table II–4, p. 20.

11. Compare T. D. Ellsworth, D. Benjamin, and H. Radolf, "Impact of Long Island Centers on Shopping Habits," *Journal of Retailing,* New York University, Fall 1957, pp. 109 ff.

12. These figures are derived from estimates of county-by-county distribution of (1) jobs and (2) employed residents, in 1955, in the Regional Plan Association's Bulletin 87, Tables 26, 27. If for each county its share of the Region's *jobs* is j, and its share of the Region's *employed residents* is r, the *minimum* fraction of all workers in the Region working in a county other than that where they live is given by $\frac{1}{2} \sum |j - r| = 0.26$. The other limit cited in the text—the proportion commuting across county lines if the workplace pattern were the same for em-

ployed residents of each county—is given by the formula: $1.00 - \Sigma jr = 0.86$.

13. A recent U.S. Census sample survey found a corresponding percentage of 11.5 for all U.S. employed workers in September 1954, and 38.5 for all employed residents of New York City. Bureau of the Census, Current Population Reports, Series P–20, No. 60, August 17, 1955: *County of Work and County of Residence, September 1954.*

14. In the distributions as tabulated from survey responses, there was a conspicuous hump in the 60–79 minute time class, and a dent in the preceding 50–59 minute class (after the obvious adjustment to the different sizes of the class intervals). We suspect that this reflects respondents' inability to estimate their commuting time precisely, and a resultant tendency to favor the response of "an hour," which would inflate the 60–79 minute class at the expense of the 50–59. Our smoothed distribution, therefore, may give a more accurate idea of actual commuting times than the crude reported figures do.

15. The median was employed in Tables 30 and 31 as a measure of the length of the representative journey, since arithmetic averages are affected by a few extreme items and since the longest time-interval was open-ended. The arithmetic means, as estimated from survey results, run consistently higher than the medians, because of the influence of these few very long journeys. This is especially the case with commutation to jobs in Staten Island, where the water barriers impose particularly long times for those coming from anywhere outside the borough, and particularly for those coming from Manhattan.

16. Intracounty flows account for about 46 per cent of the total. Flows to Manhattan from within the Region account for about 41 per cent. Eliminating the overlap (Manhattan intraborough, 7 per cent), we have 80 per cent of the total commuting within the Region accounted for as Manhattan-bound or intracounty.

17. In this respect, it is well to note, Essex County commuters behave very much like Core residents; many of them travel considerable distances daily from the western portion of the county into downtown Newark.

18. Much more complex concepts of the access factor's role in shaping the Region are, of course, possible. One could, for instance, calculate an "access rating" for any point in the Region that would take account of its distances from all other points in the Region where jobs or other access attractions exist.

This is the "potential" type of measure, which has attained some currency in recent regional-science literature.

CHAPTER 7: WHO LIVES WHERE AND WHY

1. On the importance of occupational type as a basis for residential distribution and the formation of homogeneous neighborhoods, see Otis Dudley Duncan and Beverly Duncan, "Residential Distribution and Occupational Stratification," *American Journal of Sociology*, March 1955, pp. 493–503.

2. The eight categories which appear in Table 32 include all occupations reported in the U.S. Census of Population except farm employment, which we ignored throughout.

3. A full explanation of the construction of these indices appears in Appendix L.

4. The relative concentration of "sales" jobs in Monmouth County is, one may surmise, a special case involving the ocean-side resort development in that county. There is a very slight relative concentration of sales employment among the residents of Monmouth as well, the residence index being 101.5.

5. The relative concentration of craftsmen-foremen among residents of Suffolk County can be associated with a moderate relative concentration of jobs of that type in both Nassau and Suffolk, with indices of 118 and 106 respectively.

6. Here, as in the case of the craftsmen-foremen, we can associate a residence concentration in Suffolk County with moderate relative concentration of the corresponding type of jobs in both Nassau and Suffolk; the index for laborers' jobs is 108 in each case.

7. Employment in wholesale trade, by contrast, is heavily centralized. See Chapter 4.

8. There are, however, a number of white-collar communities with substantial proportions of multifamily housing. Most of them are in Westchester or close to Newark, and net densities are generally moderate or even low. Examples are Tarrytown, Bronxville, Irvington-on-Hudson, Dobbs Ferry, and North Pelham (all in Westchester County), and Montclair and East Orange in Essex County.

9. Some of the differences in income level between groups, of course, reflect large differences in the proportion of the sexes. The sales and clerical groups, in particular, show a marked contrast in relative income standing among males and among females, and the clerical group stands out as the only one with a preponderance of women.

10. Any statistical comparison of levels of income between areas as different as the Core and the rural suburbs gives of course a quite imperfect measure of relative levels of well-being or styles of life. On the characteristic pattern of income levels in U.S. metropolitan areas, see U.S. *1950 Census of Population,* Special Report P–E No. 5A, *Characteristics by Size of Place;* and O. D. Duncan and A. J. Reiss, Jr., *Social Characteristics of Urban and Rural Communities, 1950* (New York, 1956), especially pp. 129–130. The prevalence of higher income levels in the urbanized areas surrounding central cities than in the central cities is documented in the Census figures themselves. The tendency for average income to fall off again in the outermost parts of a metropolitan region is less directly documented, but appears clearly indicated by the fact that income levels run consistently higher in urbanized areas than outside urbanized areas and are also correlated positively with size of urbanized area and (outside urbanized areas) with size of place. This implies a falling-off in income levels as we get out into the "Outer Ring" type of zone that is only to a minor extent tied in with the economy of the metropolis proper. For the Chicago metropolitan area specifically, Duncan and Reiss (pp. 148–149) have shown this by using three zones—central city, "suburbs," and "fringe"—with the highest income levels in the intermediate ("suburbs") zone.

11. Chart 8 and Table 37 are based on quite different sets of data. The figures in Table 37 are estimates of average personal income per capita in 1956, while those underlying Chart 8 represent median income of families and unrelated individuals reporting income in 1949, according to the 1950 Census of Population. The radically smaller average size of household in Manhattan as compared to the rest of the Region probably means that Manhattan's relative income standing among the counties looks better on a per capita basis (as in Table 37) than on a family-and-unrelated-individual basis (as reported in 1950 Census of Population). Moreover, the peculiar distribution of incomes by size in Manhattan probably makes Manhattan's relative standing look better when the arithmetic average is used (as in Table 37) than when the median is used (as in the Census figures), since the arithmetic average is influenced by the size of the extremely high incomes. Notice also Table 51, which is comparable with Table 37.

12. Income data were reported in the 1950 Census only for urban places of 2,500 population or more, a criterion which excludes many of the new outlying communities. The income

figures used are based on median income of families and un-related individuals for each urban place, that is, the same defi-nition of income as was used on a county basis for the data in Chart 8.

13. The significance of size of a community in relation to cost and quality of municipal services is discussed in Robert C. Wood, *1400 Governments*, a book in this series.

14. For example, the very low density average of 2.23 for the bottom income fifth in access zone 4 is wholly accounted for by the small borough of Paramus in Bergen County, which had relatively low median income in 1949, but moderately large minimum zoned lot sizes, ranging from one-fourth of an acre upwards. (New Jersey State Planning Bureau, *Zoning in New Jersey, 1956*.)

15. A representative illustration is a recent slum-clearance proposal for an area of about 20 acres somewhat south of Pennsylvania Station in Manhattan. The assessed value of the land in this tract was $8.25 per square foot, but for redevelop-ment it would be necessary to acquire not only the land but also the existing buildings, thus increasing the bare land cost to $16.50 per square foot. Assuming redevelopment at 112 dwelling units per net acre, this would mean average site-acquisition and clearing costs on the order of $6,000 per dwell-ing unit.

16. Department of City Planning, New York City, *Newslet-ter*, September 1958.

17. State of New York, Temporary State Housing Rent Com-mission, *High Rent Housing and Rent Control in New York City*, April 1958, pp. 18–19.

18. The median rent per unit in the 23rd to 96th Street zone, for units completed in 1947–1956, was $219 compared with $181 for the borough as a whole. *Ibid.*, Table 2-5, p. 14.

19. *Ibid.*, Table 8-10, p. 100. Prewar statistics showed that 97 per cent of New York City's occupied units renting for $200 or more per month were located in Manhattan. The situation is not greatly different today, and the costliest housing is still being built in Manhattan. (*Ibid.*, pp. 36–38). During the first half of 1958, more than four-fifths of New York City's new apartment units renting for $50 or more per room were con-structed in that borough. (Based on data from Department of City Planning, New York City.)

20. "A survey of consumer expenditures in 1950 revealed that urban households in the United States with incomes of $10,000 or more per year allotted an average of 7.7 per cent

of their incomes to housing. . . . In New York City, households with $10,000 or more in 1950 spent an average of 9.6 per cent of their income for housing." For the families in controlled higher-rent apartments in Manhattan in 1956, the median percentage was 15 and the average roughly 16. (*Ibid.*, p. 70.) Probably the percentage runs even higher for tenants of non-controlled high-rent apartments.

21. Compare Chart 8 above.

22. For example, the average lot size in all final plats approved in Morris County in 1957 was 24,500 square feet. About 5 per cent of the lots were 40,000 square feet (1 acre) or larger, 60 per cent were 20,000 to 40,000 square feet, and the remaining 35 per cent were in plats with an average lot size between 10,000 and 20,000 square feet. In the same year the average lot size in newly filed plats in Westchester County was about 27,500 square feet net; in the northern part of Westchester it was roughly 50,000 square feet net. (Derived from Morris County Planning Board, *Annual Report, 1957*; Westchester County Department of Planning, *Subdivision Activity in Westchester*, September 1958.)

23. A recent harrowing account of the tribulations of a trainload of Fairfield County exurbanites on a winter's evening quotes one dedicated Wiltonian as saying, "The worse the service, the fewer the people to move out here. I'm in favor of bad service. . . ." (Marvin Barrett, "The Hardy Commuters of Wilton, Connecticut," *The Reporter*, May 15, 1958, p. 40.)

24. Among the households occupying controlled higher-rent apartments in Manhattan in November 1956 (which represent preponderantly households in the top tenth of the income scale), nearly 63 per cent had no children under 18 in the household. Another marked family characteristic of the higher-rent apartment dwellers in Manhattan is the advanced age of the head of the household. The median age in these households was 53.9 years in November 1956, compared with 46.4 years for the heads of household in all renter-occupied apartments in New York City in April 1950. The comparison is of course affected to some extent by changes in the age structure of the population in general between 1950 and 1956. (State of New York, Temporary State Housing Rent Commission, *High Rent Housing and Rent Control in New York City*, April 1958, p. 66; Table VI–4, p. 161; and Table 6–3, p. 65.)

25. A further factor underlying the shift of the middle income groups away from their former close-in neighborhoods is the rising trend of living standards. A middle-income house-

hold today wants and can afford a somewhat better house than did a household in a corresponding middle position on the income scale a generation ago. This factor should not be over-emphasized, however, since housing construction costs seem to have risen at least as fast as per capita disposable incomes since 1929.

26. These groups are treated at length in Oscar Handlin's *The Newcomers*, a volume in this series.

27. U.S. 1950 *Census of Population*, Special Report P–E No. 5A, *Characteristics by Size of Place*; and Duncan and Reiss (see our note 10, above), Chapters 3, 11, 12.

28. See Handlin (note 26, above).

29. Donald J. Bogue, *Components of Population Change, 1940–50: Estimates of Net Migration and Natural Increase for Each Standard Metropolitan Area and State Economic Area* (Studies in Population Distribution, No. 12, published jointly by Scripps Foundation for Research in Population Problems and the Population Research and Training Center, University of Chicago, 1957).

30. Middle-income families that already have many children, on the other hand, sometimes find that the big houses they need are available only in older neighborhoods.

31. Any impressions drawn from such small numbers of communities as appear in some of the classes in Table 41 must of course be viewed as suggestive rather than conclusive. For instance, the five communities in the lowest row of the table (low income, high proportion of children) are a very mixed bag; Glen Cove (Nassau County) Harrison (Hudson), Paramus (Bergen), Waldwick (Bergen), and Tarrytown (Westchester).

CHAPTER 8: SPREAD OF THE PEOPLE

1. These shifts are described in comprehensive statistical terms in Amos H. Hawley, *The Changing Shape of Metropolitan America* (Glencoe, Ill., 1956); Donald J. Bogue, *Population Growth in Standard Metropolitan Areas, 1900–1950,* prepared under contract with Housing and Home Finance Agency (Washington: Government Printing Office, 1953); Donald J. Bogue, *Components of Population Change in Standard Metropolitan Areas,* Scripps Foundation (Oxford, Ohio, 1957).

2. Another analysis yielding similar results, with areas classified by straight-line distance rather than time, was made on

the basis of unpublished calculations by Professor Hawley for 1920, 1930, 1940, and 1950, extended to 1955 by the New York Metropolitan Region Study. Hawley's figures for the New York Standard Metropolitan Area are included in his published density-distance tabulations for groups of United States metropolitan areas, in *The Changing Shape of Metropolitan America.*

3. The term is Dr. Hans Blumenfeld's, from his "The Tidal Wave of Metropolitan Expansion," *Journal of the American Institute of Planners,* 20:3–14 (Winter, 1954).

4. In 1910, only 16 per cent of the population of Queens lived within half a mile of rapid transit; by 1920, the percentage was 58. Consolidated Edison Company of New York, *Population Growth of New York City by Districts, 1910–1948* (New York, December 1948), pp. 20–21.

5. See note 1 above.

6. New York State Division of Housing, Bureau of Research and Statistics, *Construction Authorized or Started in New York State,* Nov. 28, 1958, Table 8, page 9. Percentages calculated.

7. The Standard Metropolitan Area used by the Census Bureau, it will be recalled, covers all of the New York Metropolitan Region except five outlying counties: Fairfield, Dutchess, Putnam, Orange, and Monmouth.

8. Calculated from data in Bureau of the Census, *1956 National Housing Inventory, Components of Change, 1950 to 1956: New York–Northeastern New Jersey Standard Metropolitan Area* (Washington, 1958). The other causes of housing inventory change, including mergers, did not appear on balance to affect the number of nonwhite-occupied units between 1950 and 1956. It should be borne in mind that the 1956 inventory survey was based on a sample, leaving a considerable margin of error, particularly in findings involving relatively small numbers of dwelling units.

9. A suggestive indication of the importance of conversions in the older neighborhoods of the Region prior to 1950 can be derived from the Census reports on housing by age of structure and the estimated number of households. Thus, the *1950 Census of Housing* reported that 3,080,865 dwelling units in the 22 counties of the New York Metropolitan Region in 1950 were in structures built prior to 1930 (almost certainly a substantial under-estimate, since it may be presumed that a high proportion of the 200,000-odd units for which no building date was reported were in old structures). It has been estimated by the Regional Plan Association (Bulletin 87, Tables 19 and 22,

pp. 26 and 39) that the number of households in the Region in 1930 was about 2,860,000. The number of dwelling units exceeded the number of households (occupied dwelling units) by only 3 per cent in 1940. It seems to follow that (despite all the demolition of old structures that must have occurred between 1930 and 1950 in the Region) there were actually a few more dwelling units in pre-1930 structures in 1950 than 1930, the increase representing the excess of gains by conversion over losses through demolition and all other causes.

10. The highest migration and moving rates are characteristically found in the 20–24 age group in both sexes. Compare Bureau of the Census, Current Population Reports, Series P-20, No. 85, *Mobility of the Population of the United States, March 1957–March 1958* (Washington, Oct. 13, 1958), Table 4, p. 11.

11. See source cited in our note 10.

12. For a further discussion of this subject, see Oscar Handlin, *The Newcomers,* another volume of this series.

13. Based on Census figures for Wards 7, 10, 11, 13, and 17, as given in Regional Plan Association, *Information Bulletin* No. 2, April 20, 1931, p. 2. Areas of population decline in the inner parts of the Region for each decade from 1920 to 1950 are mapped in Regional Plan Association, Bulletin 55 (July 1941), Figs. 5–6, and Bulletin 85 (November 1954), p. 9.

14. Based on data from U.S. *1950 Census of Population* and Special Census of April 1, 1957, and on housing data supplied by Department of City Planning, New York City.

15. The remaining Health Area showing a significant increase in population was at the lower tip of Manhattan, where fluctuations in the transient population of seamen play a major role in population change and the total population does not exceed 12,000.

16. According to a rule of thumb of the trade, a new house is within the means of a family with an annual income of at least 40 to 50 per cent of the purchase price. Compare Glenn H. Beyer, *Housing: A Factual Analysis* (New York, 1958), p. 153. Estimates of the Region's income distribution suggest that only about a sixth of the households of the Region have incomes in excess of $7,500.

17. In Manhattan, for example, about 95 per cent of the private apartment units completed during the first quarter of 1958 rented for $100 or over. In the rest of New York City, the proportion was 98 per cent. See Department of City Planning, New York City, *Newsletter,* September 1958.

18. In 1954 there were about 4,000 square miles of vacant land suitable for development in the Region's 6,914 square miles of land area. Each million new suburbanites, occupying land at a density of, say, 8 persons per gross acre, would need somewhat more than 200 square miles. This calculation is of course intended merely as a suggestion of possible orders of magnitude.

19. Areas highly resistant to obsolescence by virtue of design well adapted to evolving needs occur, for example, in Greenwich Village, Radburn, Forest Hills Gardens, and Sunnyside Boulevard Gardens.

20. Maps 4 and 5 on pages 10–11 of Regional Plan Association Bulletin 87 are particularly informative on this point. The area already "intensively developed" by 1954 appears to include virtually all the usable land within the limits of an hour's commuter journey to central or lower Manhattan; and in some sectors (for example, the south shore of Long Island and the Fairfield County shore) it extends even beyond the limits of a 1½-hour journey.

21. A recent survey of residential demolitions in New York City, covering the first quarter of 1958, shows that nearly 90 per cent of such demolitions were for public improvement purposes. Nearly half the demolitions in the City as a whole (and in Manhattan alone, nearly two-thirds) were to make way for public housing. Razing for street and highway purposes accounted for 7.8 per cent in Manhattan and nearly half the total in the other boroughs. Demolitions were heavily concentrated in the poorer portion of the housing inventory, 90 per cent of those in Manhattan being walk-up old-law tenements. This study is reported in Department of City Planning, New York City, *Newsletter,* January 1959. Compare also Table 43 above for data on characteristics of housing demolished in the Standard Metropolitan Area in the period 1950–1956.

22. The basic Manhattan street grid was adopted and published in 1811 on the basis of surveys made a few years earlier. In later years it was found possible to interpolate a few additional avenues (for example, Madison, Lexington) between the numbered ones originally provided for.

23. Regional Plan Association, Bulletin 91, *Hub-Bound Travel in the Tri-State Metropolitan Region: Persons and Vehicles Entering Manhattan South of 61st Street, 1924–1956* (New York, 1959).

24. From state motor vehicle bureaus.

25. The Staff Report (December 1957) of the Metropolitan Rapid Transit Commission Study found that the proportion of

commuters to New York who travel by train rises rapidly with increased distance, in the commuting territories of both the Long Island and the New Haven railroads.

26. It is also relevant to note that the large suburban shopping centers report sizable fractions of their business coming from city residents who drive out to the suburbs to shop.

27. One factor that may significantly restrain the growth of lot sizes is the mounting concern over the health problem raised by reliance on septic tanks and wells for sanitation and water supply. Where community sewage and water services are required, the costs of large-lot development become much greater.

28. Regional Plan Association, Bulletin 63 (November 1944), pp. 5–6. That bulletin says (on map following p. 6) that "in general close residential development consists of those areas having 5 or more houses per block and includes local business districts"—excepting main business areas in southern Manhattan. Within New York City the relation of population patterns to mass transport facilities has of course been different, with a much more pervasive network of facilities and with automobiles playing a smaller role. Thus, ". . . since 1910 and probably before, at least 84% of the population of the city [New York] has lived within one-half mile of the [rapid transit] lines. For 1910, 1920, 1930 and 1940 the percentages were 84%, 92%, 88%, and 88%, respectively." Consolidated Edison Company of New York, *Population Growth of New York City by Districts, 1910–1948* (New York, December 1948), p. 2.

29. Estimates by New York Metropolitan Region Study, deflated by the national consumer price index.

30. Edward E. Pratt, *Industrial Causes of Congestion of Population in New York City* (New York, 1911).

31. Population density and the degree of crowding in slums can of course be measured in several different ways—dwelling units per acre, persons per acre, persons per square foot of floor space, etc. Our identification of peak density areas in Table 50 was on the basis of persons per square mile of land area, and peak densities by some other measure (for example, persons per unit of floor space) might not be in the same areas. This in no way invalidates, however, our general point about the factors working toward reduced peak slum densities over the long run.

32. For the New York Metropolitan Region and for United States metropolitan areas more generally, such fragmentary evidence as is available from various surveys over the last few

decades suggests that, despite speedier transportation, people spend at least as much time as they ever did in getting to work, and probably more. Compare Leo F. Schnore, "The Journey to Work in 1975," in *Applications of Demography: The Population Situation in the U.S. in 1975,* ed. Donald J. Bogue (published jointly by Scripps Foundation for Research in Population Problems and the Population Research and Training Center, University of Chicago, 1957). Schnore observes (p. 74), ". . . we need not assume that commuting time will remain the same. Historically speaking, much of the time gained in the shortening of the individual's workday has already been spent in increased travel time, and this seems likely to continue in the future." In the New York Region specifically, a comparison of reported median commuting times in 1934 and 1955 shows residents of every New York City borough, plus Bergen and Hudson Counties, having a markedly longer journey in 1955 than in 1934, with no change established for residents of the other counties covered in 1934 (Essex and Middlesex). The 1934 data are from New York, N.Y., Emergency Relief Bureau, Works Division, *Real Property Inventory, City of New York: Residential Report* (New York, 1934), and unpublished tabulations from similar surveys in New Jersey, supplied by courtesy of the New Jersey Dept. of Conservation and Economic Development; the 1955 data are those of the sample Regionwide journey-to-work survey described in Appendix K.

33. For example, "Suburbanites Shift to Fringes of City," *New York Times,* May 4, 1958, Section 8, p. 1; "Suburban Return to Cities Is Seen," *New York Times,* June 26, 1958, p. 45; William H. Whyte, Jr., "Are Cities Un-American?" *Fortune,* September 1957 (reprinted in Editors of Fortune, *The Exploding Metropolis* (New York, 1958). A little quantitative evidence on reactions of recent migrants to the suburbs is provided in Mauri and Florence E. Edwards, "The New Suburbanite," in *Today's Living* (supplement to *New York Herald Tribune*), March 9 and 30, 1958. On page 19, March 30 issue, it is reported that in a sample of 4,000 families, "relative newcomers to Long Island, Westchester, and New Jersey," about 10 per cent of the Long Islanders reported that "if they had to do it over," they would stay in the City. The corresponding percentage was 9 in Westchester and 5 in New Jersey.

34. By about 1975 it is expected that more than two-thirds of all Americans will be living in the 200 largest Census metropolitan areas as now demarcated, and that only about 9 per cent will be living on farms. See Ray P. Cuzzort, "The Size

and Distribution of Standard Metropolitan Areas in 1975," and Louis J. Ducoff, "The Farm Population and the Agricultural Labor Force in 1975," in *Applications of Demography: The Population Situation in the U.S. in 1975,* cited in our note 32 above.

APPENDIX F: COMPUTATION OF TAX LEVELS

1. For examples based on this technique see: Joe Summers Floyd, Jr., *Effects of Taxation in Industrial Location* (Chapel Hill: University of North Carolina Press, 1952); Pennsylvania Economy League, Inc., Western Division, *The Relative Tax Cost to Manufacturing Industry* (November 1956); Commonwealth of Massachusetts, *Report of the Special Commission on Taxation,* Part IV, *The Comparative Impact of Corporate Taxes in Massachusetts* (June 1951); Clarence Heer, *Tax Bills of Selected Manufacturing Corporations in Six Southeastern States* (Raleigh: North Carolina State Planning Board, 1945). Other techniques include comparison of actual tax bills of similar firms at different locations, and comparison of tax costs of branches of the same company which are located in different jurisdictions. In both cases the problem is to find establishments sufficiently alike at different locations and thus far no investigator has succeeded in accomplishing this. For a discussion of these and other techniques see Floyd, just cited, pp. 43–44.

2. It has been suggested that the only really accurate way to determine what the assessed value of a firm would be in various communities is to construct the firm physically, from location to location, and have the local assessor assess it at each place! A study of the tax burden in Massachusetts approached this technique by providing the local officials in the jurisdictions being compared with descriptive blueprints and photographs. On the basis of this information the local assessors were asked to determine what the assessment of the firm would be were it located in their jurisdiction. Commonwealth of Massachusetts, *op. cit.,* pp. 13–14.

3. A number of localities make their own determinations from time to time of the ratio of assessed value to market value for properties in their jurisdiction, usually basing such ratios on the sale prices of properties sold in some prior period. In the case of New York City, the most recent ratios of this kind are slightly higher in some boroughs and lower in others than the state figures used in this study. The differences, however, are

not great enough to have a significant effect on the resulting tax comparisons. Although the New York State equalization figures are less current than those which might be obtained from local studies in some cases, they possess two advantages: they are determined by one agency applying uniform standards of measurement in all New York State localities; and they are based upon samples of all properties in such jurisdictions, rather than exclusively on properties sold.

4. Commonwealth of Massachusetts, *op. cit.,* p. 15.

5. James A. Arnold, Jr., "The Personal Property Tax," *New Jersey Municipalities* (October 1956), pp. 5–8.

6. Brooklyn Chamber of Commerce, *Annual Report, 1954–1955,* pp. 4–5.

INDEX

ANCHOR BOOKS

American History and Studies (continued)